LOYALTY IN THE SPIRITUALITY OF ST. THOMAS MORE

BIBLIOTHECA

HUMANISTICA & REFORMATORICA

VOLUME IV

LOYALTY
IN THE SPIRITUALITY OF
ST. THOMAS MORE

by

BRIAN BYRON

NIEUWKOOP * B. DE GRAAF

1972

Fifty copies of this book were issued as a dissertation and presented to the Faculty of Theology of the Pontifical Gregorian University in candidacy for the Degree of Doctor of Divinity.

Vidimus et approbamus ad normam Statutorum Universitatis Romae,
ex Pontificia Universitate Gregoriana
die 15 mensis Iunii anni 1966

THOMAS SPIDLIK, S.J.
EDUARDUS HAMEL, S.J.

Nihil Obstat

MONS. JAMES MADDEN, D.D.

Imprimatur

† N. T. CARD. GILROY,
Archbishop of Sydney

Die. 15 Aprilis 1971

ISBN 90 6004 293 X

Printed in the Netherlands by n.v. Drukkerij Trio, The Hague.

To my Mother and Father

FOREWORD

I wish to express sincere gratitude to all who cooperated in enabling me to produce this dissertation. His Eminence Cardinal Gilroy, Archbishop of Sydney at the time of composition, kindly granted me leave from pastoral activities so that I could further my studies in Rome. Thanks are also due to the executive of the Manly Union who awarded me the Father Philip Claver Smith Roman Bursary and to the Society of St Peter the Apostle for generous financial assistance. The Superior of the English College, Rome, kindly allowed me the use of their library which was particularly valuable for my topic. The association, *Amici Thomae Mori*, centred at Angers, France, also put at my disposal some very useful material. One of my present students, Gregory Windle, has given me great assistance in checking the text and notes and compiling the index. To Abbé Henri Gibaud I am indebted for his careful examination of my thesis which he reviewed in a most encouraging way in *Moreana*, no. 13, Feb. 1967, 89–94. He also gave me a list of *corrigenda* and several important suggestions which I have now incorporated. Another of my students, John Chalmers, also deserves my thanks for checking many details and references. My typist, Mrs Norma Sullivan, has earned my undying admiration and sincere thanks for preparing a faultless manuscript.

Acknowledgements are due to the following publishers for very generous permissions to use copyright material: – Yale University Press for quotations from *The Latin Epigrams of St Thomas More*, edited and translated by L. Bradner and C. A. Lynch; *The Selected Letters of St Thomas More*, edited by Elizabeth Frances Rogers; *Utopia*, edited by Edward Surtz S.J. and J. H. Hexter; to the Clarendon Press, Oxford, for an extract from *English Literature in the Sixteenth Century*, by C. S. Lewis; to the Council of the Early English Text Society for material from A. I. Taft's *The Apologye of Syr Thomas More;* to Sheed and Ward Ltd. for quotations from *The Fame of Blessed Thomas More;* to the Catholic University of America Press for citations from *A Translation of St Thomas More's 'Responsio ad Lutherum'*, by Sister Gertrude J. Donnelly; to The Open Court Publishing Company for material from *John Colet and the Platonic Tradition*, by Leland Miles; to Jonathan Cape Ltd. and the estate of R. W. Chambers for extracts from his *Thomas More;* to Abbé Germain Marc'hadour for many favours and especially for permission to use material from his excellent quarterly, *Moreana*.

Special thanks are due to my moderator, Fr Thomas Spidlik S.J. It was his discerning principles which guided me to such a happy choice of subject and to a fruitful programme of inquiry.   BRIAN BYRON

TABLE OF CONTENTS

BIBLIOGRAPHY

I. WORKS OF MORE

The Workes of Sir Thomas More Knyght, sometime Lorde Chauncellor of England, wrytten by him in the English Tonge, edited by WILLIAM RASTELL, London, 1557.

Thomae Mori, Angliae quondam cancellarii opera omnia, Frankfurt, 1689.

Opus epistolarum Des. Erasmi Roterdami, edited by P. S. ALLEN et alii., 12 vols., Oxford, 1906–58. It contains More's letters to Erasmus.

The Apologye of Syr Thomas More, Knight, edited with introduction and notes by ARTHUR IRVING TAFT, London, 1930.

The English Works of Sir Thomas More, edited W. E. CAMPBELL and A. W. REED, two vols., series not completed, London, 1931.

The Four Last Things, by the Blessed Martyr Sir Thomas More, Knight, edited by D. O'CONNOR, London, 1935.

Sir Thomas More: Utopia and Dialogue of Comfort, Everyman Library, London, 1910, reprinted 1937.

St Thomas More's History of the Passion, translated from the Latin by his granddaughter Mistress Mary Basset, edited in modern spelling with an introduction by P. E. HALLETT, London, 1941.

The Correspondence of Sir Thomas More, edited by E. F. ROGERS, Princeton, 1947.

The Latin Epigrams of Thomas More, edited and translated by L. BRADNER and C. A. LYNCH, Chicago, 1953.

English Prayers and Treatise on the Holy Eucharist, edited by PHILIP E. HALLETT, London, 1959.

St Thomas More: Selected Letters, edited by ELIZABETH FRANCES ROGERS, New Haven and London, 1961.

A Translation of St Thomas More's Responsio ad Lutherum, with an introduction and notes, a dissertation for degree of Doctor of Philosophy by Sister GERTRUDE JOSEPH DONNELLY, Catholic University of America Press, Washington, D.C., 1962, Book I only.

The Complete Works of St Thomas More, published by the St Thomas More Project, Yale University, New Haven and London, 1963–

—— Vol. 2, *The History of King Richard III,* edited by RICHARD S. SYLVESTER, 1963.

—— Vol. 4, *Utopia,* edited by EDWARD SURTZ S.J., and J. H. HEXTER, 1965.

—— Vol. 5, *Responsio ad Lutherum,* edited by JOHN M. HEADLEY, translated by Sister SCHOLASTICA MENDEVILLE, 1969.

Utopia, edited with Introduction and Notes by EDWARD SURTZ S.J., in series, *Selected Works of St Thomas More,* published by the St Thomas More Project, Yale University, New Haven and London, 1964.

A Dialogue of Comfort against Tribulation, edited with critical introduction and notes by LELAND MILES, Bloomington, Indiana, 1965.

—— The same in popular edition.

Sir Thomas More: Neue Briefe, edited by HUBERTUS SCHULTE HERBRUGGEN, Munster, 1966.

II. OTHER AUTHORS

BASSET, BERNARD, S.J., *Born for Friendship: the Spirit of Sir Thomas More*, London, 1965.

BECK, EGERTON, 'St Thomas More and the Law', in *Dublin Review*, no. 394, 1935, 53–72.

BELL, PHILIP INGRESS, 'The Trial of Thomas More', in *The Month*, vol. 23, 1960, 325–339.

BIETENHOLTZ, PETER G., 'Erasmus' View of More', in *Moreana*, no. 5, Feb., 1965, 5–16.

BOLT, ROBERT, 'A Man for All Seasons', in *The New Theatre of Europe*, edited by ROBERT W. CORRIGAN, New York, 1962.

BOUYER, LOUIS, *Christian Humanism*, translated by A. V. LITTLEDALE, London, 1958.

—— *Erasmus and the Humanist Experiment*, translated by FRANCIS X. MURPHY, London, 1959.

BREWER, J. S., *The Reign of Henry VIII from his Accession to the Death of Wolsey*, edited by JAMES GAIRDNER in two vols., London, 1884.

BRIDGETT, T. E., *The Life and Writings of Sir Thomas More, Chancellor of England and Martyr under Henry VIII*, London, 1891.

BRUZZO, LUIGI, *La considerazione in occasione della canonizzazione di San Tommaso More*, Rome, 1936.

BULLOUGH, GEOFFREY, (Editor), *Narrative and Dramatic Sources of Shakespeare*, London, 1960.

BUSH, D., (review of) *Utopia*, edited by E. SURTZ and J. H. HEXTER, in *Moreana*, no. 7, August 1965, 85–92.

CAMPBELL, W. E., *More, Utopia and his Social Teaching*, London, 1930.

—— *Erasmus, Tyndale and More*, London, 1949.

CAVANAUGH, JOHN R., C.S.B., 'The Stephen Motif in More's Thought', *Moreana* no. 8, Nov. 1965, 59–66.

CECIL, ALGERNON, *A Portrait of Thomas More*, London, 1937.

CHAMBERS, R. W., *Thomas More*, reprinted London, 1951.

Cobbett's Complete Collection of State Trials and Proceedings for High Treason and other Crimes and Misdemeanours from the Earliest Period to the Present Time, 'Trial of Sir Thomas More', vol. I, 386–395.

COGNET, LOUIS, *Post-Reformation Spirituality*, translated by P. J. HEPBURNE-SCOTT, *A Faith and Fact Book*, no. 41, London, 1959.

Conciliorum Oecumenicorum Decreta, edited Centro di Documentazione, Istituto per le Scienze Religiose, Bologna, Freiburg, 1962.

DANIEL-ROPS, 'Thomas More, Planiste de "L'Utopie",' *Moreana*, no. 6, May 1965, 5–8.

DERRETT, J. DUNCAN M., 'Neglected Versions of the Contemporary Account of the Trial of Sir Thomas More', in *Bulletin of the Institute of Historial Research*, vol. XXXIII, no. 88, Nov. 1960, 202–223.

—— 'Thomas More and the Legislation of the Corporation of London', reprinted from *The Guildhall Miscellany*, vol. II, no. 5, Oct. 1963, no pagination.

—— 'The "New" Document on Thomas More's Trials', in *Moreana*, no. 3, June 1964, 5–19.

—— 'The Trial of Sir Thomas More', in *The English Historical Review*, vol. LXXIX, no. 312, July 1964, 449–477.

—— 'More's Conveyance of His Lands and the Law of "Fraud",' *Moreana*, no. 5, Feb. 1965, 19–26.

—— 'More's Attainder and Dame Alice's Predicament', *Moreana*, no. 6, May 1965, 9–17.

—— 'St Thomas More and the Would-be Suicide', *Downside Review*, vol. 88, no. 293, Oct. 1970, 372–377.

DE SMEDT, Most Rev EMILE-JOSEPH, 'Religious Liberty', in *Council Speeches of Vatican II*, edited H. Küng et alii, Glen Rock, New Jersey, 1964, 237–253.

DE VOCHT, HENRY, *Acta Thomae Mori*, Louvain, 1947. (This contains an anonymous account of More's trial and death written between 1535 and 1556.)

Dictionnaire de Spiritualité Ascetique et Mystique, articles, 'Devoir', Tome III, coll. 653–672, by JEAN TONNEAU O.P.; 'Devoir d'Etat', Tome III, coll. 672–702, by RENE CARPENTIER, S.J.; 'Fidélité', Tome V, coll. 307–332, by PIERRE ADNES, S.J.

Dictionnaire de Théologie Catholique, article, 'Servet (Michel)', Tome XIV², coll. 1967–1972, by L. CRISTIANI.

Documents of Vatican II, General Editor WALTER M. ABBOTT, S.J., London, 1966.

DONOGHUE, CHARLES, *The Religious Doctrine in More's Utopia*, Rome, 1940.

EGAN, WILLIS J., S.J., *The Rule of Faith in St Thomas More's Controversy with William Tyndale 1528-1533*, Los Angeles, 1960.

ESTRADA, FRANCISCO LOPEZ, 'Santo Tomas Moro en España y en la America Hispana', *Moreana*, no. 5, Feb. 1965, 27–40.

Encyclopaedia Britannica, articles: 'Catherine of Aragon', vol. 5, 39–40; 'Luther, Martin', vol. 14, 491–498, n.n., London, 1960.

Fame of Bessed Thomas More, The, being addresses delivered in his honour in Chelsea, July 1929, by R. KNOX, HILAIRE BELLOC, G. K. CHESTERTON, Lord Justice RUSSELL, HENRY BROWNE S.J., REGINALD BLUNT, BEDE JARRETT O.P., with an introductory essay by Professor R. W. CHAMBERS, London, 1929.

GABETTI, GIUSEPPE, 'Lutero, Martino', in *Enciclopedia Italiana*, vol. XXI, pp. 692–705.

GAIRDNER, JAMES, *A History of the English Church in the Sixteenth Century from Henry VIII to Mary*, London 1924.

GIBSON, R. W., *St Thomas More: A Preliminary Bibliography of His Works and of Moreana to the Year 1750*, New Haven and London, 1961.

GOULDER, LAURENCE, *The Tower Pilgrimage*, London, n.d.

GRAHAM, HUGH, 'St Thomas More and Christian Education', *Thought*, vol. XI, 1936, 19–33.

GRISAR, JOSEPH, S.J., 'De aestimatione et fama quibus habiti sunt B. Joannes et Thomas More', in *Positio pro canonizatione impetranda*, Rome, 1934.

HAMEL, EDOUARD, S.J., *Loi naturelle et loi du Christ*, Bruges, 1964.

HARPSFIELD, NICHOLAS, *The life and death of Sr Thomas Moore, knight, sometymes Lord high Chancellor of England, written in the tyme of Queene Marie by Nicholas Harpsfield, L.D.*, edited by ELSIE VAUGHAN HITCHCOCK with introduction by R. W. CHAMBERS, and with Appendices including the Rastell Fragments, the News Letter to Paris describing the trial and death of More; More's Indictment, and More's Epitaph, *Early English Text Society*, London, 1932.

HALL, Henry VIII, edited by CHARLES WHIBLEY, two vols., London, 1904.

HOLLIS, CHRISTOPHER, 'St Thomas More, European', *Studies XXIV*, 1935, 379–390.

—— *St Thomas More*, revised edition, London, 1961.

HUGHES, JOHN JAY, *Stewards of the Lord*, London and Sydney, 1970, (especially for section, 'St Thomas More on eucharistic sacrifice', pp. 129–136.)

JANNELLE, PIERRE, 'Humanisme et unité chrétienne: John Fisher et Thomas More', *Etudes*, May 1935, 442–460.

—— 'More (Le bienheureux Thomas)', in *Dictionnaire de Théologie Catholique*, Tome X₂, coll. 2472–2482.

JARRETT, BEDE, 'A National Bulwark against Tyranny', in *The Fame of Blessed Thomas More*, London, 1929, 107–116.

KERNAN, GERALD, 'St Thomas More Theologian', *Thought*, vol. XVII, 1942, 281–302.

KNOX, RONALD, 'The Charge of Religious Intolerance', in *The Fame of Blessed Thomas More*, London, 1929, 35–50.

KÜNG, HANS, *Freedom in the World: St Thomas More*, translated by CECILY HASTINGS, London, 1965.

LEWIS, C. S., *English Literature in the Sixteenth Century*, Oxford, 1954.

LOVERA, CARLO, *Tommaso More*, Rome, 1935.

LYONNET, STANISLAS, S.J., *St Paul, Liberty and Law*, Rome, 1962.

MARC'HADOUR, GERMAIN, *Saint Thomas More*, textes traduits et presentés par GERMAIN HARC'HADOUR, en introduction: Thomas More vu par Erasme; contains, Lettre à Dorp; La Supplication des Ames; in collection, *Les Ecrits des Saints*, Namur, Belgium, 1962.

—— *L'Univers de Thomas More*, Paris, 1963.

—— 'St Thomas More', *The Month*, vol. 29, no. 2, 1963, 69–84; also in *Pre-Reformation English Spirituality*, London, 1965, 224–239.

—— 'St Thomas More patron des libres-penseurs? (réflexions sur *A Man for All Seasons*)', *Moreana*, no. 8, Nov. 1965, 28–42.

—— *The Bible in the Works of St Thomas More*, Nieuwkoop, 1969–

—— *Thomas More et La Bible*, Paris, 1969–

MARIUS, RICHARD C., 'What Kind of Man was Thomas More?', *Moreana*, no. 4, Nov. 1964, 115–117, (extract from letter).

—— Review of *England's Earliest Protestants 1520–1535* by WILLIAM A. CLESCH, New Haven, 1964, in *Moreana*, no. 6, May 1965, 69–76.

MILES, LELAND, *John Colet and the Platonic Tradition*, London, 1962.

—— 'Patristic Comforters in More's Dialogue of Comfort', *Moreana*, no. 8, Nov. 1965, 9–20.

MORE, CRESACRE, *The Life of Sir Thomas More, Knight, by his Great-Grandson Cresacre More Esq. (London MDCCXXVI)* edited and modernized by JAS. L. KENNEDY, Greenburg, Pennsylvania, 1941. (Originally written 1631).

NICHOLS, R. M. (translator), *The Epistles of Erasmus*, in 3 vols., London, 1901–1906 and 1908–1918.

O'CONNELL, JOHN R., 'St Thomas More as Citizen', *Dublin Review*, no. 394, July 1935, 37–52.

O'SULLIVAN, RICHARD (editor), *Under God and the Law*, Series 2, Papers read at the Thomas More Society, London, Blackwell, Oxford, 1949.

—— *The Spirit of the Common Law*, a representative collection of the papers of RICHARD O'SULLIVAN, selected and edited by B. A. WORTLEY, Tenbury Wells, England, 1965, especially paper 1, 'Sir Thomas More the Lawyer', 19–39.

PARMITER, GEOFFREY DE C., 'The Indictment of St Thomas More', in *Downside Review*, vol. 75, 1957, 149–166.

—— 'St Thomas More and the Oath', *Downside Review*, vol. 78, 1960, 1–13.

PINEAS, RAINER, *Thomas More and Tudor Polemics*, Bloomington, 1968.

REYNOLDS, E. E., *Saint Thomas More*, New York, 1958.

—— *Margaret Roper, Eldest Daughter of St Thomas More*, London, 1960.

—— 'An Unnoticed Document', in *Moreana*, no. 1, Sept. 1963, 12–17.

—— *The Trial of St Thomas More*, London, 1964.

—— *Sir Thomas More*, no. 178 of series, *Writers and their Work*, London, 1965.

—— *Thomas More and Erasmus*, London, 1965.

—— *The Field is Won; The Life and Death of St Thomas More*, London, 1968.

RO. BA., *The Lyfe of Syr Thomas More, Sometymes Lord Chancellor of England by Ro. Ba.*, written c. 1599, edited by E. HITCHCOCK, P. E. HALLETT and A. REED for Early English Text Society, London, 1950.

ROPER, WILLIAM, *The Lyfe of Sir Thomas Moore, Knighte*, written by William Roper, Esquire, which married Margreat, daughter of the sayed Thomas Moore, and now edited by ELSIE VAUGHAN HITCHCOCK, London, 1935; (originally written c. 1557; cf. Introduction xlv).

SEEBOHM, FREDERICK, *The Oxford Reformers*, 2nd edition, London, 1869.

SHEBBEARE, CLAUDE EUSTACE, *Sir Thomas More – A Leader of the English Renaissance*, London, 1929.

Sir Thomas More – An Anonymous Play of the Sixteenth Century ascribed in part to Shakespeare, edited in Five Acts by JOHN SHIRLEY, written c. 1593, Canterbury, n.d.

16

STAPLETON, THOMAS, *The Life and Illustrious Martyrdom of Sir Thomas More*, (Part III of *Tres Thomae*), translated by Mons. P. E. HALLETT, London, 1928; first published in Latin, Douai, 1588.

SULLIVAN, FRANK and MAJIE PADBERG, *Moreana*; *Materials for the study of Saint Thomas More*, Four Volumes, Los Angeles, 1964–1968.

SURTZ, EDWARD L., S.J., *The Praise of Wisdom, A Commentary on the Religious and Moral Problems and Background of St Thomas More's Utopia*, Chicago, 1957.

WATKINS, DAVID R., 'The Saint Thomas More Project', in *Yale University Library Gazette*, vol. 36, 1962, 162–168.

ZEEVELD, W. GORDON, review of *The History of King Richard III*, by St Thomas More, edited RICHARD S. SYLVESTER, New Haven, 1963, in *Moreana*, no. 1, Sep. 1963, 64–69.

17

ABBREVIATIONS

ALLEN   *Opus epistolarum Des. Erasmi Roterdami,* edited P. S. ALLEN et al., 12 vols., Oxford, 1906–1958.

Apol.   *The Apologye of Syr Thomas More, Knight,* edited with introduction and notes by ARTHUR IRVING TAFT, London, 1930.

BASSET   *Born for Friendship. The Spirit of Sir Thomas More,* London, 1965.

BRIDGETT   *The Life and Writings of Sir Thomas More,* London, 1891.

CHAMBERS   *Thomas More,* reprinted London, 1951.

Corr.   *The Correspondence of Sir Thomas More,* edited E. F. ROGERS, Princeton, 1947.

CWR   *The Complete Works of St Thomas More,* vol. 5, *Responsio ad Lutherum,* edited by JOHN M. HEADLEY, translated by Sister SCHOLASTICA MENDEVILLE, 1969.

Dial. of Comf.   *Sir Thomas More: Utopia and Dialogue of Comfort,* edited ERNEST RHYS, reprinted London, 1937.

DS   *Enchiridion Symbolorum Definitionum et Declarationum de Rebus Fidei et Morum,* edited HENRICUS DENZINGER and ADOLPHUS SCHÖNMETZER, editio XXXIV, Rome 1967.

DSAM   *Dictionnaire de Spiritualité Ascétique et Mystique,* Paris, 1932–

DTC   *Dictionnaire de Théologie Catholique,* Paris, 1903 ff.

English Prayers   *English Prayers and Treatise on the Holy Eucharist,* edited by PHILIP E. HALLETT, London, 1959.

Epig.   *The Latin Epigrams of Thomas More,* edited and translated by L. BRADNER and C. A. LYNCH, Chicago, 1953.

EW   *The Workes of Sir Thomas More, Knyght,* edited by WILLIAM RASTELL, London, 1557.

EW 1931   *The English Works of Sir Thomas More,* edited by W. E. CAMPBELL and A. W. REED, London, 1931.

HARPSFIELD   *The Life and Death of Sr. Thomas Moore, Knight,* edited by ELSIE VAUGHAN HITCHCOCK, London, 1932.

Hist. Pass.   *St Thomas More's History of the Passion,* edited by P. E. HALLETT, London, 1941.

Moreana   *Moreana: Bulletin Thomas More,* a quarterly of the Association: *Amici Thomae Mori,* Angers, France, 1963–

Op. Om.   *Thomae Mori, Angliae quondam cancellarii opera omnia,* Frankfurt, 1689.

Resp.   *A Translation of St Thomas More's Responsio ad Lutherum,* translated by Sister GERTRUDE JOSEPH DONNELLY, Washington D.C., 1962.

REYNOLDS   *Saint Thomas More,* New York, 1958.

REYNOLDS, *The Trial*
      The Trial of St Thomas More, London, 1964.

ROPER   *The Life of Sir Thomas More, Knighte,* edited by ELSIE VAUGHAN HITCHCOCK, London, 1935.

SL   *St Thomas More: Selected Letters,* edited ELIZABETH FRANCES ROGERS, New Haven, 1961.

STAPLETON   *The Life and Illustrious Martyrdom of Sir Thomas More*, translated by
              P. E. HALLETT, London, 1928.
Ut.   *The Complete Works of St Thomas More*, vol. 4, *Utopia*, edited by EDWARD
              SURTZ S.J. and J. H. HEXTER, New Haven, 1965.

INTRODUCTION

That a great public servant should be put to death for treason is irony enough, but that he should be canonized for it requires explanation. Such is the challenge we take up when we look for loyalty in Sir Thomas More – a man listed among those beheaded as traitors on Tower Hill. Four hundred years later, he was enrolled among the saints. Normally it is possible for a Christian to obey both God and Caesar (Mk. 12:13–17), but, being human, Caesar sometimes errs, and this can present a dilemma. The object of this thesis will be to study the policy More adopted when he found himself confronted with conflicting demands on his loyalty. It is a theme which hitherto has not been studied in detail on a theological level.

More has always been popular. Especially today many feel the attractions of this towering figure, this mundane saint and martyr. The fact of a huge revival in the study of his life and works – a revival of such proportions that it has been termed 'a Morean Renaissance' – is indicative of his relevance to our own day. Interest in More is shown by the following facts: for the first time ever the whole of More's works, both Latin and English, are being published in a single series by Yale University. In 1965 three independent editions of *Utopia* were published in English, as well as the *Dialogue of Comfort* in a double format to cater for the student and the ordinary reader. *Moreana*, the organ of the association, *Amici Thomae Mori*, issued quarterly from its centre at Angers, France, gives overwhelming evidence of unparalleled activity in this field. In yet another area, there has been the immense success of Robert Bolt's drama, *A Man for All Seasons*, which has brought More very much into the public eye.

What is the reason for this great interest? The question leaves room for speculation. The programme of religious renewal envisaged by the Christian humanists was interrupted by the Reformation. Their apparent lack of success, together with the reluctance of many to accept change, provoked the more drastic methods of the early Protestants. There followed the lamentable fragmentation of Christianity which our own age finds such a scandal. There has been recently a greater appreciation of the ideals of the humanists: the return to the sources, the stress on positive theology, the scientific study of Scripture and the Fathers, the suspension of remote speculation, the study of secular culture in order to understand and express better the content of Revelation. By the beginning of the sixteenth century the 'new learning' was making considerable headway. In the forefront of the movement was Thomas More. Even

21

in the realm of spirituality the humanists had something to offer to the modern world. Erasmus in particular outlined a way of life with a simple biblical basis that was intended for the Christian in the world[1] – a lay spirituality, even a spirituality of marriage and the family. The sanctification of the secular, which was proposed by Erasmus, was effected by More.

Biographies of More are easily obtainable, so it will be unnecessary to give many details. The sources for this thesis are More's own writings, as well as those of his contemporaries in so far as they shed light on More's thought. (See Bibliography).

The canonization of Thomas More attests authentically for a Catholic that he achieved heroic sanctity by his acceptance of martyrdom. How he developed to this height of perfection is a study in Spiritual Theology, and it is in this section of Theology that I present this thesis. Spiritual Theology has been defined as a theological discipline which is founded on the principles of divine revelation and the experience of the saints; it studies the organism of the spiritual life and the consciousness which we have of it; it explains the laws of its progress and evolution; it describes the process which souls follow from the beginning of the Christian life right up to the summit of perfection.[2] The experience of the saints is a source peculiar to this branch of theology: hence this thesis legitimately considers not only More's doctrine, but also his experience, and his consciousness of the spiritual conflict in his life, particularly at the end. However, neither space nor time allows a full treatment of More's spirituality. It is a subject with many fascinating aspects. So we must limit ourselves: we must choose one facet and resist all others. The garden-paradise of More's soul is full of trees laden with enticing fruits, but for us they are all forbidden. We must seek the tree of life that stands in the midst of the garden. We must find a central theme which will limit our inquiry, yet give it meaning.

Beginning from the obvious fact that More was a lawyer, one is led to suspect that law played a part in his spiritual life. Moreover, even a superficial knowledge of his history reveals a strong sense of duty. His readiness to die rather than yield on a matter of principle bespeaks a devotion which is heroic. A man so devoted to law and duty is a loyal man. If More was such, it is a safe guess that the concept of loyalty will be a profitable vein in the voluminous output of his pen.

What precisely do we mean by loyalty? It is a complex notion which includes the ideas of obedience, devotion to duty, fidelity.[3] It is a natural virtue which can be elevated by grace. In one of his books, E. E. Reynolds states that the old Roman virtue of *pietas* was strong in More as evidenced by his relations

1. Especially in *Enchiridion Militis Christiani* (1503) and *Christiani matrimonii institutio* (1526).
2. Cf. ANTONIO ROYO MARIN O.P., *Teologia de la perfección cristiana*, B.A.C. 4th. ed., Madrid, 1962, p. 34.
3. The *Concise Oxford Dictionary* defines 'loyal': 'True, faithful, to duty, love, or obligation; faithful in allegiance to sovereign, government, or mother-country', and 'loyalty' as 'Loyal temper or conduct'. See also JEAN TONNEAU O.P., 'Devoir', in *DSAM*, Tome III, coll. 653–672; PIERRE ADNES S.J., 'Fidelite', ibid. Tome V, coll. 307–332.

with his father, his family, and his prince.[4] However, the English word 'piety' has a different meaning. 'Loyalty' has the sense I seek, providing it is given a Christian dimension.

In the first chapter of my thesis I deal with More's description of the historical phases of law, particularly in relation to religion. In the second chapter I deal with his idea and practice of duty – the concrete application of obligation in particular cases. In the third chapter I treat of the great problem of conflicting laws and duties which brought about his downfall and finally his execution.

The lesson of Christian loyalty is relevant to our day. There is a tendency nowadays to minimize law, to extol freedom, to despise what is of obligation. St Thomas More was confronted with similar ideas. He was an intelligent and holy man, and his opinion will therefore be of interest to us.

The task I set myself, therefore, was to discover the extent to which the concept of loyalty played a conscious part in More's spiritual life. The indulgent reader is invited to cross the threshold and judge the results for himself.

4. *Thomas More and Erasmus*, London 1965, pp. 21, 116.

CHAPTER I

MORE'S CONCEPT OF LAW

According to its etymology, the word 'loyalty' is derived ultimately from the Latin word *lex* through the French *loi*. But the connexion between 'loyalty' and 'law' is not merely nominal; the dictionary definition of 'loyalty' contains the idea of obedience to law. If even this general notion of loyalty denotes a relationship with law, we will expect that the nexus between the two terms will be more pronounced in a lawyer, especially in an outstanding one such as St Thomas More, who rose through the ranks of legal practice and administration to the very summit of his profession. To obtain an adequate appreciation of the virtue of Christian loyalty in this man, it is necessary to understand how he himself conceived the idea of law. With this object, we will consider first More's division and description of law; then we will investigate the reasons why man should obey law; then the relation of law and conscience, and finally the question of the balance of law and freedom. The overall result of this chapter will be an understanding of the attitude that St Thomas More had to law.

ARTICLE I

THE HISTORICAL PHASES OF LAW

Among the writings of St Thomas More there is no treatise which discusses law in the philosophical or theological manner of the Schools, and consequently there is no analysis of the concept of law into the usual divisions, although of course he was familiar with them.[1] More dealt with law in his books when he was provoked to do so by a particular situation, in *Utopia*, for example, because of the unjust conditions under which many lived at the time, and in his controversial works because of the new theology of law put forward by the Protestant Reformers. In these works, More described law in its various historical phases, so it will be convenient to divide our material accordingly and it will also provide an approach to the subject in harmony with that of More himself.

A The Beginning of Law

Historically, law came into human society at the very beginning when God first spoke to His human creatures at their creation. More describes the primitive

---

1. *Corr.* 493.

law under which our first parents and the patriarchs lived in his *Apology:* '. . . at our creation He gave but two precepts or three, by His own holy mouth to our first parents.'[2] He also implanted reason in man's mind so that they had sufficient warning of their other obligations. The knowledge of the primitive revelation was passed from generation to generation, from father to child. The content of revelation was increased and clarified as time went on: men were told of a future Redeemer, they were given special messages concerning God's will in matters which nature and reason could not tell them. Most of these revealed commands were written in Scripture, but probably not all of them.

Even before the coming of Christ man had knowledge of divine sanctions, of the immortality of the soul, of reward and punishment, and even of Purgatory, by reason alone.[3]

B The Mosaic Law

The next phase in the development of law was the period in the history of the Chosen People under the law of Moses. More's comments are usually comparisons with the New Law to which it is inferior. 'The law of Moses', says Hythlodaeus in the *Utopia*, was '. . . severe and harsh, being intended for slaves, and those a stubborn breed.'[4] Later, in his *Dialogue concerning Heresies*, More declares that the Ten Commandments were given to the Jews because their passions had obscured the law of reason. The other prescriptions of the Old Law were to keep them from straying off the path upon which God had set them: this is the reason for the 'great heap of laws and ceremonies' that affected their lives in such detail. The Church buried the ceremonies of the Jews' synagogue with honour and reverence.[5]

C The Law of Christ

In his *Utopia* More described the spirit of the Gospel through the mouth of Hythlodaeus as the new law of mercy in which God gives commands as a father to his sons.[6] In comparison with the Old Law, the law of Christ is characterized by a more intimate and personal relationship with God the Father. The prophet Jeremy had foretold the inner nature of the New Law: 'I shall give My law in their minds, and I shall write it in their heart.'[7] This was fulfilled by our Saviour Christ who redeemed us and left us his new law. More argued from the personal nature of the Gospel law to the convenience of a living witness, so that it is something more than what is written in the books of

2. *Apol.* 274.
3. *EW* 315.
4. *Ut.* 73. Hythlodaeus is a fictitious traveller who has just returned from the newly discovered island of Utopia which is of course also only a product of More's imagination.
5. *EW* 307; *EW 1931* II, 94.
6. *Ut.* 74.
7. *EW* 307.

the evangelists: it is the substance of our faith, written in men's hearts by the operation of God and His Holy Spirit which brings man to justification. The first communication of the New Law, after all, was not made in writing: in fact it seems to have been made even without words, as for example when St Peter received the knowledge of heavenly mysteries not from flesh and blood but by secret inspiration of the Father. 'And so it was convenient for the law of life rather to be written in the lively minds of men than in the dead skins of beasts.' [8]

In conjunction with 'the secret inspiration of God' there was the activity of Christ himself through his preaching 'by His blessed mouth through the ears of His apostles.' [9] Not all of this oral deposit of Christ was written in the Scriptures. To prove this point, More argues that individual evangelists omit important doctrines, so it is probable that something important was not recorded by any of them. He argues also from various texts of the New Testament itself, viz. John 16:12–13; 20:25; I Cor. 11:34. [10]

The law of Christ is contained in both Scripture and Tradition. As a Christian humanist, More was an ardent advocate of the study of the original sources of Catholic doctrine, the Bible and the Fathers. He was a keen supporter of Erasmus in his work of editing the Greek New Testament and of giving a fresh translation into Latin. [11] He also advocated the publication of authorised vernacular Bibles. [12] He condemned theologians who never condescend to search the Scriptures. For More, the Bible is 'the venerable queen of all letters', and 'the very lovely, wholesome meadow' through which one may stroll leisurely from beginning to end with profit. [13] But the chief reason for More's devotion to Scripture is that it is the primary source whence one can discover the New Law of Christ, by which we are saved. This is why Holy Scripture is the highest and best learning that any man can have, 'if one take the right way in the learning.' [14]

After the Scriptures the next source of knowledge of the law of Christ is 'their ancient interpreters' whom More quotes frequently as 'the old holy doctors'. The Fathers are to be taken as a moral unity because individual Fathers could err and in fact did. [15] More himself had a wide knowledge of the writings of the Fathers. As a young man he lectured on St Augustine's *City of God* 'to his no small commendation, and to the great admiration of all his audience'. [16] His familiarity with patristic writings is evidenced by the fact that in his *Dialogue concerning Heresies*, for example, he quotes as authorities Origen,

8. Ibid. 95.
9. Ibid. 95.
10. *EW* 459; TAFT'S notes in *Apol.* 277.
11. Letter to Dorp, *SL* no. 4, Especially p. 42 ff.
12. *EW* 241–6.
13. *SL* 28, 33, 35.
14. *SL* 36–7; *EW* 162–3.
15. *SL* 36–7.
16. HARPSFIELD, 13.

Cyprian, Lactantius, Eusebius, Basil, Gregory Nazianzen, Ambrose, John Chrysostom, Jerome, Augustine, Cassian, and Gregory the Great.[17]

More's notion of tradition includes also the ordinary living practice of the faith, 'the common practice handed down from the early Fathers.'[18]

The law of Christ is propounded unerringly by the Church. It can be known first from the ordinary teaching and reception of doctrine among its members, secondly by the Church's magisterial pronouncements.[19] When we deal with the subject of the formation of conscience we shall see that for More one of the norms for its formation is the teaching of the universal Church, especially in the decisions of a General Council. For the moment we prescind from purely ecclesiastical law and consider the Church's function in relation to the deposit of faith.

In reply to the Protestants, More concedes that Christ could have arranged matters so that each person might come to a knowledge of the truth by interior inspiration. But as a matter of fact, God gave the charge of teaching to the Church and whoever condemns it in favour of his own ideas is deluding himself that he is singularly favoured by God in opposition to the Church.[20] In this present dispensation by the positive will of God the Church is necessary to interpret Scripture and Tradition. It is the Church's task, in the first place, to determine the canon of Scripture, and she carries this out with the assurance of God's guidance, thereby exercising her infallibility in one of the most fundamental questions of the whole of our religion: it is 'one of the great foundations of all Christian faith'.[21] Even when the canon has been fixed, there remains the question of interpretation, especially in the case of difficult books such as the Apocalypse, 'the book sealed with the seven seals . . . which the Lamb seals and no one opens'.[22] Not that the Church must interpret every point of Scripture, but only those 'concerning some necessary point of our faith'.[23] Even Christ did not interpret the whole of the Bible for the Apostles either personally or through the Holy Spirit after his Ascension.[24] But Christ promised to be with his Church till the end of the world, so that as the requirements of history demand, the Church under his guidance avoids error, interprets Scripture and distinguishes Tradition. Christ remains faithful to his promise to be with the Church in spite of the sins she may commit: he does not disown her 'because of the cockle flourishing amidst the wheat in this the growing time.' The net remains Christ's even when it holds bad fish. The Church is his Spouse; she sins, but she is chastened; he watches over her so that she will not fall into the

17. G. KERNAN, 'St Thomas More, Theologian', *Thought* vol. XVII, June 1942, 291.
18. *SL* 36.
19. For notion of *ecclesia discens* and *ecclesia docens* see *EW* 633; also WILLIS J. EGAN, *The Rule of Faith in St Thomas More's Controversy with William Tyndale 1528–1533*, Los Angeles, 1960, 66.
20. *Resp.* 194; *CWR* 205.
21. *EW* 170, 319.
22. *SL* 33.
23. *EW* 170.
24. *SL* 34.

fornication of false worship. Through the Spirit of Truth, he cherishes and instructs her so that she will not err in faith.[25]

To exercise her function as the permanent and infallible teacher of Christ's law, the Church must be distinguishable from false teachers: she is a visible Church, or as More calls her, 'a known church'; she is founded by Christ on the Apostles, governed by his Vicar, the successor of St Peter,[26] and remarkable for the unity of her faith. More describes this unity as a distinguishing mark of the true Church, the Mystical Body of Christ. That Church is the Catholic Church 'be it never so sick, whereof the principal Head is Christ'. God provided that we would have security in our faith, and the proof of His fidelity is found in the unity of Catholics which can be attributed to the work of the Holy Spirit who animates the Body and inspires the members to consent together to all necessary truths. So the Church may be found with ease and her judgments on truth and error may be accepted with confidence.[27]

The 'obedience of belief' which the Christian owes to Christ and his Church is seen by More as a suitable balance to the 'disobedience of God with inordinate desire of knowledge like unto God' of our first parents:[28]

> God hath ever kept man in humility, straining him with the knowledge
> of confession of his ignorance, and binding him to the obedience of
> belief of certain things whereof his own wit would verily ween the
> contrary.

Heretics, says More, are guilty of disobedience because of their pride. But they are building a Tower of Babel which will lead to dissension and division, so that their falsity is evident to all: '. . . the damned devil of hell . . . so entangleth their tongues and so distempereth their brains, that they neither understand well one of them another, nor any of them well himself.'[29]

Although charity is the badge of Christians, it should not be concluded that true jurisdiction does not exist in the Church. All jurisdiction in the Church arises from charity, but this does not mean that authority in the Church is nothing else but fraternal charity. There is real authority of a public nature in the Church as in civil society, and whoever resists it resists an ordinance of God. More proves this from the fact that Christ himself taught obedience to the 'Scribes and Pharisees sitting on the Chair of Moses'; he exercised it himself when he cast the money-changers out of the temple; the very words of Christ, 'Feed my sheep', denote real authority as the Greek verb of the Gospel means 'to govern'.[30]

25. *Resp.* 149, 195–6; *CWR* 117, 205–7.
26. *EW* 185.
27. Ibid. 527–8; KERNAN, op. cit., 299–300; Abbé GERMAIN MARC'HADOUR, 'St Thomas More', *The Month*, vol. 29, no. 2, 1963, 4, note 4: 'More's intense devotion to the Mystical Body is undoubtedly the most striking feature in his own spiritual portrait and the central piece of his doctrinal construction.'
28. *EW 1931* II, 112.
29. *Apol.* 44–5; for full treatment of distinguishing the true church from false ones see *EW* 177–185.
30. *Resp.* 189; *CWR* 197.

The concept of the law of Christ outlined in the above paragraphs contains elements which are to be blended into a harmonious whole. For the humanists the truth lay in moderation and balance. The promise of Christ to send the Paraclete concerned an interior operation: 'He will guide you, that is, he will mould you within, and with his breath he will direct your hearts to all truth.' But his witnesses are to be public figures: Christ spoke to his Apostles when he said: 'I am with you to the consummation of the world',[31] that is he spoke to the official teaching Church.

D The Law of Christendom

Christ gave to his Church the power of making laws. The laws made and accepted in the Church constitute, in More's terminology, the law of Christendom.

In the early Church the Apostles collectively and individually made laws. For example, the Apostles gathered at the Council of Jerusalem made laws under the guidance of the Spirit to regulate the practices of gentile converts. St Paul by himself devised for the Corinthians laws for the ordering of their church services. Moreover, lest anyone dispute the wisdom of his directions, he used his authority and silenced opposition.[32]

More attributed to St Peter a special place in the Church as constituted by Christ: he was the 'stone' upon which it was built. Commenting on Peter's action in cutting off the ear of the High Priest's servant, More takes the opportunity of putting advice for Peter into Christ's mouth: Christ is loath that Peter should fight with the temporal sword; Peter may use two spiritual swords: one is the 'terrible and dangerous sword of excommunication' which he should always keep 'within the scabbard of mercy and pity, till an urgent and wondrous necessary cause enforce [him] to draw it out'; but Peter is to bestir himself valiantly in wielding his principal weapon, 'the sword of God's word' which can be as salutary as a lancing knife.[33]

On his own admittance, More's opinion concerning the origin of the Pope's Primacy evolved during his controversies. He had apparently been of the opinion that it was of merely human institution, but when the subject came under keener discussion he gave the matter deeper thought and concluded that it was a continuation of the office of Peter with the same divine authority. In 1534 he wrote to the King's secretary, Thomas Cromwell, saying how Henry himself had brought the matter to his attention. The King had been writing his book against Luther, the *Assertio septem sacramentorum*, in which he strenuously argued to the divine institution of the Roman Primacy. More's first reaction had been to advise the King 'either to leave out that point, or else to

31. *Resp.* 140; *CWR* 101.
32. *Apol.* 112–3.
33. *Hist. Pass.* 104.

touch it more slenderly' because of the possibility of future conflicts with the Pope, who was also a secular prince. His Grace had refused to make the change, thereby influencing More to give closer study to the subject. Having read the writings of the Fathers and the decrees of the Councils, More realized that he could not in conscience 'deny the primacy to be provided by God'.[34] Nevertheless, although these proofs were certain as far as he was concerned, he realized that they were not universally accepted, especially since the doctrine had not as yet been defined. But even so, he argued, the primacy was at least 'ordained by the Church' and therefore must be accepted in practice. It is surprising for us to find that More thought that the Pope was subject to a General Council: one Pope could be deposed and another substituted in his place. It is also interesting that More pointed out that there is no necessary link between the Holy See and the city of Rome. Everyone knows, he says, that it was once in a different place. In His providence, God seems to have chosen Rome 'as the most celebrated spot in all the world', but it does not follow that it must always be there: 'wherever the Chair of Peter is transferred, to that spot also is transferred his authority.'[35]

Both in his *Responsio* and his letter to Bugenhagen, More argued that the unworthiness of some few Popes does not imply necessarily that the office itself is bad. Good Christians should pray that God will raise up Popes who befit the dignity of the Apostolic office: men who despise riches and honour, who will promote piety and peace among the people and exercise their authority against the oppressors of the weak.

A General Council not only declares authentically the law of Christ but is also the supreme authority in ecclesiastical law. We will see later, for example, how much More adhered to the decrees of a Council in carrying out the suppression of heresy.

The other members of the clergy, the Bishops taken individually and the priests, have their authority from God through the medium of the Church, and also 'by the grant of kings and princes'. And because they have the assistance of the Holy Spirit, as Christ promised, 'men ought with reverence, and without resistance, grudge, or argument to receive them'.[36]

More also attributed the force of law to custom in ecclesiastical matters.[37]

E The Law of the Land

When More dealt with civil law he had in mind the concrete codes of life adopted in the various countries that made up Christendom until the outbreak of the Reformation. It was assumed that these countries were based on Christian principles, that they recognized officially the law of Christ and the fact that all

34. *SL* 212.
35. *SL* 213–4; *Resp.* 175; *CWR* 167.
36. *Apol.* 112–3.
37. Ibid. 118; *Op. Om.* 99; *CWR* 415.

belonged to the family of nations which made 'up the corps of Christendom':[38]

> And therefore sith all Christendom is one corps, I cannot perceive
> how any member thereof may without the common consent of the
> body depart from the common head.

Even when More discussed the laws drawn up by his Utopians by the unaided efforts of reason, he had in mind a comparison with existing conditions in Christian countries. In many respects the Utopians were *naturaliter Christiani* and their rather orthodox religion played the predominant role in their concept of law.

The *Utopia* was More's first attempt to evaluate the wisdom of contemporary laws by contrasting prevailing conditions and social evils with the peace and prosperity of an imagined island inhabited by pagans.[39] We must hasten to add that More himself did not necessarily subscribe to the legal system of his creatures. Their extreme views were meant to instigate thought and discussion so that the purpose of law would be understood and so that current laws could be judged in a clearer light. The perennial debate concerning the book is the question of how much More meant to be taken seriously and how much was merely satire.[40] The book has been a success because it achieved what its author intended: it has caused endless discussion because More asked the right questions.

The teachings of Luther and Tyndale also occasioned remarks from More on the nature of civil law. More of course was not a sympathetic reader of either of these thinkers, and did not pretend that he could see any sense in the Lutheran paradox of freedom and law, or any consistency in Tyndale's rejection of Church authority and exaggeration of royal authority.[41] As far as he was concerned, Luther's concept of freedom undermined all authority, both of Church and State, and the upheavals in Germany were the logical outcome of his heresy. Tyndale's distinction was invalid because the authority of the Church came from God as did the State's: the rejection of the former would ultimately lead to the collapse of the latter.

When More himself discussed the moral obligation of the law of the land, he gave much the same answer as would at least some Catholic moralists. All civil laws bind 'upon some temporal pain', and many bind 'upon pain of God's displeasure too'. This seems to imply that in More's opinion some laws were merely penal. However, he gives no examples or principles for deciding.[42]

In the *Utopia* More suggests that laws should not be endlessly multiplied.

---

38. *SL* 213.
39. A recent critique by DANIEL-ROPS, 'Thomas More, Planiste de l'*Utopie*', *Moreana,* no. 6, May 1965, 5–8.
40. The *Utopia* was taken so seriously that it was used as a practical handbook in a Mexican settlement, and was put onto the Index in Spain; see FRANCISCO LOPEZ ESTRADA, Santo Tomas Moro en España y en la America hispana', *Moreana* no. 5, Feb. 1965, 29.
41. RICHARD C. MARIUS, review of *England's Earliest Protestants*, by WILLIAM A. CLESCH, *Moreana* no. 6, May 1965, 69–76.
42. *Corr.* 524.

The Utopians have few laws, while other countries have 'almost innumerable books of laws and commentaries' which are still not sufficient. They consider it unfair that people should be bound by laws which are so numerous and so obscure that they cannot understand them. Such laws also make it possible for clever lawyers to manipulate cases and quibble about fine points. By contrast the Utopians forbid anyone to practise as a lawyer: each man argues his own case, with the result that there is better hope of arriving at the truth.[43] Luther had perhaps read the *Utopia*,[44] and one wonders if it influenced his opinion that after the advent of the Gospel detailed laws should be unneccessary because good and honest magistrates would be sufficient to administer justice. His remark brought out More's real opinion: citing Aristotle as his authority, he points out the wisdom of making laws as detailed as possible. In the first place, laws are drawn up at the discretion of many wise legislators, not just by one particular judge. The more definite they are, the less is left to the discretion of the individual judge. Moreover, clear laws are a shield to the judges themselves because they can point to them to show that their verdicts are based on law and are not the result of personal animosity. Even after the reception of the Gospel, laws are still necessary. If the law of the Gospel forbids theft, the human law which punishes it is useful. Moreover, some things are not settled by the Gospel, such as the division of property according to fixed convention. More knew human nature well from his long practice as a lawyer and a judge, and he remained too much of a realist to agree with Luther that crime would stop if society did away with laws and kept only the Gospel as its legal code.[45]

As we would expect in a man of his character and position, More was always anxious to eliminate bad laws and promote good ones. In *Utopia* Hythlodaeus bitterly attacks the social evils resulting from defective legislation and passionately urges reform. He pleads for the prevention of monopolies, for the sharing of ownership among the people: a system of justice that can only boast that it punishes crime while not touching the causes is not real justice but a sham. More returned to the same theme years later when writing his *Dialogue of Comfort:* he criticises severely legislators whose target is small criminals or even the innocent while the worst malefactors escape like bumble bees breaking through cobweb but little gnats and flies get caught. Laws are meant to protect the innocent, not to wound them.[46]

In the criticism of already existing laws, More advised caution and discretion. *Utopia* itself was written in Latin and was never published in English during More's life-time. It was intended as a thought-provoking essay to be read by the educated audience of international scholars, and was certainly not calculated to stir up revolt among the populace. The danger of tumult was the very thing that More objected to in his *Apology* in which he attacked the

43. *Ut.* 195.
44. Germain Marc'Hadour, *L'Universe de Thomas More*, Paris, 1963, 261.
45. *EW 1931* II, 188; *Resp.* 231; *CWR* 275-7.
46. *Ut.* 69; *Dial. of Comf.* 289.

anonymous author (now known to have been the lawyer, Christopher St German) who had published two pamphlets, *Spirituality and Temporality*, and *Salem and Bizance*, in which he called for reform in the law regarding the trial of heretics and other procedures especially those involving the clergy. In his reply, More sets out his principles for bringing about changes in law, and discusses the important point of a subject's reaction to a law repugnant to the law of God. He was prepared to defend publicly already existing laws if he thought them good, but if he thought them 'nought' he would give his advice and counsel in favour of a change, not publicly, but 'in place and time convenient': he certainly would not 'put out books in writing abroad among the people against them' as the 'Pacifier' (St German) had done. If certain laws are not against the law of God, even though they could be improved, it is better to offer advice quietly in the right quarters and to endure them till a change is made, rather than stir up trouble publicly and bring the law under which people live into derision. After all, the 'reformer' may well be quite wrong himself. If a particular law were against God's law to the extent that to observe it would endanger one's salvation, even then it is better to avoid causing chaos and sedition by keeping one's advice for discrete discussion. [47]

At this point we can consider More's attitude to the king, the head of state, who initiated legislation in the English Parliament and who was the highest authority in the administration of law. Was More an absolute believer in the divine right of kings? [48] Or was he at heart a republican? [49] In his youth More gave a good deal of thought and emotion to the question of tyranny. Among the twenty-three Latin epigrams he wrote dealing with kings and government, his favourite concern is for the difference between a good king and a tyrant. A good king, he says, is a father, not a master; he is the head of his people; he is a sheep-dog, whilst a bad king is a wolf. [50] This pre-occupation with tyranny may have owed its origin to the impression made upon More's youthful mind by the former kings, Richard III and Henry VII. More's *History of Richard III* (written c. 1513–1518) was responsible for the unfavourable characterization of Richard found in Shakespeare's play which has become the traditionally accepted image of that monarch. [51] More seems to have incurred the displeasure of Henry VII, and on his death and the accession of his son, More, to mark the occasion, composed an epigram in which he expressed himself with daring frankness: 'This day is the limit of our slavery, the beginning of our freedom. [52]

47. *Apol.* 108.
48. REYNOLDS, *The Trial* 141.
49. *Epig.* xxvii; cf. PETER G. BIETENHOLZ, 'Erasmus' View of More', *Moreana no.* 5, Feb. 1965, 8.
50. *Epig.* 172–3.
51. W. GORDON ZEEVELD, review of More's *The History of King Richard III*, ed. RICHARD S. SYLVESTER, New Haven, 1963, in *Moreana* no. 1, Sep. 1963, 68; G. BULLOUGH (ed.), *Narrative and Dramatic Sources of Shakespeare*, London 1960, vol. III, 9: 'In this work (Richard III) . . . men saw a new combination of didactic principle and a sense of causation, human and divine, with orderliness, factual accuracy, and characterization.'
52. *Epig.* 138.

34

While he was still uninvolved in public affairs, More allowed himself the liberty of speculation in politics. In another epigram he asked: what is the best form of government?[53] The same question occupied him in *Utopia* (whose full title includes the words, 'the Best State of a Commonwealth'). The island is a representative democracy: the officials are elected annually, except for the head of state, the governor, who holds office for life 'unless ousted on suspicion of aiming at tyranny'. Speaking of kings in general, Hythlodaeus says that people choose a king for their own sake, and not for his; it is his duty to take more care for the welfare of his people than for his own.[54]

As he was drawn deeper into the responsibilities of high office, More gave up this theoretical speculation and confined himself to the task of making the machinery of the existing state function as it should. But he never changed his opinion that the king derives his authority, mediately indeed from God, but immediately from the people through their representatives in Parliament. This was commonly believed at the time: it was the premise of the whole conversation held between More and Rich in the Tower. More agreed that he would be bound to accept Rich as king if Parliament so decided.[55] We may conclude then that More was not a believer in absolute monarchy, even though he admitted that the authority of the head of state came indirectly from God. The selection of the ruler and his decisions are subject to a representative body, in the case of England, the Parliament. We may note a parallel between this and his opinion that the Pope is subject to a General Council.

No king has the right to give his country to the Pope, or even to allow the exaction of tribute from his people to the Pope. According to More, the collection of Peter's Pence was given by the English people to the Pope by way of gratitude and alms.[56]

ARTICLE II

REASONS FOR OBSERVING LAWS

A person living in a Christian country at the time of More would be bound by the law of reason, the law of Christ, the law of Christendom, and the law of the land. Since all these are ultimately founded on divine authority they form a unified body, and hence there can be a unity among the motives which will move a person to observe them. More has scattered references to motive throughout his works. This article is an attempt at systematizing this part of his thought.

Some of the motives suggested by More could be termed positive, others negative. The positive ones are the goods to be obtained by observing law; the

53. Ibid. 204.
54. *Ut.* 123, 95.
55. W. E. CAMPBELL, *Erasmus, Tyndale and More*, London 1949, 255.
56. *EW* 296.

negative are the evils that are incurred by breaking law. Some of these motives, both positive and negative, arise from temporal considerations, others from considerations of eternity.

The temporal end of law is to provide an order in which man may lead a life in conformity with his dignity as a rational being, and in a Christian state as a member of the Mystical Body. Normally this will imply a state of peace, a sufficiency of goods, and freedom to fulfil one's duty to God and man. A just social order will permit and encourage man to develop all his faculties, especially his intellect. This is one of the main topics brought up for discussion in *Utopia*.

The Utopians debate the question as to what it is that constitutes a happy life. They rather incline to the view that happiness is to be found in pleasure – not in every type of pleasure, but only in that which is good and decent according to the dictates of reason, and above all they place the pleasures of the mind. Authors agree that their moral philosophy was a form of hedonism. [57]

More's view is not necessarily the same as the Utopians, but there is an indication of his opinion, not so much in the details, but in the overall effect of the book. Remembering that he is contrasting Utopia with existing conditions, we can see that he is criticizing the state of affairs prevailing in Europe, especially in England. He is advocating laws which will ensure employment for all; he is advocating the rationalization of labour, the sharing of wealth and leisure and universal education. The laws of Utopia were not necessarily meant to be a solution: they were an example designed to promote questions concerning the purpose of human society. The desire for the good life engenders a search for good laws and a motive for abiding by them.

The immortality of the soul induces man to look beyond death for further motives. The Utopians, even without the aid of revelation, were certain of this doctrine of the soul's immortality and believed also that human law would collapse if men did not believe it. They looked forward to the future life as a reward for fidelity to their Creator's will in this life. [58]

The Christian will observe law for the happiness of having a good conscience, for the hope of heaven, for the winning of Christ. But the highest motive of all will be that of disinterested love of God. [59]

By negative motives, we mean the fear of punishments, human and divine. Again in *Utopia* there is a questioning of the purpose of penal law and a plea for a rational gradation of punishment. Hythlodaeus complains of the severity of current laws, for example the hanging of thieves, especially because many are deprived of the opportunity of making an honest living. Moreover, he argues, it is bad policy to have the same penalty for theft as for murder: instead of merely robbing his victim, a robber will be induced to kill him, since, if he is caught, the penalty is no greater, and the chances of his being captured are less

57. *Ut.* 161–3. See Index for references to *hedonism*.
58. *Ut.* 163.
59. *Corr.* 509; *English Prayers*, 18.

because the principal witness is out of the way. Hythlodaeus points out too that the commandment, 'Thou shalt not kill', applies to the State as well as to individuals. If the State makes exceptions to that command, what stops it from going further and allowing rape, adultery and perjury? It is different where God Himself has set a precedent, but God nowhere allowed the death penalty for theft. The law of Moses, he continues, punished theft by fine, not by death, so surely in the new law of mercy Christian brethren, children of a common Father, should not be more cruel to one another. [60]

In Utopia there are no fixed penalties for most crimes: the judges consider each case on its merits. But there are rather severe penalties stipulated for a few crimes: e.g. relapsed adulterers and uncontrollable prisoners are put to death; slavery with hard labour is mandatory for adultery on the first offence. [61]

More himself does not question the benefit of reasonable punishment. Punishment can be salutary: a kind father will chastise his child for his correction. Moreover, the punishment of criminals will deter others from committing crime. More justified the punishment by death of heretics whom he considered the worst criminals of all because they brought men to temporal and eternal ruin. Such executions were necessary to rid society of a great evil, to deter others and as retribution that would be followed by the eternal punishments of God. [62]

Man ought also obey law from the fear of divine retribution. The Utopians feared the wrath of God. More believed that God punishes sin even in this life, but mercy tempers justice: just as He rewards us above our merits, He punishes us far below what we deserve. More had a very real belief in Purgatory which made him desire to do his penance on earth and to avoid sin so as to minimize the time he would have to spend in its flames. [63]

Hell too played an important part in More's motivation. About 1522 he wrote *The Four Last Things* for the spiritual benefit of his family. In the *Dialogue of Comfort* too he gives a vivid description of the pains of hell: [64]

> . . . . . your soul first, and after that at the final judgment, your body
> too be driven down deep toward the centre of the earth into the fiery
> pit and dungeon of the devil of hell, there to tarry in torment world
> without end.

All the pleasures of this world would not compensate for one hour of hell, let alone an eternity.

There is copious evidence in More's writings that he recommended the motives I have outlined, and that he used them himself. Because of man's weakness and the gravity of the temptations to which he is subject, wisdom dictates that he make use of all motives which will help him to be a law abiding

---

60. *Ut.* 61, 73–4.
61. *Ut.* 191 ff.
62. *EW* 326; the prosecution of heretics is treated below.
63. *Dial. of Comf.* 297; *English Prayers* 13, 21; *EW* 314.
64. *Dial. of Comf.* 297.

Christian. The gradation n More's own motives s shown in the following prayer: [65]

> Give me, good Lord, a longing to be with Thee, not for the avoiding of the calamities of this wretched world, nor so much for the avoiding of the pains of purgatory, nor of the pains of hell neither, nor so much for the attaining of the joys of heaven in respect of my own commodity, as even for a very love of Thee.

ARTICLE III

THE INNER LAW OF CONSCIENCE

The question of conscience did not receive detailed attention from More until he himself was a conscientious objector to the divorce proceedings of the King. During the last two years of his life the term 'conscience' is mentioned frequently in his writings, especially in his letters. From these sources we can discover his thought on the nature of conscience. We will consider it under the two principal headings of its formation and its examination.

A The Formation of Conscience

1. Individual Responsibility

St Thomas More pointed out again and again that he, and he alone, was responsible before God for the stand he had taken on the Oath of Succession and the Act of Supremacy. In a matter involving his eternal salvation he would rely on no one else and in turn would not accept the responsibility of the salvation of others. Admittedly the situation was rather extraordinary and unusual factors were involved, but they helped to bring out the basic issues.

More would not take the oath because his conscience would not allow him to do so. On the other hand, he did not blame others who took the oath, he did not doubt their sincerity or criticize their learning. He would answer to God for his own soul, but for no one else's. [66]

The individual's responsibility is brought out very clearly in the conversation between More and his daughter Margaret, and recorded by her. Perhaps the dialogue was deliberately staged to give More the opportunity of answering the objections which people were making to him and members of his family. Margaret put a series of suggestions to her father and recorded his answers. Some people, she began, were saying that he was blindly following the lead of Bishop Fisher. More replied that although he considered the Bishop the most

65. *English Prayers* 18.
66. *SL* 232–3.

38

learned and virtuous man in the realm, he was not merely imitating him, as appeared from the fact that he had clearly refused the oath before it was offered to the Bishop, and the Bishop had proposed to take the oath in another form which was different from the form More was willing to use. The following words bring out More's determined independence:[67]

> Verily, daughter, I never intend (God being my good Lord) to pin my soul at another man's back, not even the best man that I know this day living: for I know not whither he may hap to carry it.

Margaret then put it to her father that he would be justified in taking the oath because nearly everyone else had taken it. Such a reason More replied, would not help him before God. He told her the story of the dissenting juryman who would not agree with the other jurymen for the sake of 'good fellowship' just as he would not expect them, for the sake of fellowship, to accompany him to hell to which he would be condemned for voting against his conscience. Margaret protested that she meant he could follow the example of the others, not merely to keep them company, but because they were wise and virtuous. But even this consideration, said More, would not absolve him from a personal decision especially since he was well instructed in the issues involved. Margaret pressed her point by adding that the men she was talking of were not merely private individuals, but they constituted Parliament, which More was bound to obey. More replied: some laws of the land bind only under 'temporal pain' although others bind 'upon pain of God's displeasure'. But, he went on, this does not mean a man must swear that any point of the law 'is well made', nor may a man keep a law which is 'unlawful' (i.e. before God).[68] So the individual is not free to follow blindly the legislation of Parliament, but must exercise his own critical judgment concerning its morality.

2. According to Reason and Faith.

From the very beginning of his conflict with the law, More made it clear that his conscientious objections were based, not on some vague feeling nor mere stubbornness, but on diligent research and deep reflection on the matter. When he first refused the oath at the palace of the Archbishop of Canterbury at Lambeth, he informed the Commissioners that he could not swear because in his conscience 'the truth seemed on the other side'. He had not formed his conscience 'suddenly nor slightly but by long leisure and diligent search for the matter'. More was aware he must make use of his learning to a degree in keeping with his intelligence and education: he described himself realistically as 'being at the leastwise somewhat learned'.[69]

In a letter to Margaret from the Tower, More described the conflict he was experiencing between the fear of death and his obligation:

---

67. *Corr.* 516.
68. *Corr.* 524.
69. *SL* 221; see also 210, 215, 220, 243, 244.

... in that conflict the Spirit had in conclusion the mastery and reason
with the help of faith finally concluded that for to be put to death
wrongfully for doing well ... it is a case in which a man may lose his
head and yet have none harm.

Elsewhere too he insists that where a man sees moral danger he is bound 'by
learning and good counsel' to form a certain conscience. [70]

As was expected, More was accused of being 'stubborn and obstinate'. We
will consider his answer in greater detail later. Suffice it to say that he claimed
his refusal to swear was based on a 'timorous conscience' and not 'of any
obstinate mind or misaffectionate appetite'. He claimed to have kept his mind
open to argument: his mind was 'as toward and as conformable as reason could
in a matter disputable require'. [71]

3. According to the Teaching of the Universal Church

When the possibility of a national independent English Church was first
discussed, More looked for a certain and objective norm of belief, and decided
that the most authentic guide in matters of faith was the teaching of the universal Church, particularly as declared in a General Council. Before the Act
of Succession was passed he wrote to Cromwell giving a thorough explanation
of his thought on the matter of the Pope's primacy. Then he went on to the
decisions of General Councils. The definitions of lawfully assembled councils
concerning 'truths to be believed and to be standen to .... ought to be taken
for undoubtable, or else were therein nothing no certainty'. If the authority of
Councils were overthrown, Christendom would be thrown into turmoil,
'continual ruffle and confusion', because everyone would be propounding his
own private opinion. [72]

More insisted continually that Christendom is one corps, it is kept in unity
by the Holy Spirit, and no one may lawfully abandon the faith of the universal
church. This was the argument he used several times against the objection that
he ought to conform to the law of Parliament which had the support of the
Lords (including the Bishops) and the Commons of the realm: 'I am not then
bounden to change my conscience and confirm it to the council of one realm,
against the general council of Christendom.' When later he refused to break his
silence concerning the King's Supremacy, he was accused of inconsistency
because he had, as Chancellor, allowed the Bishops to exact a precise answer
from heretics concerning the primacy of the Pope. In reply More observed
rather facetiously that Cromwell gave him great praise above his deserving.
But the cases were different, because 'as well here as elsewhere the Pope's power
was recognized for an undoubted thing which seemeth not like a thing agreed in
this realm and the contrary taken for truth in other realms'. [73] Again when

70. *Corr.* 542, 547.
71. *SL* 210.
72. *SL* 213.
73. *SL* 221–2; 251–2.

discharging his conscience after the verdict at the trial, he based his stand on 'the general law of Christ's universal Catholic Church'.[74]

4. Conscience and Salvation

The ultimate criterion for judging one's actions, in More's opinion, is whether one's conduct 'may stand with his salvation'. This formula he uses several times in his last letters, showing that he considered the correct formation of conscience on important matters to be vital for salvation. If a person has not certainty, he must form his conscience again 'by learning and good counsel'; he must ask for the grace to conform his mind unto the high pleasure of God.[75]

B The Examination of Conscience

The examinaton of conscience is the act of the intellect by which a person judges the morality of past actions. In a balanced mind the same criteria will be used as in the prior act of the formation of conscience. St Thomas More dealt briefly with the examination of conscience in his ascetical writings, for example in his *Treatise on the Holy Eucharist*. He understands St Paul's 'Let a man prove himself' as referring to an examination of one's state of soul. He adduces Scriptural authority to show it is 'not only right hard, but peradventure impossible' to have certainty concerning one's state of soul 'without special revelation of God'. He quotes St Paul again: 'In mine own conscience I know nothing, but yet am I not thereby justified.' Nevertheless, he goes on, God in His goodness is content 'if we do the diligence that we can'. If we have done our best in the search of our conscience, God will not impute to our charge 'any such secret lurking sin', and if we go to Communion the reception will not be unworthy, but the strength and virtue of the Sacrament 'purgeth and cleanseth the very soul'.[76]

Between his condemnation and his martyrdom, More composed *A Devout Prayer*, addressed to the Holy Trinity and asking mercy for his sins. He indicates the examination of conscience on particular points: 'In my childhood, in this point and that point, etc. After my childhood, in this point and that point, and so forth by every age, etc.' He asks for the grace to repent his sins 'and utterly to forsake them'. He then returns to the matter of forgotten and unrecognized sins. He indicates sorrow for such sins and for the fault of allowing one's reason to become so blinded with sensuality as not to discern them or to forget them.[77]

These extracts point to the fact that More's conscience was meticulously honest and discerning, but not scrupulous. Scrupulosity implies a lack of balance, of objectivity, and is frequently accompanied by a wrong concept of

74. HARPSFIELD, 193–4.
75. *Corr.* 547; cf. 528, 538, 559.
76. *English Prayers* 34–36.
77. Ibid. 15.

God's justice. More certainly saw the possibility of scruples, he had dealings with scrupulous people, he had great sympathy for their plight, but there is no proof that he himself ever gave way to unbalanced judgments. In the *Dialogue of Comfort* he goes into the subject of scruples in quite a lot of detail. This does not necessarily mean that he experienced them habitually: he was a man of wide experience of human nature and he had a lively imagination. In his writings he describes many situations, feelings, temptations, which he imagined, but of which he did not necessarily have first-hand experience. So it does not follow from his description of scruples that he was himself scrupulous. On the contrary, there is a mountain of evidence to show that More's judgment was habitually based on objective norms, and he believed God's justice would not demand more than was humanly possible in the examination of conscience.[78]

A favourable examination of conscience will result normally in a happy and peaceful state of mind. More several times speaks of the satisfaction derived from a good conscience even in a person suffering adversity for justice' sake. His uncanny power of foretelling the future is shown in the following passage which turned out to be a close description of his own trial:[79]

> For surely if a man may (as indeed he may) have great comfort in the clearness of his conscience, that hath a false crime put upon him, and by false witness proved upon him, and he falsely punished, and put to worldly shame and pain therefor: an hundred times more comfort may he have in his heart, that where white is called black, and right is called wrong, abideth by the truth, and is persecuted for justice.

During his imprisonment, More confessed to anxiety, but he felt beneath it a fundamental joy because of the certainty of his innocence: '. . . the clearness of my conscience hath made my heart hop for joy.'[80] More's satisfaction at having done what his conscience demanded was noticed on two famous occasions by his son-in-law, William Roper: the first time was when he was 'merry' because he had passed 'the point of no return'; the second was when he sadly tore himself away from his family as he left his home for the last time. He said quietly to Roper: 'Son Roper, I thank our Lord the field is won.'[81]

ARTICLE IV

LAW AND FREEDOM

To penetrate more deeply into More's thoughts on loyalty, law, and conscience, to bring out more clearly the difference between his refusal to obey the Act of

78. For a different opinion see BASSET, 69–76; ibid. for the story of the scrupulous man from Winchester.
79. *Dial. of Comf.* 148.
80. *Corr.* 540.
81. Cf. HARPSFIELD, 160, 166.

Succession and his application of penal laws to other religious dissenters, it will be of value to study his debate with the Reformers on the role of law in the Christian life. The nature of Christian freedom has been constantly discussed from the time of St Paul's manifesto, but the debate reached its highest pitch with the appearance of Martin Luther. The problem was at the heart of the Reformation and it is still high on the agenda of ecumenical discussion. Dialogue has now replaced controversy, but not before many bitter words were spoken and many stinging insults hurled. Our object in reviewing the battle is to seek ideas, not to cheer our champion's blows.

They were two mighty warriors that took the field: Luther, who had given up law to enter the monastery; Thomas More, who had abandoned the idea of the cloister to become England's most renowned lawyer. More was undoubtedly the leading figure on the English scene to take up the defence of the Church: Luther was his first opponent.

A The Role of Law after the Gospel

1. The Reformers' Doctrine of Law

The Reformers of the 16th century all agreed in rejecting the legislative authority of the Church. After this, however, there were differences of opinion among them and evolution of thought in individual Reformers.

In 1520, Martin Luther published his three famous reform pamphlets: *Address to the German Nobility*, *The Babylonian Captivity*, and *The Freedom of the Christian Man*. He denied the authority of the Church to impose laws binding in conscience and called upon the secular power to reform religion. In 1523 he composed the tract, *On Civil Power*, in which he distinguished the political sphere from the spiritual, the 'interior man' from the 'exterior man'. The latter is the man of flesh bound to live in community and therefore to abide by civil law. However the civil law has a value that is merely profane, and has no bearing on man's salvation. The 'interior man', the spiritual side of man, is bound by no law. The function of law is to show man his impotence. [82]

Luther's ideas on freedom and law had a big influence on the English Reformers with whom More clashed a few years afterwards. One of the greatest of these was William Tyndale who carried on his campaign from exile in the Low Countries. He also denied the validity of Church Law, but his theology of biblical law evolved into a fore-runner of Puritanism, a legalistic 'theology of contract' which was a complete reversal of Luther's doctrine. [83] Tyndale strenuously upheld the divine origin of the authority of civil rulers. He called upon them to reform religion; he taught that all must obey them, but they themselves are answerable only to God. It is of interest, however, that he

---

82. See articles on Luther, *Encyclopedia Britannica*, London 1960, vol. 14, 491–8; *Enciclopedia Italiana*, XXI, 692–704.
83. MARIUS, op. cit.

opposed Henry's divorce: even the King must learn from 'the spiritual officer' what to believe, how to live and how to rule.[84]

2. More's Answer to the Protestant Attack

Luther's treatise, *The Babylonian Captivity*, provoked a rejoinder from a surprising quarter, indeed from no less a person than the King of England, Henry VIII. Himself an amateur theologian, Henry published with the assistance of advisers including Sir Thomas More his *Assertio septem sacramentorum* (1521) for which he received from the Pope the title *Defensor Fidei*. In his reply to the King's book, Luther used such scurrilous language that it was beneath the royal dignity for the King to continue the debate in person.[85] Two men took over the task: Bishop John Fisher and Thomas More, who wrote under the pseudonym of William Ross. His book, *Responsio ad Lutherum* (1523) contains Henry's text, Luther's criticism, and then More's counter comments.[86]

Both Henry and More understood Luther's remark that neither man nor angel can place a law over a Christian as implying he rejected all law, both ecclesiastical and civil. More quotes Henry's proofs from the New Testament and tradition: St Paul tells us to obey those placed over us, he himself made laws concerning the election of bishops, about widows, about women keeping their heads covered in church. The same Apostle said 'the Law is good', and the Law is the bond of perfection'.[87] St Augustine spoke of the good purpose of the power of the king, of the books of his torturer, of the severity of a good father. St Ambrose too made a law forbidding the marriage embrace during Lent. These arguments, said More, stand despite Luther's reply.[88]

More then added his own arguments from experience. The law of the Gospel and the law of reason are not sufficient in all civil matters: the division of property, for example, is not explicitly covered by either law, but can only be achieved by custom, contract or public law. Nor can everything be left to the discretion of magistrates, as we saw in the previous article. Such a suggestion would not make the people more free: it would be slavery, because they would be subject, not to fixed and certain rules, but to the whims of magistrates.[89]

More understood Luther as saying that law binds a Christian only if he

---

84. CAMPBELL, op. cit. 114.
85. BRIDGETT, gives the following examples: 'The king is "rex infelix, stolidissimus, delirus, nugigerulus, sceleratissimus, sacrilegus; latro, asinus, porcus, truncus, antichristus, stultitiae monstrum; rex mendacii, damnabilis putredo, faeces latrinae etc".'; p. 211.
86. This method of letting the opposition speak for itself was characteristic of More's method of debate. He either quoted the words of an opponent or used a form of dialogue to allow opinions to be fairly stated. See TAFT's notes to *Apol.* 261: 'No other controversialist of the period, I believe, approaches More in accuracy or in extensiveness of quotation from the works of opponents.'
87. Actually Col. 3:14 calls *charity* the bond of perfection. See GERMAIN MARC'HADOUR, *The Bible in the Works of St Thomas More*, Nieuwkoop, 1970, Part III, 118.
88. *Op.Om.* 74–5; *CWR* 273.
89. *Resp.* 232; *CWR* 277.

44

consents to it. More had no difficulty in showing that as far as civil law is concerned this would be thoroughly unworkable: thieves and cut-throats would never consent to laws which would punish them. Moreover, each time a new citizen arrived laws would have to be suspended until he consented to them.[90]

In the same work More takes Luther to task for confusing the personal character of officials with the office they hold and basing his argument against the office on the unworthiness of the person holding it. If Luther rejected the papacy because of the vices of some popes, he would logically have to reject also all other offices, kingship, dictatorship, consulate, magistracy, and the people would be without law and order. It looked as though Germany would find out by hard experience that it is better to have bad rulers than none at all.[91] The *Responsio* ends with a prophetical warning to the Germans. Luther's spiritual doctrine will bring about social disaster. Many of the Princes applaud the apostacy of the clergy and the rejection of papal supremacy because they wish to seize the Church's possessions. But they are deluding themselves: if the people throw off the law of the Church it will not be long before they throw off the yoke of the Princes too; anarchy will reign, they will slaughter the nobles, and, following the doctrine of Luther, they will trample all law underfoot; finally they will turn on each other and bring about their own destruction. 'I beg of Christ', concludes More, 'that I may be a false prophet.'[92]

Later events proved More to be a very accurate prophet. In his letter to the Protestant Bugenhagen he points to the eruptions that followed Luther's preaching in Germany as proof of his error. He indignantly describes Luther's agitation of the peasants to rebel, and then his villainous and treacherous desertion of them. He denounced Luther's action in calling upon the nobles to tear the peasants to pieces and his later efforts to smother the odium that was felt against him for the slaughter of which he was the sole cause. After what had happened in Germany, More was flabbergasted that anyone could still believe Luther's doctrine. How could anyone equate the Gospel with the rioting, slaughter, plunder and burnings that Luther's ideas had caused? How could anyone claim that the profession of the Gospel means destruction of the sacraments, insulting the saints, blaspheming the Mother of Christ, despising the Cross of Christ, breaking vows, defiling virginity consecrated to Christ, exhorting monks and virgins to perpetual whoredom, not only by words but by shameful example?[93]

Tyndale's theory was somewhat different from that of Luther, but More did not appreciate this fact. This is not surprising since Tyndale's thought was still evolving, even as a result of More's criticism, and in a slogging match such as

90. *Resp.* 233; *CWR* 279.
91. *Resp.* 162; *CWR* 141.
92. *Op.Om.* 110; *CWR* 693.
93. Corr. 328; *EW* 305: More attributes to Luther's account the deaths of over 60000 peasants slain in Germany in one summer.

45

this was, More could not be expected to cater for the niceties of difference in his opponent's changing position. In any case, his arguments were framed to cover those who rejected the Church's authority. More could see what logically followed once this step was taken: if the Reformers differed among themselves, it was because they were not logical.

In his *Confutation* (1533) More quotes Tyndale as arguing that any ecclesiastical law added to the law of God is evil because it would imply that God's law, being insufficient, is not good. More replies that this argument, if true, would destroy all law, of both Church and State, with lamentable consequences. Although Tyndale clearly upheld civil law, More asserted that it was the intention of the Reformers, 'if they plainly durst speak it out', to throw out all law. This followed from their arguments against the Church. Such was the intention of Tyndale, his master Martin Luther, 'and all the serpentine seed that is descended from them':

> For Luther saith that we need no more laws, but only the gospel, well
> and truly preached after his own false fashion. And he babbleth also
> in his Babylonica that neither man nor angel hath any power or
> authority to make any law, or any one syllable of a law upon any
> Christian man, without his own agreement given thereunto.

Nor may anyone compel a Christian to keep laws of the Church, said Tyndale: he may only as a brother exhort him to keep the law of Christ. The use of force is tyranny. Again, More replies, this principle could be used to destroy all law, which is really what the Reformers want, because 'all laws are lets, as they take them, to their evangelical liberty'.[94] Their doctrine would lead to anarchy, to 'heaps of heavy mischief', and it would take a long time to undo the damage and 'set the world in order and peace again', Without penal laws, 'with fear of punishment once taken away', everyone would do what he liked and chaos would follow. This proves that the Reformers lack all sense of responsibility, it proves they are dishonest and insincere. For them Christian freedom means throwing off all restraint so they can enjoy themselves by riotous living:[95]

> And this they call the liberty of the Gospel, to be discharge of all order
> and of all laws, and do what they list, which be it good or bad, be, as
> they say, but the works of God wrought in them. But they hope by this
> means God shall for the while work in them many merry pastimes.

It is clear then that in More's thought the Christian is bound by law. In what sense is he free? We will try to find More's opinion by discussing his treatment of the question of religious freedom, first under ecclesiastical law, then under civil law.

B Christian Freedom and the Law of the Church

In this section we shall examine More's arguments that the laws of the Church

94. *EW* 618–620.
95. *EW* 274.

46

are the guarantee of the Christian's freedom. *Sub lege libertas* is the ideal of a healthy society, and this is the view More took of Church law.

1. Disorder is not Freedom

The fact that the Church is a visible society demands that it should have rules and customs to regulate its activities in an orderly way. More quotes Luther as boasting that his church has Communion at any time of the day or night, with no restrictions about vestments, place or rite. More resorts to rather vulgar language in rejecting this ceremonial freedom of the Lutherans:[96]

> All things are free to you. It does not matter to you where, when or how
> you sacrifice; by day or by night, in light or darkness, drunk or sober,
> clothed or naked, clean or dirty, on an altar or as a rascal on a W.C.!

In other words, certain regulations are necessary to ensure that divine worship is carried out with fitting decorum. More goes on to point out that community life in the Church demands certain conventions, such as agreement on the time of celebrating various feasts and liturgical seasons: Luther's freedom from all law and custom is preposterous:[97]

> What then! So that when one is celebrating Christmas, another is
> holding Easter; while religious people are observing the Lenten fast,
> Father Tipsy and his tipsy companions are celebrating Bacchanalia!

In his reply to the King's book, Luther instanced examples of customs in the early Church which were contrary to the contemporary laws of the Church. But the fact that certain things were once allowed (e.g. the marriage of priests, Communion without fasting) does not prove they are always allowed, More replied. For example, he says, St Paul had St Timothy circumcised, but that does not prove circumcision is still necessary because shortly afterwards the enforcement of circumcision was forbidden.[98]

More resumes the polemical tone as he goes on to reject any freedom which involves separation from the Mystical Body. For Luther each individual must be free to receive directly the Word of God, without any intermediary. This private interpretation, More considers, is the cardinal point of Luther's theology of freedom:[99]

> So he calls the whole Church Babylon and the faith of the Church he

---

96. *Op.Om.* 99, my translation: 'Omnis tibi libera sunt: nec tua refert, ubi, quando, quomodo sacrifices: noctu ne, an interdiu, in luce ne, an in tenebris, ebrius, an sobrius, vestitus, an nudus, cultus, an sordidus, super altare, an super foricam furcifer.' *CWR* 419.
97. *Op.Om.* 100: '...quid ni? ut dum unus natale celebrat, aluis faciat Pascha, et dum religiosi jejunant Quadragesimam, Pater potator interea, cum suis compotoribus, celebrat bacchanalia.' *CWR* 429.
98. *Op.Om.* 99; *CWR* 409.
99. *Op.Om.* 105: 'Ita totam Ecclesiam appellat Babylonam: Ecclesiae fidem vocat servitutem; & homo misericors offert libertatem omnibus qui velint ab Ecclesiae separari, & istius putridi & abscissi membri contagione corrumpi. At quibus modis invitat in hanc plusquam servilem libertatem, operae pretium est cognoscere. Magnam censet ac primariam rationem: quod verbis divinis non est ulla facienda vis, neque per hominem, neque per Angelum.' *CWR* 453.

calls slavery! And this merciful man offers freedom to all who wish to be separated from the Church and be corrupted by the contagion of this rotten amputated limb! And how he invites us into this freedom worse than slavery is worth knowing: he considers his first and primary reason to be this – No violence is to be done to the Word of God, neither by man nor by angel.

2. 'Deo servire regnare est.'

More could see no indignity in observing the commandments of God or of the Church of Christ. For More, the will of God is uppermost: to observe it is to achieve our destiny and reign. To reject Christ's yoke is to adopt the freedom of the devil which is nothing but the worst slavery: 'To serve God, through the laws and customs of Christian people, is to reign!' [100]

3. Christian Liberty: Freedom from Sin

In his *Dialogue of Comfort*, written while he was a prisoner, More returns to the question of freedom. He rejects again the notion of freedom as consisting in doing what one pleases, showing that *de facto* we are continually subject to restriction and limitation while we are in this world. The worst bondage of all affects nearly everyone, viz. the bondage of sin: [101]

Let every free man that recknoneth his liberty to stand in doing what he list, consider well these points, and I ween he shall then find his liberty much less than he took it for before.

And yet have I left untouched the bondage that almost every man is in that boasteth himself for free, the bondage I mean of sin, which to be a very bondage, I shall have Our Saviour Himself to bear me good record. For He saith: . . . . . Every man that committeth sin is the thrall or the bondman of sin.

It follows from this that one of the elements of Christian freedom will be freedom from sin, which in turn implies the keeping of the Commandments and of laws which bind in conscience.

4. Christian Liberty and the Sweet Yoke of Christ

The complex question of the mixture of joy and sorrow, of ease and hardship, of freedom and of service, constituted a paradox which occupied More's mind again and again as he engaged the Reformers in controversy. He treats the problem at length and very beautifully in the *Dialogue concerning Heresies*. [102] The Messenger says on behalf of the Protestants that Christ came to call us to

---

100. *Op.Om.* 98: 'Nam ut legibus & moribus Christiani populi, Deo servire regnare est, ita leges & mores abrumpere, quos populum suum Christus voluit observare, & suave jugum excutere, quod Christus voluit suum gregem portare, quid aliud est, quam servum Deo fugitivum esse, ut libere vivas Diabolo? Imo libertatis specie, servitutem servias miserrimam.' *CWR* 415.
101. *Dial. of Comf.* 309–310.
102. *EW* 142; *EW 1931* II 68–9.

the law of liberty, to give us an easier yoke and a lighter burden, 'which he had not done if he would load us with a fardel full of men's laws, more than a cart can carry away'. More replies that the laws of Christ and the Holy Spirit are designed 'for the governance of his people', and are by no means as difficult as the laws of Moses. The same is true of the laws of the Church: 'You would, I ween, rather be bounden to many of the laws of Christ's Church than to the circumcision alone.' In fact, the laws of the Church are less difficult than the laws of Christ. In the first place Christ commands us to avoid all sin, not just mortal sins. In a sense it is easier to avoid the big sins than the smaller ones, yet we are commanded not to swear at all, we are not to be angry, we are to pray always, we are to avoid every idle word. These laws of Christ are more exacting than those of his Church. Secondly, More continues, there is the grave obligation that Christ put on his disciples to endure even death for his sake:[103]

> What ease also call you this, that we be bound to abide all sorrow and shameful death and all martyrdom upon pain of perpetual damnation for the professoin of our faith? Trow ye that these easy words of his easy yoke and light burden were not as well spoken to his apostles as to you, and yet what ease called he them to? Called he not them to watching, fasting, praying, preaching, walking, hunger, thirst, cold and heat, beating, scourging, prisonment, painful and shameful death?

This passage and similar ones, especially in the *Dialogue of Comfort* which also discusses the themes of persecution and martyrdom, reveal in More a keen awareness of all that was to be involved in his own passion. One of the key ideas for understanding his death is this: the martyr is not being called upon to perform some work of supererogation; he is faced with the ultimate alternatives, heaven or hell. The force of the argument is that this duty to confess Christ is a law, a command, a strict obligation binding under pain of eternal damnation, and it is imposed by Christ himself. It is not a counsel proposed for free acceptance or rejection by Christians. So the law of Christ can be the hardest thing a man can be called upon to obey.

The next step in the argument is that if Christian liberty is compatible with such a strict obligation as that of undergoing death and all suffering for Christ's sake, *a fortiori* it is compatible with the comparatively easier obligations made by human law. When the Reformers deny the moral obligation of these lighter laws, they are not bearing the easy yoke of Christ, but putting the yoke off altogether. For them the burden is not light: they have put the burden down. Finally, even Saints Peter and Paul, who understood the meaning of Christian liberty better than these Protestants, nevertheless commanded us to be obedient to our superiors and rulers.

In what sense then is the Christian free? In what sense is his yoke easy and his burden light? More's answer is found in these words taken from the same passage:[104]

103. Ibid.
104. Ibid.

> The ease of His yoke standeth not in bodily ease, nor the lightness of
> His burden standeth not in the slackness of any bodily pain, but it
> standeth in the sweetness of hope, whereby we feel in our pain a pleas-
> ant taste of heaven.

The Christian life is not one that is easy for the flesh. What makes it easy is
'the sweetness of hope', the hope of the happiness of heaven. It is this hope that
gives us the motivation, the encouragement to bear the burden and to keep the
commandments. With the goal before us, the difficulties appear less. The
stronger our hope the more eagerly we undertake whatever is nesessary to
achieve our destiny.

  In another treatise written in his last years, More puts before us the example
of Christ's obedience to the will of his Father, especially in regard to his Passion, both as a proof that we too must obey, and as an encouragement in the
trials of the life of the Christian. The death of Christ was the supreme act of
obedience, it was the epitome of all his moral teaching. Christ speaks: [105]

> All My life hitherto hath been a pattern of obedience and a sample of
> humility. Was there ever anything that I have either oftener or more
> earnestly taught ye, than to be obedient to your rulers, to honour your
> parents, to yield unto Caesar what belongeth unto him, and to God
> likewise whatsoever is due to Him?

These words sum up the greatest lesson More learnt from his Master.

  Fr Hans Küng writes that for St Thomas More Christian freedom consists
in complete spiritual detachment from all created things, even from life itself. [106]
This thesis is supported by the very facts of More's life and death, and is
implicitly contained in his teaching on the necessity of detachment. It was a key
point in the spiritual instruction of his family. Roper recalls that More prepared
his family for the troubles ahead ('quia spicula praevisa minus laedunt') by
speaking to them of the joys of heaven, the pains of hell and the sufferings of
the martyrs, saying 'what an happy and blessed thing it was, for the love of
God, to suffer loss of goods, imprisonment, loss of lands, and life also'. [107] The
same lesson is implied in More's writings: 'Now because that this world is . . .
not our eternal dwelling, but our little while wandering, God would that we
should in such wise use it, as folk that were weary of it.' [108] The same theme
runs through his famous prayer: [109]

> Give me Thy grace good Lord to set the world at nought,
>   To set my mind fast upon Thee. . . .
> Of worldly substance, friends, liberty, life, and all,
>   To set the loss at right nought for winning of Christ.

The idea of detachment is certainly an important part of More's spirituality,

105. *Hist. Pass.* 107.
106. *Freedom in the World: St Thomas More*, London 1965, 26–31.
107. Roper, 55.
108. *Dial. of Comf.* 153–4.
109. *English Prayers* 13–4.

as it is an important part of the teaching of Christ. However, More himself does not explicitly identify Christian freedom with detachment.

From this study it emerges that More does not say explicitly what constitutes the freedom of a Christian. The nearest he comes to an explicit statement is in the passage we have examined where he rejects the Protestant explanation of evangelical liberty, and places the lightness of our burden in Christian hope.

In the paradox of liberty and obligation, More puts greater emphasis on the latter, as was natural in the circumstances, seeing that the Protestants were challenging the doctrine of the moral obligation of human law. He clearly vindicates the Catholic doctrine of obedience from the teaching of Christ, the Apostles and tradition. But he does not precisely define the nature of Christian freedom. For him, law defines duties rather than rights. The only rights he seems to think are important are God's claims on our service. Man's right to be free is not absolute. Even when More mentions that man is not bound by a human law which is against the law of God, he does not think about it so much in terms of being free, but as being bound by a prior law of God.

To summarize: For St Thomas More Christian freedom does not consist in disorder; it consists in being free from sin, in reigning in God's service under the sweet yoke of Christ with the hope of heaven to come.

C Religious Freedom under Civil Law

The question of religious freedom in civil law is one which still concerns modern society. Religious toleration has long been preached by various denominations, it has been proclaimed in the constitutions of different countries, it has been upheld by the Charter of the United Nations, but on the other hand it has not been universally practised. The lively discussion on the *Declaration on Religious Freedom* in the second Vatican Council shows that the question is difficult and complex. [110] An examination of More's thought on the subject will not only help the aims of our thesis as stated at the beginning of this article, but will throw light on the history of the question.

We shall discuss More's opinion under three headings, viz. religious freedom in a pre-Christian society, in a Catholic society, and in a post-Reformation society. [111]

1. Religious Freedom in a Pre-Christian Society

The early part of the sixteenth century was comparatively free from religious strife. It was in such a relatively calm atmosphere that More *ex professo* dealt with the matter of religious freedom in a society which lacked the benefit of Christian revelation when it drew up its laws. But does More's description of

---

110. Cf. speech of Most Rev. E. J. DE SMEDT, 'Religious Liberty', in *Council Speeches of Vatican II*, ed H. KÜNG et al., Glen Rock, New Jersey, 1964, 237–253.
111. CAMPBELL, op. cit. 153–4: 'For More there were two kinds of state: a Catholic state, and a state that was not Catholic.'

Utopian toleration really represent his own view,[112] or is it merely a device to allow the introduction of Catholicism on the arrival of Hythlodaeus?[113] First, let us see exactly what measure of freedom was permitted in Utopia in the matter of religion. More deals with the subject under the heading of 'Utopian Religions' in the second book of *Utopia*.

The island of Utopia allows freedom of religion within certain limits. The citizens are free to worship the sun, moon, planets, the heroes of the past, the Supreme Being. (In fact they all agree that there is a Supreme Being Who is Creator and providential Governor of all things.) The laws of Utopia were drawn up by its founder, King Utopus. For the sake of peace and the good of religion he ordained that it should be lawful for every man to follow the religion he chose. It was to be lawful to attempt the conversion of others by quiet, modest and reasonable discussion, but violence, abuse and scorn were strictly forbidden: they were punishable by exile or enslavement. Hythlodaeus himself tells how one of the Utopians who had been converted to Christianity incurred the penalty of exile. Immediately after his baptism he began to preach his new religion 'with more zeal than discretion'; he began to condemn other religions and their followers as impious and sacrilegious. He was arrested, tried and convicted, 'not for despising their religion, but for stirring up a riot among the people'.[114] This reservation concerning the manner of proselytising was a serious element in More's thought. We will see that he later censured the Reformers because of the way in which they preached their doctrine.

More also describes a doctrinal limit to Utopian toleration: King Utopus strictly forbade that anyone should deny the immortality of the soul and the providence of God. He believed that the doctrine of sanctions after death was necessary even for the laws of society. An unbeliever would keep civil laws only out of fear, and if by chance this motive were removed, he would seek his own private ends without care for the common good. Nevertheless, anyone holding these opinions is not subject to physical punishment, but suffers severe moral disadvantages: public infamy, exclusion from office, and enforced silence concerning his opinion. Such penalties are necessary because these doctrines are the foundations of public morality, and society must protect itself against those who do not believe them. Mere disbelief was not punishable by itself, but discussion was forbidden, except with the priests. Any who murmured against the imposition of silence were also punished.[115]

Utopus made laws to protect the right of citizens to quiet and reasonable discussion of religion because he firmly held that truth would eventually

112. D. Bush, review of *Utopia* ed. E. Surtz and J. H. Hexter, in *Moreana* no. 7. Aug, 1965, 87; Chambers, 256–282.
113. Leland Miles, *John Colet and the Platonic Tradition*, London 1962, 176: 'The toleration advocated in More's fictitious *Utopia* must be understood as the only means of introducing Catholicism into that pagan land. In Catholic England More advocated no such toleration.'
114. *Ut.* 219 ff.
115. *Ut.* 223.

emerge by its own natural force. Even the madness of the unbelievers mentioned above would give way to the reasoning of the priests. So if one religion alone is true and all the rest false, it will become conspicuous before long.

The desire for objective truth is found also in the Utopians' worship. They pray that all men, including themselves, may be brought to the truest form of religion; but there is a thought-provoking proviso: if variety itself is not more pleasing to God. The Utopians keep their minds open to truth, or at least try to do so. The fact that they did not all immediately accept the Christian faith of Hythlodaeus' missionaries shows More's realism.

I have said before that we must be on our guard against attributing to More the opinions of the Utopians. However, it seems in this case that we do have More's true concept of religious liberty at least in a pre-Christian society.[116] The accent on reason, on calm discussion, on objective truth on the one hand, and the condemnation of violence and bitterness on the other, are typical of More. Negatively, in the dialogue between himself and Hythlodaeus in the book itself, More does not voice any opposition to these laws, as he does to other aspects of Utopian life, such as their communism, pre-marital inspection etc.[117]

2. Religious Freedom in a Catholic Society

Any consideration of the opinion of St Thomas More or of anyone else in a similar position in this question of religious toleration should take into account the historical context. More expressed his opinion in his defence of a society which had been Catholic for over a thousand years. He was writing as a controversialist, and not in a vacuum, but rather amidst bitter religious turmoil. The anti-heresy laws in question had been in force in England for over a hundred years and were similar to those in use in a big part of Christendom.

During the reign of Henry IV (1399–1413) the heresy of Lollardism began to spread in England and the bishops felt unable to cope with the situation. The Act, *De heretico comburendo*, was consequently passed through Parliament. This Act was extended in the reign of Henry V (1413–22). It was repealed in the reigns of Henry VIII (1509–47) and Edward VI (1547–53), but revived under the Catholic Queen Mary (1553–58).[118] It may also be recalled that even though the Protestants taught private interpretation of the Scriptures, it was not understood by the majority of them as implying religious toleration in the modern sense. Catholics were put to death under Henry VIII, Edward VI, Elizabeth I (1558–1603) and James I (1603–25), not under heresy laws it is true, but as traitors for denying the royal supremacy of the English Church. Apart from this, anyone who did not practise the established religion was subject to fines and other disadvantages. The *Catholic Emancipation Act* was not passed till 1829. On the continent Calvin did not allow religious freedom, and condoned

116. CHAMBERS, 129–131.
117. *Ut.* 103 ff.; 189.
118. LAURENCE GOULDER, *The Tower Pilgrimage*, London n.d., 13.

the burning of a Spaniard, Miguel Serveto, for denying the doctrine of the Trinity. [119]

St Thomas More considered it his duty to carry out the requirements of law against heretics. As an officer of the realm it was his duty to apprehend them, hand them over for trial to the ecclesiastical court, and to execute the sentence imposed. On becoming Chancellor he would have had to take the oath 'to give his whole power and diligence, to put away, and to make utterly to cease and destroy, all manner of heresies and errors, commonly called Lollardies, within the precincts of his office and administration, from time to time, with all his power'. [120] The fact that he took the oath is sufficient proof in his case that it was not contrary to his conscience. Now let us try to discover the reasons which satisfied his conscience.

In his *Confutation*, More tells us why he feels bound to suppress heresy, which he compares to a carbuncle. If it is incurable, it must be cut clean out: he is bound to take this action, first because of his oath, as do all officers of justice in England, then 'by reason and good congruence', and also 'by plain ordinance and statute'. [121] Anyone who really knows More would not seek to excuse him merely on the grounds that he was carrying out the civil law. [122] He did not conscientiously object to the law. In the place to which we have just referred, he does put more emphasis on the fact that he was following the law, but he was speaking to his fellow countrymen who were ultimately responsible for their laws. And he does state too that the laws are valid because they are in accord with 'reason and good congruence'. The reason he gives is that it is better to cut out an infected area rather than let it destroy the whole organism. Notice too that he mentions a condition before the extreme penalty is to be invoked: 'if it haply be incurable'. More lenient measures should be adopted first.

In his *Apology* More claims the support of the whole Catholic Church for the methods used under his jurisdiction. We have already seen that for More one of the norms for the formation of conscience was the belief of the universal Church. He states that neither 'the Pacifier' (St German) nor anyone else can bring forward a case in which even an obstinate heretic has not been treated with 'charity and justice, according to the common laws of all Christ's Catholic Church, and the laws of this realm. .'. [123] So More considered that justice and charity to dissenters were required by national and international law.

The lawyer Christopher St German in his anonymous work mentioned earlier advocated the repeal of heresy laws, alleging occasional instances of

119. CAMPBELL, op. cit., 153–4; TAFT's introduction to *Apol.*, lxxxv; *DTC*, article, 'Servet', XIV², col. 1967; FRANÇOIS WENDEL, *Calvin*, London 1965, 93–9; WENDEL, a Protestant, after discussing this incident, judges Calvin in a way similar to my conclusion about More.
120. *Apol.* footnote, xxxiv.
121. *EW* 351.
122. As against MILES, op. cit. 176, footnote 21.
123. *Apol.* 102.

injustice. More's reply enumerates his reasons for supporting the existing legislation. It is an important passage so we will quote it in full: [124]

> ... if he but to the very principal point alone, wherein he laboureth to change and put away those good laws .... in that point alone, I say, we lay against him the common consent of this realm. And he layeth his own reason against it. We lay against him the consent of the General Council. And against this he layeth his own reason. We lay against him the general approbation of all Christian realms. And against this he layeth his own reason. And what is his own irrefragable reason that he layeth against all this? Surely no more, as you see, but that by those laws an innocent may sometimes take wrong. Against this reason we lay him that if this reason should stand, then against malefactors there could no law stand. We lay against it also that by his devices, if they were followed, by the increase of heresies many innocents must needs take much more wrong. To this answereth he that he will not answer that.

So the reasons behind the law against heretics are: the common consent of the realm, the consent of a General Council, the general approbation of all Christian realms, and finally the wrong suffered by innocent parties if heresy is allowed to spread.

We have already seen the fact that English law commanded the suppression of heresy. To which General Council did More allude? Among the Acts of the IV Lateran Council (1215) there is a section which deals with the treatment of heretics. It is the third constitution, *De haereticis*. [125] This constitution treats not only of the ecclesiastical penalties, but describes the punishments to be enforced by civil authorities. Heretics condemned by ecclesiastical courts are to be handed over to the secular arm to be punished with due penalties. Their goods are to be confiscated. Those under suspicion of heresy are to be 'smitten with the sword of anathema', they are to be shunned by everyone, and if they persist in excommunication for a year, they are to be treated as heretics and condemned. Moreover, the secular authorities are to be warned, induced and even, if necessary, compelled by ecclesiastical censure, to take an oath that they will use all their power to exterminate all heretics within their jurisdiction and indicated to them by the Church. The pertinent chapter of the Council's Acts must be signed *amodo quandocumque* with an oath by anyone taking a spiritual or temporal office. If a temporal officer neglects this duty of 'purging his territory of the rottenness of heresy' he is to be excommunicated. If he does not repent within a year, this fact is to be notified to the Supreme Pontiff so that he may release his vassals from their allegiance and give the territory to Catholics who, having exterminated the heretics, may take possession of it. By way of encouragement, it was also decreed that Catholics who undertook this crusade

124. *EW* 1031.
125. *Conciliorum Oecumenicorum Decreta*, ed. Centro di Documentazione, Istituto per le Scienze Religiose-Bologna, Freiburg, 1962, 209–211.

to exterminate heretics would receive the same Indulgence and privilege as those who actually went to the relief of the Holy Land. There follow further warnings, especially to judges and lawyers, against defending or favouring heretics.

St Thomas More took the oath mentioned in this constitution as he assumed the various offices through which he graduated to the Chancellorship of England. We have seen that he formed his conscience according to certain objective norms, one of which was the decisions of an ecumenical council of the Church. The mind of IV Lateran could hardly have been clearer. On this score then we can safely say that he had no conscientious objections against this oath. We may add that More was possibly acquainted with the Bull of Leo X, *Exsurge Domine*, which condemned the errors of Luther, including number thirty-three: 'Haereticos comburi est contra voluntatem Spiritus.'[126]

More supported his arguments from authority with reasons: if heresy is not checked, many innocents will suffer. The rights of heretics to freedom and to life itself yield to the prior rights of society, both spiritual and temporal.

Society has the duty to safeguard those conditions which are necessary for the spiritual welfare of the community. More considered that it was necessary to belong to the body of the Church and to have right faith in order to be saved. By their very existence and especially their preaching the Reformers would confuse the more simple members of the community, weaken the unity of the true faith, thereby causing some to leave the Church or to become indifferent, so that they would lose their souls. More prayed for the Reformers, 'the prodigal children', that they would return to their mother the Church, to the true faith, so that all would be knit together in mutual love and charity, and would 'as His true members, attain unto the glory of our Captain and Head, which whosoever hopeth to have out of His Body, the Church, and without right faith, doth with a vain hope lewdly deceive himself'.[127] Spreading heresy meant to More spreading damnation among human souls. It was the State's duty to prevent this from happening.

Society also had the right to protect itself against civil disorder. More believed that heresy implied civil strife, first because of its inherent repudiation of authority, secondly because the Reformers advocated the violent overthrow of Catholicism. What grounds did he have for these beliefs?

In the first place, heresy was always associated in More's mind with civil strife.[128] We have already seen how he prophesied that Luther's theories would bring ruin to Germany and how his prophecies were in fact fulfilled. He naturally foresaw similar experiences in store for England if heretical ideas spread there. He associated the atrocities of the imperial forces during the sacking of Rome in 1527 with the German Lutheran contingent. In an unquot-

---

126. *DS* n. 1483.
127. *Hist. Pass.* 97–98; TAFT's introduction to *Apol.*, lxxxv.
128. RONALD KNOX, 'The Charge of Religious Intolerance', in *The Fame of Blessed Thomas More*, London 1929, 44.

able passage he describes the 'exquisite cruelties' perpetrated by the imperialists in order 'that ye may perceive by their deeds what good cometh of their sect. For as our Saviour says 'Ye shall know the tree by the fruit'.' [129] *De facto*, the Reformers were, thought More, violent and abusive. Naturally such conduct would disturb the peace because Catholics would defend themselves with violence and abuse. We will see in another place some examples of the virulence of the Protestant attack, and also of the strong language More felt entitled to use against them. Some of the heretics advocated violence especially against the clergy. [130] These facts justified for More the terrible death penalty attached to the crime of heresy. In the hypothesis of non-violent heresy he would have allowed less serious penalties: 'The fear of these outrages and mischiefs . . . . have been the cause that princes and people have been constrained to punish heresies by terrible death, whereas else more easy ways had been taken with them.' [131] Whether these 'more easy ways' meant something less than the death penalty he does not say, but it seems a reasonable supposition. However, later he seems to think that heresy should be punished for its own sake, not merely to deter people from it or to cure them of it. Its punishment is also retibutive: heresy is 'well worthy to be as sore as any other fault, since there is no fault that more offendeth God'. [132]

In the *Dialogue concerning Heresies*, the intermediary between More and the Protestants, the Messenger, suggests a truce between Catholics and Reformers, so that both may preach their doctrines in a reasonable and peaceful manner. More declines to approve such an arrangement. He agrees that it 'were per-adventure no evil way' to allow Turkish missionaries into Christendom, if the Turks would allow Christian missionaries into Turkey, 'violence taken away by assent on both sides'. This would be a fair arrangement because each side would stand the chance of both gaining and losing, and More was confident that the truth of the Christian religion would eventually win out. But there would be no similar compensating advantage for Christendom, united in the Catholic faith, if heretics were allowed to start preaching and dividing that unity. The heretics would have everything to gain and nothing to lose, while Catholics would gain nothing and could only lose in the confusion of ideas that would follow. [133] This rather pragmatic argument would appeal to the common man with a sense of what constitutes a fair deal.

While St Thomas More accepted in principle that heretics could be prosecuted under the prevailing circumstances, he did not necessarily approve of every jot and tittle of the laws themselves. He did not criticize these laws in public, but he was called upon to answer the arguments of Christopher St German. This lawyer had argued that the laws and processes affecting the

129. *EW* 258–9; *Apol.* lxxxiii.
130. *EW* 291; CHAMBERS, 265.
131. KNOX, op. cit., 44.
132. Ibid.
133. *EW* 275–6; CHAMBERS, 265.

crimes of murder, heresy, treason and felony did not give any protection against biased judges and false witnesses. More answered that in proving too much he proved nothing, because the same could be said about all processes. [134] In particular the 'Pacifier' disagreed with the practice of allowing certain people to act as witnesses in these four cases who were debarred in other cases, viz. those under the punishment of infamy and even infidels. The Messenger joins forces with St German and rejects the explanation that serious crimes need more rigorous methods: such may be true after the crime is proved, but certainly not before it is proved. In fact 'the more heinous, odious, and abominable that the crime is, the more slow should we be to believe it, and the more sure and plain proof should we have, ere we should judge any man for so evil to commit it'. More answers that in fact the testimony is carefully sifted and further safeguards may be provided at the judge's discretion. But the reason why even the infamous and infidels are allowed as witnesses in these cases is that this type of criminal usually makes sure that no honest person is there to witness his crime: such people, knowing that they would face the death penalty if discovered, 'do not use commonly to take a notary and honest witness with them to make an instrument thereof . . . . but use to do it as covertly as possible'. [135] More lumped heretics together with murderers, thieves and traitors in this matter particularly, because he considered them utterly unscrupulous in their contempt of law, especially in that they were untrustworthy in the matter of oaths: [136]

> For never could I find heretic yet that any conscience had in any oath.
> And of truth Tyndale in his answer to my Dialogue teacheth them
> that they may break their oath and be forsworn without any scruple
> at all.

In practice More found himself dealing with individual heretics who were guilty of deception, treachery and perjury. [137] Some went so far as to commit sacrilege in their hatred of the Catholic faith. [138] Added to this, the political history of heresy, in the case of the English Lollards under Henry IV and Henry V as witnessed by the statutes of Parliament, as well as in the case of the German Lutherans, convinced More that it would be better to retain the existing laws.

More could not believe that most of the Reformers with whom he had to deal were in good faith. So he seemed rather perplexed when he came up against an apparently sincere person such as John Frith. He admits that he

134. *Apol.*, 154.
135. *EW* 210. Ironically, More himself when indicted for treason came under this procedure: the court could legally accept the evidence of one witness.
136. Ibid. 345.
137. Ibid.; *Apol.*, lxxxiv: '. . . More had seen little to inspire respect for their beliefs. Most of them had been persuaded to renounce their utterances. Of the few who had been brought to the stake almost all had previously recanted; two or three recanted again, when recantation could no longer save them. In More's official dealings with individual heretics he had repeatedly found them guilty of deception, treachery toward one another and perjury.'
138. Ibid., lxxxix.

feels sorry for the young man, as do other temporal and spiritual officers, but they cannot favour him on principle: '. . . no man can show him the favour that every man fain would, without the displeasure of God and peril of their own souls and many other men's too.'[139] But Frith was an exception so far as More's experience was concerned.

To recapitulate: St Thomas More believed that the penal laws against heretics were necessary and justified by reason, faith and the decrees of a general council, and that officers were bound under peril of their salvation to carry them out. If he thought there should be any change in the law, he would not discuss the matter publicly but would give his opinion 'in place and time convenient'. But he rejected the reasons of St German as invalid.

3. Religious Freedom in a Post-Reformation Society
Would Thomas More have allowed religious toleration in circumstances different from those he knew? The question remains largely hypothetical. However, Roper reports a conversation had with More which throws some little light upon the subject. Roper had been expressing his happiness about the state of England, with its 'catholic prince', its virtuous and learned clergy, its sound nobility and its 'loving, obedient subjects, all in one faith agreeing together'. More brought him down to earth with one of his prophetical sayings:[140]

'Troth it is indeed, son Roper, I pray God', said he, 'that some of us, as high as we seem to sit upon the mountains, treading heretics under our feet like ants, live not the day that we gladly would wish to be at a league and composition with them, to let them have their churches quietly to themselves, so that they would be content to let us have ours quietly to ourselves.'

This passage has been mis-interpreted as indicative of cruelty and intolerance. Even Stapleton appears to have been embarrassed by it and changed it:[141]

'. . . but a time will soon come when you will see all this zeal for religion, together with us and others who cultivate it, brought under contempt and despised, and made of no more account than we make of these poor little ants.' As he spoke he scattered with his foot an ant-hill that he happened to see on the way.

Roper's account is of course to be preferred, being the original and by an actual witness, and also because it contains the difficulty. But a closer examination of Roper's account reveals neither cruelty nor intolerance. More envisaged a situation in which heresy has been so widely accepted that the only solution would be an agreement to live and let live. He prays that the situation in which there is such a large body of Protestants will never come about, not that such a solution will not be agreed to. In other words, he hopes that society will remain Catholic, but if large sections of the community adopt other beliefs,

139. Ibid., 101.
140. ROPER, 35.
141. STAPLETON, 81.

then he would prefer toleration to continual discord. The phrase 'treading heretics under our feet like ants' appears to me to indicate sympathy rather than cruelty. It may also have been that More was considering the possibility of allowing Protestants to practise their religion 'quietly'.

D A Judgment on More's Doctrine of Religious Liberty

In the light of the *Declaration on Religious Freedom* issued by Vatican II, what are we to say on the doctrine we have been discussing? In the first place, it seems clear that More's thought on the compatibility of Christian freedom with the moral obligation of following the truth and obeying lawful authority is in accord with the Consiliar pronouncement.[142] Before passing judgment on the orthodoxy of his doctrine on religious freedom under civil law, another question must first be considered, viz. the relationship between *Utopia* and More's later writings wherein he defends the current anti-heresy laws.

We have said that *Utopia* certainly gives More's thoughts on a pre-Christian society, but to accept this as a complete answer would be unrealistic, because it does not tell us why he raised the question in the first place. More was a practical man and was not given to imagining purely hypothetical situations for their own sake. *Utopia* is essentially a satire and critique of current society, and the very fact that he raised the matter of religious tolerance for discussion bespeaks dissatisfaction or at least doubts about the wisdom and justice of the treatment of religious dissenters in sixteenth century Europe. Does this mean More was inconsistent when he later took up the defence of the *status quo*?[143] According to the *letter* there is no contradiction, because in *Utopia* he merely made a tentative suggestion to which he did not commit himself. But there is definitely a change in *spirit* because he later upheld those laws which he had implicitly questioned. This change can be partially explained by the change in circumstances: *Utopia* was written in a pacific atmosphere for a select audience, whereas later he was engaged in a violent controversy against a definite class of heretics, viz. people whom he believed to be preaching doctrines which had caused such chaos elsewhere that neither religious nor civil peace and freedom could exist. It seemed to him that it was not a time for compromise.

But what are we to say of these laws? *Utopia* was years ahead of its time, and undoubtedly helped the cause of religious toleration. Nevertheless, Utopian laws err on the side of intolerance in discriminating against and unjustly penalizing those who do not believe in the immortality of the soul and divine providence.[144] The anti-heresy laws which More defended in his controversial

142. 'A Declaration on Religious Freedom', in *The Documents of Vatican II*, ed. WALTER M. ABBOTT S.J., London, 1966, 677.
143. CHAMBERS, 274.
144. 'A Declaration on Religious Freedom', paragraph 2: '... the right to this immunity continues to exist even in those who do not live up to their obligation of seeking the truth and adhering to it. Nor is the exercise of this right to be impeded, provided that just requirements of public order are observed'; *The Documents of Vatican II*, 679–680.

60

works erred in failing to distinguish the case of those who were prepared to practise their religions with regard to the common good and with respect for the religious belief of others. Those responsible for these laws failed to appreciate the dignity of man and religion which demands that man should practise his faith freely, with personal responsibility and without coercion.[145]

In defending these laws, More exaggerated the need of right faith for salvation in that he did not accept the possibility of the salvation of Christians sincerely in error. He also appears to have exaggerated the necessity of belonging to the Body of the Church in order to be saved.[146]

We may conclude then that the laws were unjust and More erred in defending them. The error of those responsible for those laws probably contributed to the violent turn which the Reformation took as there was no outlet for legitimate dissension. Nevertheless, it also emerges that More was sincere in his opinion but in the circumstances it was difficult to distinguish the truth.

CONCLUSION TO CHAPTER I

Our study of More's doctrine on law reveals a synthesis which is intrinsically related to the Christian life. His existential approach to the subject is ideally suited for a spirituality of law. He preferred to describe law's practical role in the history of man's salvation. More had in mind the Christian, who is bound by the law of Christ, the law of Christendom and the law of the land, all of which pre-suppose the law of reason. Among these laws there is a hierarchy: in religious matters, the Christian is bound by the law of reason, the law of Christ and the law of Christendom, and since these laws are of divine origin or have the guarantee of divine assistance, there can be no conflict between them. The law of the land in purely civil matters is subject to the law of reason; it also is based on divine authority but has not the guarantee of God's infallible guidance, and therefore may come into conflict with the other types of law. Law is essentially the will of God and therefore is intelligent: it provides the order which is in accordance with man's nature elevated by grace. In this order man achieves his temporal and eternal destiny. This provides man with his motives for obeying law: it is the will of his Creator, it is good for man himself, both here and hereafter; disobedience, on the other hand, brings temporal and eternal punishment. There is also a hierarchy among these motives, but maximum motivation is obtained by remembering all of them. Subjectively, law is to be found in conscience, but man must conform his conscience to objective norms. By providing justice and truth, by excluding violence and error, law guarantees the freedom of the innocent to pursue a happy and useful life, to fulfil his duties to God, to himself and to his neighbour, and thereby to achieve his eternal salvation.

145. Ibid. paragraphs 2 and 4.
146. 'Decree on Ecumenism', ibid. pp. 345–6.

CHAPTER II

MORE'S CONCEPT OF LOYALTY
AND THE FULFILMENT OF DUTIES

We have said that the concept of loyalty includes the notion of fidelity to duty, and so in this chapter we shall pursue our investigation by examining More's understanding of the fulfilment of various duties to God, the Church, the State, family, friends, opponents and himself. Duty is a legitimate study for spiritual theology, because in fact man makes his individual way to God by discovering and fulfilling God's will as manifested in the concrete situation in which he exists.[1]

ARTICLE I

DUTIES TO GOD

A In General

The doctrine that man's most serious duty is to God is one which underlies the whole of More's spiritual life and doctrine. It will be sufficient therefore for us to treat it briefly and generally. More's prayers, his last letters from prison, his ascetical works such as *The Life of John Picus* (c. 1505), *The Four Last Things* (c. 1522), the *Treatise on the Passion* (?–1534) and the *Dialogue of Comfort* (1534), are all concerned with the duty of man to adhere to God in preference to all created things.

In a verse paraphrase of a prayer of Picus, More speaks of our duties to God as servants and as children: we are His servants by nature, but children by His grace. He prays for the grace to respond to God's loving invitation by dutifully renouncing sin and by loving God in return:[2]

Grant me, good Lord and Creator of all,
The flame to quench of all sinful desire,
And in Thy love set all mine heart afire.

Elsewhere he prays for the grace 'to set the world at nought, to set my mind fast upon Thee'; he asks that he may fix his heart firmly upon God 'with little respect unto the world'; he prays for 'a full faith, a firm hope, and a fervent

---

1. For the role of duty in the spiritual life see J. TONNEAU, op. cit. For duty as concrete manifestation of God's will, RENE CARPENTIER S.J., 'Devoir d'Etat', in *DSAM*, Tome III coll. 672–702.
2. *English Prayers* 21–4.

charity, a love to the good Lord incomparable above the love of myself; and that I love nothing to Thy displeasure, but everything in an order to Thee'.[3]

In the *Dialogue of Comfort* the whole basis of the discussion is that man's primary duty is to obey God and in that obedience he will find his true happiness. However, More stresses the fact that our service of God must be wholehearted and undivided: there is no fellowship between light and darkness, between Christ and Belial; no man can serve two masters, so we must obey Christ in all his commandments: 'Break one of His commandments, and break all. Forsake one point of His faith, and forsake all, as for any thanks you get of Him for the remnant.' We may not bargain with God as to what we shall do and what we shall not.[4]

In the same work, More for the last time brings up the controversy concerning faith and good works. It is an important passage in the evolution of the debate. As a practical man, More declares that he can see little difference between the teaching of some of the Protestants that good works will automatically follow true faith and the Catholic doctrine of the necessity of both faith and good works: the difference, he says, is a 'narrow point' and a 'sharp subtle thing'. He grants that all man's works are 'his bare duty', that none of them are rewardable in heaven of their own nature, 'but through the mere goodness of God', and that man can do no good work 'without God work with him'.[5]

More's daughter, Margaret, bears witness to his efforts to live his principles. Love of God and detachment from all worldly things are the marks in his character which she specially mentions in a letter to him in prison: '. . . you have abjected all earthly consolations and resigned yourself willingly, gladly and fully for His love to His holy protection.'[6]

When St Thomas More entered the service of King Henry VIII the harmony that existed between Church and State enabled him to live peacefully in good conscience. According to More, the King himself said to him that he should serve God first, and after God, the King. More remembered these words and brought them to the King's attention later when the occasion demanded.[7] His loyalty to Henry would be limited by one thing only: his prior duty to God. According to the *Paris News Letter* they were More's last words: he prayed for the King 'protesting that he died his good servant and God's first'.[8]

B In Particular: More's Idea of Martyrdom

We single out for special consideration the ultimate loyalty of martyrdom, be-

3. Ibid. 13; 15–20.
4. *Dial. of Comf.* 293.
5. Ibid. 152.
6. *Corr.* 510.
7. Roper, 49; *SL* 209, 229, 250.
8. Harpsfield, Appendix II, 266: 'Apres les exhorta, et supplia tres instamment qu'ils priassent Dieu pour le Roy, affin qu'il luy voulsist donner bon conseil, protestant qu'il mouroit son bon serviteur et de Dieu premierement.'

cause More deals with the subject very beautifully and because he progressively realized ever more clearly that he himself could be called upon to lay down his life for his beliefs.

More considered it the duty of all to accept death with equanimity. Even the Utopians were expected to die willingly because of their strong faith in future bliss: '. . . they suppose that God will not be pleased with the coming of one who, when summoned, does not gladly hasten to obey but is reluctantly drawn against his will.' In Utopia no one mourns the death of anyone who dies cheerfully. More returns to this same point with a touch of humour in the *Dialogue of Comfort:* 'Hard it is for him to be welcome that cometh against his will, that saith unto God when He cometh to fetch him, welcome my Maker magry my teeth.'[9]

More spent much time analysing the situation of the martyr. He first asks the question whether it is right to worry about the course we would take in the event of persecution. Some say we should not even consider the matter, but, says More, 'to counsel a man never to think on that case is in my mind as much reason, as the medicine that I have heard taught one for the toothache, to go thrice about a church-yard, and never think on a fox-tail.' It is more realistic to say that a Christian should be disposed to undergo with the help of grace any persecution that God will allow to befall him. So it seems to More necessary for Christians to think often on the subject and if their hearts shrink at the thought of pain, they should remember how much Christ suffered for them and confide in the grace that God would be sure to send them.[10] He imagines Christ saying to the trembling soul: 'Pluck up thy courage, faint heart . . . be of good comfort, for I myself have vanquished the whole world.'[11]

More had a great admiration for the martyrs, and especially for the proto-type of all martyrs, Christ Himself. Christ's Passion plays a most important role in More's spirituality: he meditated on it frequently, he wrote a treatise, the *History of the Passion*, he mortified his own body in imitation of Christ. According to More, Christ suffered more than any of the martyrs, even though the external pains of some of them seemed greater, because of the more acute 'inner anguish' that he felt.[12] Moreover, the sufferings of the martyrs have value because through them they are incorporated as closely as possible into the suffering Christ. The association of his own martyrdom with the doctrine of the Mystical Body was prophetically described when he wrote:[13]

> Now to this great glory can there no man come headless. Our Head is Christ: and therefore to Him must we be joined, and as members of His must we follow Him, if we will come thither. . . . Knew you not that Christ must suffer passion, and by that way enter into His kingdom?

9. *Ut.* 223; *Dial. of Comf.* 180. 'Magry', i.e. 'in spite of.'
10. *Dial. of Comf.* 268–9.
11. *Hist. Pass.* in *EW* 1357–8.
12. *Hist. Pass.* 49.
13. *Dial. of Comf.* 349.

Martyrdom ranks first among human good works. So meritorious is it that the martyr goes straight to God: 'So say we that martyrs, as soon as they be dead, go up straightways to heaven.'[14] More had discussed martyrdom as a good work in his book against Luther. Man is incapable of good works, Luther had asserted, because he is so poor and needy and can give nothing to God. Even in the Mass, said Luther, God is giving His grace to man, so, he concluded it is not a good work on man's part. But, objected More, this was not what Luther had set out to prove (which was that every act of man is a sin). Again, according to Luther's opinion, even martyrdom would not be a good work, which seems absurd, because, as God Himself has declared, Mary Magdalen performed a good work when she annointed the Lord. *A fortiori* the martyr, who 'merely gives back that unhappy and brief life that he has received on loan in order to obtain a blessed life that will never end' is performing a good work.[15] Moreover, no prayer is more acceptable to God than the prayers of those who are suffering persecution:[16]

> And these prayers of our Saviour at His bitter Passion, and of His holy
> martyrs in the fervour of their torment, shall serve us to see that there
> is no prayer made at pleasure so strong and effectual as in tribulation.

Many of the Utopians were converted by the 'wonderful constancy of the many martyrs whose blood freely shed had drawn so many nations far and wide into their fellowship'.[17] Even in the case of Christ, said More, there was more merit in His Passion than 'in His maundy'; similarly 'one inch' of the prayer of the martyrs in pain is worth a 'whole elle and more even of their own prayers prayed at some other time'.[18]

For Thomas More martyrdom was no mere abstraction. His writings clearly show his insight into the mental and physical anguish that may precede and accompany the martyr's death. He discusses the shame that may be attached to such a death but derives comfort from Christ Who 'through shame ascended into glory'. We should be mad if 'for fear of a short worldly shame' we should risk falling into 'everlasting shame, both before heaven and hell'. Then he deals with the physical sufferings, because, as Vincent says in the *Dialogue of Comfort*, 'all the pinch is in the pain'. Anthony rejoins that a man may have his leg cut off at the knee and feel no pain 'if his head be off but half an hour before'.[19] Nevertheless, More admitted that he feared death and torture. He was familiar with the forms of execution in use at that time: decapitation and the terrible hanging and quartering usually prescribed for treason. In every case, however, God would be faithful to His promise to strengthen His children at times of persecution: 'He will not suffer us to be tempted above our power.'[20]

14. *Hist. Pass.* 38.
15. *Op.Om.* 118; *CWR* 531.
16. *Dial. of Comf.* 172.
17. *Ut.* 219.
18. *Dial. of Comf.* 172.
19. *Dial. of Comf.* 336. Anthony and Vincent are the fictitious characters in the dialogue.
20. Ibid.

Both the *Dialogue of Comfort* and the *History of the Passion* contain penetrating studies of the psychology of martyrdom. In these books he deals with the fear and the joy that constitute the paradox of the martyr's experience. He begins by speaking of 'the great horror and fear that our Saviour had in His own flesh against His painful passion'. This example of Christ is a source of comfort to the persecuted Christian 'shrinking at the meditation of pain and death' so that he will not succumb to fear, 'but resist it and manly master it'. Christ will give the grace to submit and conform to God's will; he will send the Holy Ghost as Comforter 'that you shall as His true disciple follow Him, and with good will without grudge do as He did, and take your cross upon your back and die for the truth with Him, and thereby reign with Him crowned in eternal glory'.[21]

The fear of pain and death is natural. Some may be more acutely sensitive to it than others. Normally therefore we should not put ourselves forward as martyrs: this would be presumption and we could find the burden so great we could fall under its weight. A man must be certain that it be God's will he aspire to the crown of martyrdom. He must be 'such a man as the mighty hand of God encourageth to martyrdom: which thing must either by some secret means perceived, or else by some other reasonable ways be well tried and known'. On the other hand, the Christian is at liberty to flee persecution: '"For if they persecute ye" saith He, "in one city, get into another".'[22]

Why it is that some martyrs receive more comfort than others is due to the fact that God accommodates His graces to the circumstances and needs of particular times and places. Some He allows to go to death without any signs of consolation, with apparent fear and suffering. Others seem to embrace their cross from the start and die joyfully. Others again start out along their *via crucis* with strong forebodings, but in the moment of their triumph they are suddenly flooded with gladness and die happily:[23]

> . . . some joyfully speed them towards their death apace, and some other right sore afraid creep faint and softly thither . . . how many . . . which though they come to it, as we see, with much anguish and dread, do yet in conclusion manfully pass through those horrible strong stops of weariness, fear and heaviness, and so, stoutly breaking all those violent lets, do gloriously conquer death, and mightily get up into heaven.

Roper tells us that More prepared his family for the dark times ahead by speaking to them of the sufferings of Christ and the martyrs. Roper also preserved the account of his comment when from the Tower he witnessed the Carthusian martyrs 'cheerfully going to their deaths as bridegrooms to their marriage'.[24] The loyalty of Christ and his martyrs was More's greatest inspiration.

21. Ibid. 304.
22. *Hist. Pass.* 38; 15; cf. Matt. 10 : 23.
23. *Hist. Pass.* 51–3.
24. ROPER, 55; HARPSFIELD, 179.

Our saint saw the workings of divine providence in his own tribulation. When he was imprisoned, he told his daughter that he did not consider it a 'high displeasure' because, had it not been for his family responsibilities, he would long ago have closed himself 'in as straight a room, and straighter too'. Now that he was there, God would make provision for his family. In fact, the hermit's life in a prison cell so suited his own wishes that he felt himself being 'spoiled' by God: 'Methinketh God maketh me a wanton, and setteth me on His lap and dandleth me.'[25]

A study of More's writings in prison reveals a variation of mood between a joyful, and at times jocular acceptance, and a serious realism. Contributing factors to these changes were, firstly, the fact that at the beginning of his imprisonment he thought he would not be subject to further penalties; secondly, his health deteriorated rapidly while he was in prison. He was also saddened because his enemies perverted the use of law by attempting to trap him with it.

The prospect of suffering, combined with the uncertainty of his perseverence, had the result of sobering the tone of his last letters. 'I have not been a man of such holy living as I might be bold to offer myself to death, lest God for my presumption might suffer me to fall, and therefore I put not myself forward, but draw back.' Nevertheless, in the balance, confidence in God wins out: 'Howbeit, if God draw me to Himself, then trust I in His great mercy, that He shall not fail to give me grace and strength.'[26] His sense of humour reasserted itself only when the legal duel was over and he set out for the scaffold. This diffidence of More must not be interpreted as irresolution: he assured Margaret solemnly of his effective resolve to stand by his convictions: 'I assure you, Margaret, on my faith, I never have prayed God to bring me hence nor to deliver me from death.'[27] This resolution developed into an active desire for heaven, out of weariness for the ills of this world, but more because of his wish to be with God: 'I would be sorry if it should be any longer than tomorrow, for it is Saint Thomas' even, and the utas of St Peter, and therefore tomorrow long I to go to God, it were a day very meet and convenient for me.'[28] His wish was granted.

As in the case of good works in general, More looked upon martyrdom as a bare duty. It is interesting to find this sense of obligation attached in More's mind even to the heroic sanctity required in martyrdom. As we have seen, More used it to prove the compatibility of freedom and obligation in the Christian life:[29]

> What ease also call you this, that we be bound to abide all sorrow and shameful death and all martyrdom upon pain of perpetual damnation for the profession of our faith?

25. ROPER, 76.
26. *SL* 253; cf. also 228.
27. *SL* 238.
28. *SL* 257. 'St Thomas' even', i.e. the eve of the feast of the transfer of the relics of St Thomas of Canterbury; 'the utas of St Peter', i.e. the octave of the feast of Sts Peter and Paul, 29 June.

ARTICLE II

LOYALTY TO THE CHURCH

A The Communion of Saints

Even though St Thomas More laid down his life out of fidelity to God, the occasion of his martyrdom was his loyalty to the doctrine of the unity of the Church.[30] We have already seen something of More's lofty idea of the nature of the Church as the Mystical Body of which Christ is the Head and which is preserved in unity by his Spirit of truth. However his total concept of the Church went beyond the pilgrim or militant church and embraced in a very real way the full notion of the Communion of Saints. More had a very strong sense of the community spirit. In his youth he felt a strong attraction to the life of a religious community. When he married he built up quite a large community, and later even kept his children's families in his own home in a type of patriarchal society. More's creatures, the Utopians, were voluntarily communists, and one of the things they found most impressive in the Christian religion was that the early Christians' 'common way of life had been pleasing to Christ and that it is still in use among the truest societies of Christians'. The Utopians too had a very firm conviction of the Communion of Saints. Those who die well go to God, but remain interested in those still on earth. They are free to visit their friends and are able to protect them as they go about their affairs. The Utopians are aware of this presence which is a great source of comfort and confidence to them.[31] Erasmus tells us of the easy familiarity with which More spoke of the future life – a familiarity which gave the impression of real conviction.[32]

In his controversial works More took up the defence of this doctrine of the Communion of Saints. *The Supplication of Souls* (1529) is a defence of the financial support given to monasteries and is based on the fact that the monks fulfil a very serious obligation of the Christian community to pray for the dead. The plea, for dramatic purposes of presentation, is put into the mouths of those in Purgatory. They speak of the relief they obtain from the good works of the faithful, and especially from the oblation of the Holy Mass. They also have the help of the prayers of 'Our Lady, with such glorious saints as either ourselves with our own devotion while we lived, or ye with yours for us since our deceases and departing, have made intercessors to us'. Then there are 'the blessed spirits of our own proper good angels'. They go on to appeal to the readers to continue to pray for them: 'Remember what kin ye and we be together, what familiar friendship hath ere this between us, and what sweet

30. CHAMBERS, 366.
31. *Ut.* 127; 225.
32. ALLEN IV, no. 999.

words ye have spoken, and what promise ye have made to us... Remember how nature and Christendom bindeth you to remember us.'[33] Just as the saints in heaven are concerned for the souls in Purgatory, so they are interested in the Church militant: 'When saints were in this world at liberty and might walk the world about, ween ye that in heaven they stand tied to a post?'[34] These passages are a reflection of the devotion of More to Our Lady, the angels and saints, and of his sense of responsibility towards the Holy Souls.

B The Church Militant

Always within this context of the Communion of Saints, More preached and practised loyalty to the Church on earth.

1. The Teaching Church

As we have said, the reason for More's martyrdom was his loyalty to the unity of the Church. The occasion for his defence of that unity was the attack on the Primacy of the Pope as implied in the Supremacy of the King over the Church of England. We have already seen More's concept of the Primacy, and something of the evolution of his thought. His opinion was settled by 1528 when he wrote:[35]

> ... this is the very church; and thus hath begun at Christ and hath had
> Him for their head, and St Peter His vicar after Him, the head under
> Him, and always since the successors of him continually.

Yet in most of the writings of this period he deliberately avoided the question at the desire of the King. Even though the matter was clear to him, he realized that others were not sure the papacy was of divine institution. Consequently he based his position on the more obvious truth of the unity of Christ's Church: since there is only one Church, there can be only one head. Even if that head were chosen by the merely human law of Christendom, its authority was nevertheless legitimate. No single nation could elect its own supreme head because this would automatically entail independence of the whole, and therefore schism. We shall examine later the course More adopted when it became illegal to deny the King's Supremacy.

More clearly distinguished between the Pope's spiritual office as Head of the Church and his temporal activities as the head of the papal states. We have seen also how he distinguished the Pope's public office and his personal merit. On this point his observations are of some value. His 'exquisite discernment' is most remarkable when we remember some of the disreputable Popes who had ruled the Church even in More's own life-time.[36] More's pain at their un-

---

33. *EW* 338–9.
34. *EW* 188.
35. *EW* 185; cf. also 326 and EGAN, op. cit. 65.
36. BEDE JARRETT, 'A National Bulwark against Tyranny' in *The Fame of Blessed Thomas More*, London 1929, 113.

worthiness and at the ridicule directed at them, as well as his own attitude, is brought out in this passage:[37]

> I doubt not that Christ would have long ago looked down upon the pastor of His flock, if the Christian people had prayed for the salvation of their father, rather than persecuted him, if they had hidden his nakedness, rather than laughed at his shame.

Against Luther More advanced the goodness and holiness of many past Popes, and pointed with pride to the 'blamelessness of life and election' of the reigning Pope, Leo X.[38]

We have seen also that for More the highest authority in the Church and the ultimate norm in the formation of conscience was the body of Catholic Bishops, especially when gathered in a general Council.

Although simple priests and religious as such do not constitute a part of the 'teaching Church' in the technical sense, they do in fact have official standing in the Church as distinct from the faithful. Priests in particular exercise a function as an extension of the Bishops. Leaving aside for the time being More's detailed defence of the clergy and religious against the Protestants, we shall now consider his overall attitude to them throughout his life. We shall be seeking principles common to all phases of More's life, as a humanist, as a controversialist and as a spiritual author.

a. The State of Religion. As we would expect, More had the greatest respect for the state of religion. In *Utopia* we find that the people have the greatest reverence for priests and ascetics. The priests in Utopia are 'of extraordinary virtue, and therefore very few'. Their judgments on morality are taken very seriously. They are entrusted with the education of children and youths. They are esteemed even by foreign nations because of their restraint and humanity towards the defeated in war. In short 'to no other office in Utopia is more honour given, so much so that, even if they have committed any crime, they are subjected to no tribunal, but left only to God and to themselves'.[39]

In the *Apology* More speaks of the duty of the faithful to honour the clergy and religious. He is discussing the criticism of the clergy made anonymously by St German when he asserts that good Christian people are accustomed to give honour, as they are bound to, 'to their prelates and their curates, and to priests and religious persons' because of their devotion and duty 'to the holy profession of their godly state of living'. In the same book he expresses surprise that his adversary should suggest, even implicitly, that religious occupy a state of less perfection than do 'secular priests that have temporal lands of their own purchase or inheritance, or that serve some chantry or live upon trentals abroad'.[40]

37. *Resp.* 162; *CWR* 143.
38. *Resp.* 129–30; *CWR* 81.
39. *Ut.* 227–231.
40. *Apol.* 79–80; 70.

Writing in his prison cell, More expresses admiration for those religious who voluntarily limit their freedom of movement:[41]

> Holy monks I mean of the Charterhouse order, such as never pass their cells, but only to the church, set fast by their cells, and thence to their cells again. And Saint Bridget's order, and Saint Clare's much like, and in manner all those religious houses.

In his youth More felt the attraction of the monastic life, and even though he married, he looked forward to the time when he would be sufficiently free of family responsibilities to enjoy at least some of its benefits.[42] As a layman he protested his love for religious orders. In his *Letter to a Monk* he affirms that all good men cherish religious orders, he himself has ever loved and venerated them, and he wishes everyone else to do so too because their merits deserve the deepest charity. Moreover, the misery of the world is diminished by the unwearied prayers of so many thousands of devout religious.[43]

b. Criticism of Clergy and Religious. This basic attitude of More towards those in religion does not mean to say that he was blind to their faults or errors. At times he considered it his duty to comment on certain things which he thought out of keeping with their state in life. Writing as a humanist in the pre-Reformation years, he indulges in criticism of churchmen with a certain amount of gusto, indeed with a freedom which perhaps he later regretted when he saw the spread of the Reformation.[44] In those days before it was realized what a disaster was to follow, bad and ignorant churchmen were regarded as fair game for the enlightened humanists. Five of More's Latin epigrams deal with unworthy churchmen. One speaks of a 'certain mean and very stingy bishop' who, although very rich, kept his wine under lock and key. Another speaks of a certain fat priest whose habit it was to say: 'Learning puffs up.' Still another is on a friar who objected to comparing friends with brothers: 'We have a large and crowded monastery with more than two hundred brothers, but if from among the two hundred you can find two brothers who are friends, then I am a corpse!'[45]

This freedom in criticising priests, monks, theologians etc. was characteristic of all humanists. It is to be found throughout More's humanistic writings, e.g. in his correspondence, especially the letters to a Monk and to Dorp. The first book of *Utopia* contains a caricature of a monk.[46] Indeed, the holiness of the Utopian priests was intended as a contrast to the many unworthy churchmen of the time.

More's chief criticism of contemporary theologians was that they placed too much stress on casuistry and speculation, and were ignorant of the sources of theology – Scripture and the Fathers.[47] He attacked both the Monk and Dorp

41. *Dial. of Comf.* 325.
42. Roper 76; *SL* 173.
43. Bridgett 99; *Corr.* no. 83, p. 194 ff.
44. *SL* 144–5; also to Erasmus, ibid. 175.
45. *Epig.* xxix; nos. 53, 158, 160, 186, 187.
46. *Ut.* 83 ff.
47. *SL* 30, 32, 35 etc.

because they opposed Erasmus' edition and translation of the Greek New Testament.

More also lamented the lack of charity in religious, especially in conversation. He spoke of their party spirit, by which they were more interested in the customs and rules of their orders than they were in the commandments of God and the good of the Church. Special blame is attached also to those who lack humility:

> ... how many, with complete reliance on their religious state, are so conceited in their hearts that they imagine themselves strolling about in the heavens, and, enthroned on the rays of the sun, looking down from their lofty pinnacle upon the people, crawling like ants upon the ground, and not only upon the lay people, but upon all priests outside the fold of the cloister!

In the same letter he scoffs at the stupidity and stubbornness of a monk who preaches the certainty of salvation for anyone who says the full fifteen decades of the Rosary each day.[48]

When the Reformation broke out and the clergy were subjected to wholesale defamation, More spoke on their behalf, not with the intention of absolving them from all blame, but to see justice and truth preserved. He showed he realized the current religious problem was due to some extent to the laxity of the clergy, and no one regretted this more than he did. He deplored the fact that so many unworthy candidates were elevated to the dignity of the priesthood and called for the application of the laws of the Church regarding their selection. One passage dealing with the subject shows his sadness, but is relieved with a typical touch of humour:[49]

> 'The time was, I say, when few men durst presume to take upon them the high office of a priest, not even when they were chosen and called thereto. Now runneth every rascal and offereth himself for able. And where the dignity passeth all princes, and they that lewd be desireth it for worldly winning, yet cometh that sort thereto with such mad mind that they reckon almost God bounden to them if they vouchsafe to take it. But were I Pope –'
>
> 'By my soul', quoth the Messenger, 'I would ye were, and my lady your wife Popess too!'
>
> 'Well', quod I, 'then should she devise for the nuns! And as for me, touching the choice of priests, I could not well devise better provisions than are now by the laws of the Church provided. But for the number, I would surely see such a way therein that we should not have such a rabble, that every mean man must have a priest in his house to wait upon his wife, which no man almost lacketh now, to the contempt of the priesthood.'

48. *SL* 128–9; 132.
49. *EW* 219–220.

When More laid down the pen of controversy and gave himself over to meditation and the composition of ascetical works, he looked back to review the experiences of those troubled years. He must have wondered what had brought about the disasterous division of Christendom and left his own country in a state of schism. In the *History of the Passion* his homiletic reflection on the Apostles sleeping during Christ's agony in the garden reveals his condemnation of careless, or worse, evil-intentioned pastors. Some bishops, he says, sleep soundly and carelessly 'while virtue and true religion are like to run to ruin'. Even worse are those who slumber, 'not for sorrow and heaviness as the apostles did, but like a sort of swine wallowing in the mire, lie fast slugging in dead sleep of their mischievous blind affections, as men all drowned and drunken with the pleasant must of the devil, the flesh and the world'. In the same treatise, he compares with the traitor Judas those priests who 'consecrate the holy Body of Christ, and afterwards by false doctrine and evil example of living, kill Christ's members'. The 'lewd example of naughty priests' left the way open to heresy. [50]

The fact that More made the clergy and religious the butt of some of his 'merry tales' in his controversial books shows he appreciated the legitimate criticism of clerical failings, but at the same time it reveals a sense of perspective. For instance there is the story of the friar who, having preached for an hour, noticed a woman whispering to her pewfellow. The friar reprimanded her angrily: 'Hold thy babble, I bid thee, thou wife in the red hood.' But the church rang with her equally angry reply: 'Marry, sir, I beshrew his heart that babbleth most of us both. For I but whisper a word with my neighbour here, and thou hast babbled there all this hour!' But More was conscious of the graver faults of some priests as is shown by the tale of the poor man who 'found the priest over-familiar with his wife'. Because he 'spake it abroad and could not prove it, the priest sued him before the bishop's official for defamation'. His punishment was to make a public denial of his charge before the congregation at Sunday Mass. So on the Sunday he stood up and said: 'Mouth, mouth, thou liest!'; but shortly afterwards, he put his hands over his eyes and said: 'But eyes, eyes, by the Mass, ye lie not a whit!' [51]

In his letter to Dorp, More defends the methods by which Erasmus carried out his attacks on decadent churchmen, particularly in *The Praise of Folly*. He points out that ridicule of some churchmen did not necessarily entail ridicule of all. Moreover, Erasmus did not identify anyone he attacked by name or place, but only by the characteristic of 'sophistic nonsense'. [52]

More himself criticized by name on a few occasions. There is an account of a speech made by More when he took office as Chancellor, in which he condemned his predecessor Cardinal Wolsey. He was speaking on behalf of the King and in his capacity as head of the judiciary about someone who had been found

50. *Hist. Pass.* 56; 84–85; 77.
51. *EW* 948; 127.
52. *SL* 25, 54 ff.

guilty of misconduct.[53] He also condemned priests who had fallen into heresy and had been excommunicated by the Church, e.g. Luther and Tyndale. An interesting case is that of the 'Nun of Kent', Elizabeth Barton. In his direct contact with her he treated her with the greatest courtesy and reverence, and seemed to find her deserving of it. But when she was found guilty by her own confession he spoke harshly of her, describing her as 'a false deceiving hypocrite'.[54] We may conclude from these instances that he was prepared to speak when necessary of the faults of named individuals who had been found guilty of some crime by the appropriate authority.

c. *Reverence for Individual Religious and Clerics.* To the modern reader, the expressions of mutual esteem and reverence found in the letters of the humanists may appear unnatural and overdone. But even when this is taken into account, More's letters to John Colet, Erasmus, Tunstall, Warham, Fisher, Wolsey, Wilson etc. show a habitual and genuine reverence for them. In *Utopia*, More goes out of his way to pay tribute to Cardinal Morton.[55] Even when addressing those with whom he disagreed he spoke respectfully.[56] When speaking to or about those whom he genuinely admired, he does so with a warm love.[57]

Summary: From what we have said, it is apparent that More had the greatest respect and reverence for the state of life of priests and religious. He honoured those who lived up to the ideals of that state. On the other hand, he recognised that some were a discredit to their calling through their ignorance or moral failings. But he did not blame all for the faults of some. Nor did he publicly condemn any by name, unless they had previously been publicly convicted by the proper authority and there was reason for him to do so. After the advent of Protestantism, he regretted the extent to which he and Erasmus had ridiculed the faults of churchmen before Luther's outburst. Here is More's own summary of his attitude to the 'Spirituality':[58]

> The whole sum effect therefore of my mind in this matter is that as touching the Spirituality, I bear a tender mind of truth toward (I say) the body, not toward those that are nought therein. And this mind is everyman bound to bear. . .

2. The Worshipping Church

According to his early biographers, More was most assiduous in his practices of piety, both in the liturgy and in popular forms of devotion. He used to serve the priest at Mass, carry the cross in processions, and take part in the Rogation ceremonies. He donated the south aisle of the Chelsea parish church. He

---

53. CHAMBERS 240.
54. *SL* nos. 47, 50, 51; quotation from p. 199.
55. *Ut.* 59.
56. *SL* no. 26, to a Monk; cf. p. 37.
57. *SL*, letters to clerics mentioned above; p. 125 for eulogy of Fisher and Colet.
58. *Apol.* 190.

confessed frequently, and received Holy Communion especially when undertaking some important business. [59]

3. More as Spokesman against the Reformers

Because Lutheran ideas were infiltrating into England, Bishop Tunstall wrote to More asking him to read and refute the heretical books. He singled out More for the task because of his ability and prestige, and because of his eloquence in English. [60] More's response to this commission was the composition of eight books which make up his English controversial works. It was a huge output, being in excess of the original composition of even the energetic Erasmus. [61]

In most respects this choice of More was a good one. In the controversy with Luther, as well as in his professional career, he had shown himself to be a gifted debater. He had an excellent knowledge of Scripture and of the Fathers, and was in other respects also a competent theologian. He was one of England's leading writers: at his best his prose style is superb; at his worst he is maddeningly long-winded, and this is his biggest and perhaps only serious fault. It meant that this books were too long and too expensive to be read by the common people, who were the audience which Bishop Tunstall had in mind. His opponents, especially Tyndale, were able pamphleteers who hit with swift, sharp blows. This question of More's prolixity has been dealt with by not a few authors, and by More himself. It was due in part to his fairness in quoting his opponents at length, in part to his thoroughness, and in part to the natural advantage which the attacker always enjoys over the defender, namely, that it takes much longer to refute a charge than it does to make it: as More says in his *Apology:* 'the most foolish heretic in town may write more false heresies in one leaf, than the wisest man in the world can well and conveniently by reason and authority soyle in forty.' [64] Nevertheless, it should be admitted that he would have fulfilled his duty more successfully had he restricted himself to shorter compositions.

The quality and quantity of More's controversial work is an indication of the zeal with which he undertook his task. It is true that his later books show signs of weariness, of loss of concentration and a lack of humour. But on the whole he writes with the zest of a combatant who is sure of himself and his position, and who is certain that he is doing something worthwhile in bringing down heresy. He wrote about 1528 to John Cochlaeus: 'I wish, my dear Cochlaeus, I had the requisite knowledge in Scripture and theology to be able to write an effective rejoinder to those baneful curses.' [65] He was being modest

59. E. g., STAPLETON, 68–72.
60. REYNOLDS, 162; *Corr.* 387.
61. REYNOLDS, *Thomas More and Erasmus,* 205.
62. KERNAN, op. cit.; cf. also DONNELLY's introduction to *Resp.*
63. REYNOLDS, *Sir Thomas More*, London 1965, 32.
64. *Apol.* 7; 'soyle', i.e. answer.
65. *SL* 168.

in speaking so disparagingly of his competence, as Erasmus testifies when he describes More: 'A man of incomparable genius, a most happy memory, a most ready eloquence . . . in divinity he has made so much progress that he is not to be despised even by the most eminent theologians.'[66]

Roper tells us that the English Bishops were so grateful for More's efforts that they organized the collection of a large sum of money as a reward. More refused to accept the gift, saying he would rather see it cast into the Thames than he or any of his family should take one penny from them. Even though the offer was 'friendly and honourable', he would not have lost so many nights' sleep for mere profit, even for a far greater sum than what they were offering.[67] More realized the effectiveness of his work would suffer if it were known he was in the pay of the Bishops. This charge was actually made against him but he was easily able to dismiss it.[68]

Even though his defence of the Church was wholehearted, More at the same time wished his efforts were not necessary. As far as he was concerned, people were wasting their time reading both his and the Reformers' books. He would gladly see all his books burned and his labour lost 'upon condition that all heresies were suppressed'.[69] This statement sheds light upon More's motives in accepting the commission. He was not writing for money or for his own personal honour, but purely in defence of the Church. Bishop Tunstall's letter was for him a sign of his duty before God.

Did St Thomas More, in his loyal defence of the Church, maintain at least a just attitude towards his opponents? Leaving aside for the time being the question of abusive language, let us enquire into More's personal regard for the Christian welfare of the Reformers.

In another letter to Cochlaeus in 1532, we find More rejoicing over the death of two Reformers, Zwingli and Oecolampadius: that they had done so much damage to the Christian faith was a cause for sadness, but the fact such savage enemies of the Church were dead was a cause for rejoicing.[70]

About the year 1533 More sent to Erasmus a copy of his epitaph, in which he described himself as a 'source of trouble to thieves, murderers and heretics'. In the accompanying letter he commented that he made the reference to the heretics 'just to be smart'. He was so appalled by the ruin they were causing that he wished to be as hateful as possible to them.[71]

More considered right faith necessary for salvation. A person who has wrong faith, therefore, cannot be saved and must be guilty and hateful in the sight of God. The Christian should conform his mind to God's: what is hateful to God should be hateful to the Christian. The Reformers with their false faith put

66. ALLEN, IV, 1117, tr. DONNELLY, *Resp.* 1.
67. CHAMBERS 255.
68. *EW* 867.
69. CHAMBERS 255.
70. *SL* 177.
71. *SL* 180–1.

themselves into this category. Worse still, they try to spread their doctrines thereby bringing other souls to ruin, damaging both Church and State. This then is the root of More's antagonism to Reformers. They were for him a legitimate object of contempt.

On the other hand, More exercised basic charity towards Reformers in that he prayed for their salvation. He wrote of Frith:[72]

> I fear that Christ will kindle a fire of faggots for him here, and send his soul forever into the fire of hell. Now in these words I did not mean that I would it were so. For I would gladly undergo more labour, loss, and pain than many men might suppose to win that young man to Christ and His true faith again.

At the end of the *Dialogue concerning Heresies* he prays that 'God may give these seditious sects the grace to cease, and the favourers of these factions to amend'.[73] This prayer is elaborated in the conclusion of *The Answer to the First Part of the Poisoned Book* where he asks that the Reformers will be given the grace to turn from their heresies before it is too late so that they would be 'knit unto God' together with the Catholics in one Church, in one faith, good hope, and their 'sister, well-working charity', that they all may share in the one Eucharist, the 'very flesh and blood' of Christ, so that finally all may be 'incorporate in Christ in His eternal glory. Amen'.[74] More's refusal to compromise on matters of faith sprang from his loyalty to the truth as delivered by God to the Church. Without this faith in all the teachings of the Church, and without the sacraments, More considered it impossible to be saved. The greatest good, then, he could wish for the Reformers was that they should accept this full Catholic doctrine and be incorporated into Christ's Mystical Body and thereby attain heaven.

How can we balance the hatred and charity of More for the Reformers? More deals with the point in his *Apology* as he had been criticised for the violence of his attacks on them. 'As touching heretics, I hate that vice of theirs, and not their persons; and very fain would I that the one were destroyed, and the other saved'; this was true, he writes, no matter what 'these blessed new brethren' say to the contrary, and he had witnesses to prove it. Any Reformer who had amended he had treated 'not as an evil man or an abject, nor as a stranger neither, but as a good man and my very friend'. On the other hand, More does not wish to take more credit than is due to him, so he puts it on record for all the world to know that if a Reformer proves to be incurable and thereby is a danger to others, he 'would rather be content that he were gone in time than overlong to tarry to the destruction of other'.[75]

The modern reader is somewhat shocked when he reads the abuse which sixteenth century controversialists hurled at one another. The shock is in-

72. Ibid.
73. *EW* 288.
74. *EW* 1138.
75. *Apol.* 190–1; see REYNOLDS, *Thomas More and Erasmus* 205.

creased when we find it in the writings of a canonized saint. The point is discussed by several authors from the literary and moral points of view.[76] It is our intention to deal with it briefly in relation to loyalty and spirituality.

On more than one occasion More apologises to his readers for the use of such language, but he feels justified, and indeed compelled to do so under the circumstances. In the first place he contends that the Reformers themselves set the tone of the controversy. He was merely giving them back some of their own treatment to bring them to their senses. Possibly More's most virulent work was the *Responsio ad Lutherum*. In it he apologises for material which may have offended the modesty of the reader; he explains that it annoyed him to have been forced to use such improper language, but it was unavoidable: 'How could I possibly answer in pure, clean terms the impure words of this impure wretch when I undertook the refutation of his scurrilous lies?'[77] So much was the tone determined by the Reformers that More on several occasions declares he will treat them with 'words as fair and mild as the matter may suffer and bear', if they on their part will 'be reasonable heretics, and honest, and write reason and leave railing'.[78] He had made a similar offer at the end of the *Responsio*, but unfortunately he surrounded it with so many insults his opponent would hardly have accepted it. Evidently More did not really expect any softening on the part of the Reformers. He did not wish to take the initiative in an offer to lay down the weapons of abuse, but he did wish to intimate, in a very blunt way it is true, that on his part he was prepared to debate dispassionately: if Luther will withdraw his lies and false accusations, if he will stop his foolish and furious raging, cleanse the filth from his tongue and pen, he will find disputants who will discuss his problems with the seriousness the matter demands. But, on the other hand,[79]

> if he goes on with his scurrility and madness as he has begun, with his calmunious attacks, his inept folly, his stupid rage and his vulgar buffoonery, if he will use no language but that of the sewer . . . then – let others do what they will – we will decide . . . either to drag out the madman from his stronghold and show him his true colours, or to leave our raving friend with all his Furies . . . covered with his own filth.

We have already seen that Luther replied to the King's book in very scurrilous terms. Some of the other Reformers were almost as bad, for example Barnes, who attacked Catholic Bishops in these words: 'You worms' meat, you stinking carrion, you nourishment of hell-fire.'[80] More imagines Luther and his *compotatores* holding a council of war to devise a way of refuting Henry's book:

76. See DONNELLY's Introduction to *Resp.* where she has gathered a good number of comments; CHAMBERS 265; J. S. BREWER, *The Reign of Henry VIII from his Accession to the Death of Wolsey*, London 1884, I, 608–9.
77. *Resp.* 256; *CWR* 685.
78. *EW* 866.
79. See STAPLETON 34.
80. Quoted by TAFT, *Apol.* 285.

since they cannot use reason, they resort to foul language and mocking jests. Luther sends out his henchmen to every conceivable place of ill repute to note down every opprobrious term they hear: they gather bold, shameful, base and obscene language from harlots, procurers, bath-keepers and lavatories:[81]

> ... insults, quarrels, buffoonery, jests, boldness, baseness, filthiness, mire, dirt, dung! this entire mess was stuffed into that foulest of sewers, the mind of Luther! This whole mixture, like digested dung, Luther vomits back through that impure mouth straight into his insulting book.

Authors have remarked on the much milder tone More used against John Frith, an attractive and sincere person who was himself comparatively restrained.

There was another important factor which influenced More and made him feel compelled to write as he did: Luther had insulted the King of England. Not only as a Catholic, but as a loyal Englishman, More saw it as his duty to give this heretic such a whipping that he would be the laughing-stock of Europe and so the King's honour would be avenged. That national loyalty came into the matter is brought out in the following extract:[82]

> Luther's words: ... this damnable rottenness and very worm: it is right for me, for the sake of my King, to sprinkle this English Majesty with mud and filth, and to trample underfoot that blasphemous crown of his which attacks Christ.
>
> [More:] ... But meanwhile, for as long as it will take your Paternity to lie impudently about this, too, others will be permitted, for the cause of His English Majesty, to throw right back into your Paternity's filthy mouth, of all dung, the very dunghill, all the mud and filth which your damnable rottenness deserves! May they pour out all the sewers and latrines on your crown, deprived as it is of the dignity of the sacerdotal tonsure, as you also decreed the kingly crown should be mocked.

It has been pointed out that if More called Luther by bad names, it was in good Latin, according to the humanist code. When estimating any scandal caused by his book, we should recall that it was available only to scholars, virtually all of them male, who were familiar with polemical devices. The book has been translated into English only at the present day.

The forensic tone of the *Responsio* has been remarked upon. More, like an advocate cross-examining a 'truculent and wooly-headed' witness, proves to the court that Luther's statements contain a thousand inconsistencies and contradictions, and moreover, he is nothing but a scoundrel.[83] Certainly in the case of this book, the abuse is inextricably tied in with his purpose.

It was not only the attack on the King which moved More to retaliation

81. *Resp.* 117; *CWR* 61. More himself was Commissioner of Sewers in 1514.
82. *Resp.* 251; *CWR* 311.
83. A. Cecil, *A Portrait of Thomas More* London 1937, 201.

80

against the Reformers: they were guilty of wholesale slander and irresponsible abuse against the Catholic clergy and religious. More did not care about himself: they could call him what they liked, in fact the worse they called him the more pleasure it would give him, but he would brook no insults against others. If they forbear insults against others, he will speak fairly to them; if they will not leave their railing, he will use like language to them, even though he could not match them. He concedes them the mastery in bad language, but in any case 'to match them were more rebuke than honesty'.[84]

Another reason put forward by More to justify his bad names is that he is bound to tell the truth. He is not always being facetious when he says this. In his *Apology* he denies having said that the heretics lacked wit and learning. But the more wit and learning they have, the more they show foolishness: 'the more appeareth the feebleness of their part and the falsehood of their heresies.' Then he tells a story from Plutarch of some soldiers who deserted their own king and went into the service of Philip of Macedonia. Whenever the soldiers quarrelled among themselves, the Macedonians would call the newcomers traitors. These complained to Philip, who answered: 'Good fellows, be not angry with my people, but have patience. I am sorry their manner is no better . . . their nature is so plain, and their utterance so rude, that they cannot call an horse but an horse!' More applies the parable: '. . . even as the Macedonians could not call a traitor but a traitor, so can I not call a fool but a fool, nor an heretic but an heretic.'[85]

In a passage in the *Dialogue concerning Heresies*, he calls Luther more than a heretic, but he does so first, because what he says is true, secondly because it is necessary that Luther be exposed for what he is. If the Church's doctrine is true, 'as indeed it is', so that 'St Paul would not give an angel of heaven audience to the contrary', it would be unwise and disloyal to give hearing, 'not to an angel of heaven, but to a fond friar, to an apostate, to an open, incestuous lecher, a plain limb of the devil, and a manifest messenger of hell'. Luther, both untruly and without necessity, rails against those whom he should reverence. More, on the other hand 'between us twain' calls Luther only what he has proved himself to be 'in his writing, in his living, and in his mad marriage', and he does so only because it is necessary to save the public from the madness of the fables that contradict the truths given to the Church by the Holy Spirit, proved by miracles and martyrdoms, by the virtuous lives of confessors, the purity of chaste widows and undefiled virgins, 'by the wholesome doctrine of so many holy doctors, and by the consent of all Christian people for fifteen hundred years'.[86]

Finally, in justification of his raillery, More appealed to the precedent in the earliest Christian tradition: St Paul, he says, called 'his carlish keepers dogs'; he called 'a chief priest a whited wall (which was a spiteful word among them)';

84. *EW* 865–6.
85. *Apol.* 46.
86. *EW* 247.

St Polycarp called the heretic Marcion 'the devil's eldest son'; and was our Saviour railing 'when He called the scribes and the Pharisees hypocrites'? Is it railing 'to give evil names to such folk as are evil indeed'?[87]

More's use of scurrility was therefore a pre-meditated and carefully considered tactic. The reasons he gives for its use amount to these: the heretics started it and a taste of their own medicine may bring them to their senses; he was defending others, especially the King and the clergy; what he said was true and there was necessity to publish it; there was a precedent for speaking as he did in the conduct of Christ and his saints.

What are we to think of these reasons? In the milder climate of our ecumenical era, we may wonder what would have been the effect of a more charitable approach. Some have expressed regret that More wrote the way he did. The Victorian Brewer wrote: 'That a nature so pure and gentle, so adverse to coarse abuse ... should soil its better self with vulgar and offensive raillery ... shocks and pains, like the misconduct of a dear friend.'[88] On the other hand, C. S. Lewis considers that[89]

> from a moral point of view no very serious charge can be made; More is not much more scurrilous, only more amusingly scurrilous, than many of our older controversialists ... the chief and often the only merit of these works is the gusto of their hard-hitting, racy, street-corner abuse. It was More's business to appeal to the vulgar, to play to the gallery, and it suited one side of him extremely well ... to rebuke magnificently is one of the duties of a great polemical writer.

In the introduction to her translation of the *Responsio*, Sister Gertrude Donnelly considers the whole question and the opinions and reactions of various authors and finally gives her own verdict:[90]

> We do not contend, then, that More was blameless on the matter of scurrility in the *Responsio*, but merely that he did not begin to compare with the volcanic eruptions of Luther.

An objective decision is difficult and perhaps impossible, but it may be worth remembering that Luther himself apparently enjoyed manly, earthy humour. Our own purpose was to show that More acted as his conscience allowed and required after he had formed it by objective reason and recourse to precedent.

4. Defence of the Church's doctrine

In the four and a half years of his controversy with the English Protestants, More defended the Church in almost every arena of discussion. The quantity of his writings (about 900,000 words in that period) is some indication of the

87. Ibid. 939; the reference to St Paul and his keepers has not been traced, cf. *Moreana* no. 1, Sep. 1963, 89, but it may have been a mistaken allusion to Phil. 3 : 2; the story of Polycarp is from St Jerome's *De scriptoribus ecclesiasticis*, ch. 17.
88. Brewer, op. cit. I, 608–9.
89. C. S. Lewis, *English Literature in the Sixteenth Century*, Oxford 1954, 175.
90. Resp. 71.

completeness of his commitment.[91] It will be helpful to summarise his doctrine to bring out the extent of his loyalty to the Catholic faith, and to show that this loyalty was not blind, but based on reasonable convictions.

The subjects which More discussed were to a large extent dictated by his opponents. It soon became clear the Reformers' principles were so radical that the whole area of doctrine came under their scrutiny. Even in his first skirmish with Luther, More touched the subjects of Scripture, tradition, the marks of the true Church, the primacy of the Pope, indulgences, Communion under both kinds, the Mass, the doctrine of transubstantiation and the sacrament of orders. With the English Protestants he went into the subject of justification with all its concomitants: free will, grace, merit, predestination, satisfaction, and the sacraments.

Adherence to the living Church, the Mystical Body of Christ, is at the basis of More's system. In his opinion we must remain faithful to the Church's doctrine because of Christ's promise that he would teach the Church through the Holy Spirit and would remain with the Church till the end of the world.[92] At the head of the Church on earth is the Papacy, instituted by God, but occupied by men of free will and liable to sin: but the sinfulness of some Popes does not imply that the Papacy itself is bad. He thought the Pope subject to a general Council, and also that the Papacy is not necessarily fixed to the See of Rome. Our duty of fidelity to the Church is borne out by the Fathers, saintly men who promoted Christian piety among their people both by enlightened exposition of the Scriptures and by the goodness of their example. The Reformers have against them the perpetual consent of the whole Christian world during the centuries since Christ. This consent is inspired by the Holy Ghost, 'qui facit unanimes in domo'.[93]

More has been highly praised for his clear treatment of the doctrine of justification and predestination because he was able to see the issues so distinctly in those difficult days before the Council of Trent.[94]

If certain doctrines seem incompatible, said More, we must put it down to the feebleness of our minds: we are not justified in rejecting revealed truths because we cannot understand them. For example, we must believe that the doctrine of the necessity of God's grace is compatible with man's free will: '. . . man cannot turn unto Him without prevention and concurrent help of God's especial grace; but . . . the goodness of God provideth that His grace is ever ready to him that will use it . . .' The apparent repugnance of God's foreknowledge and human free will is due only 'to the poor blind reason of man'. If man is not free, 'Our Lord would not call upon men and exhort them to believe, as He doth in many places of Scripture'.[95] According to More, God's grace and the cooperation

91. REYNOLDS, *Thomas More and Erasmus*, 205.
92. *Op. Om.* 110; *CWR* 487; *EW* 327.
93. *Resp.* 129–30; *CWR* 129; *Corr.* 328–9.
94. KERNAN, op. cit. 285.
95. *EW* 580, 583; *Corr.* 454.

of man by faith, hope, charity and works, are necessary for salvation: St Paul sometimes speaks of justification by faith, but this must be balanced with the fact that elsewhere he inculcates the distinction between 'faith which lacks charity and the life of good works, and that which works through love'.[96] And by faith More meant right faith as is brought out in the following extract, which will also serve as an introduction to More's defence of the Eucharist:[97]

> I said in effect: If Frith labours to quench the faith that all Christians have in Christ's blessed body and blood, he shall labour in vain; and moreover I fear that Christ will kindle a fire of faggots for him here and send his soul forever into the fire of hell.

If Christians have been wrongly believing that Christ is present in the Eucharist, or if their faith in transubstantiation is something new, Christ has failed his Church and the Spirit of truth has been teaching falsehood – which is altogether unthinkable.[98] Christ is loyal to his Church and faithful to his promise.

In explaining the Real Presence, More sets out to prove that Christ is in many places at once, a thing made possible by the infinite power of God. This is a mystery, but it was clearly taught by Christ that the Eucharist is truly His flesh and blood as is evidently seen by the reaction of the people described in the sixth chapter of St John's Gospel:[99]

> Now whereas at the vine and the door they marvelled nothing, yet at the eating of His flesh and the drinking of His blood, they so sore marvelled, and were so sore moved, and thought the matter so hard, and the wonder so great, that they asked how could that be, and went almost all their way . . .

For fifteen hundred years all Christians have understood this in 'the plain literal sense'.

Concerning Baptism, More believes it to be necessary, but rejects St Augustine's doctrine that infants who die without it are consigned to eternal physical torment.[100]

Confession of sins is part of the sacrament of Penance and is to be made to priests. More rejects Luther's suggestion of confession to women because it would be a danger to the seal: before long 'all the gossips in the town' would know what had been confessed.[101]

---

96. *Resp.* 152; *CWR* 123.
97. *Apol.* 137; also *Hist. Pass.* 97–8, '. . . whosoever hopeth to have [eternal life] out [= outside] of His Body, the Church, and without right faith, doth with a vain hope lewdly deceive himself.'
98. *Op. Om.* 110; *CWR* 487. On More's treatment of the eucharistic sacrifice see JOHN JAY HUGHES, *Stewards of the Lord*, London and Sydney 1970, 129–136. Hughes concludes that More's treatment of this point did not provide an adequate reply to the theological difficulties raised by the Reformers. Hughes points out that in the *Treatise upon the Passion*, *EW* 1338, More makes use of the classical concept of representation which might have served as a starting point for a sound theology of the Mass but he failed to develop it even in his controversial writings.
99. *Corr.* 445.
100. F. SEEBOHM, *The Oxford Reformers*, London, 2nd. ed. 1869, 472 quoting 'A Letter to a Monk.'
101. *EW* 249–50.

More also defended marriage as a sacrament. Its sanctity was, he considered, at the foundation of Christian society. The Lutheran concept would lead to the ultimate declaration 'that all women ought to be common to all men'. He therefore tells Luther: 'Go teach your faithless faith and religion to the Bohemian land where matrimony is nothing but increasing and multiplying and mating like dogs in the church!'[102]

Concerning the sacraments in general, More taught that God can and does use material things to bring about a spiritual effect. The sacraments, however, are not merely signs, but causes also. Their causality is at least that which is proper to signs. He explains it with the example of a lord who gives a badge or a gown to a poor fellow, saying: 'If thou take it and wear it, I will take thee for my household servant, and in my household give thee meat and drink and wages.' The sign itself does not give meat or money, but yet it is more than a sign that he shall get them because of the lord's ordinance.[103]

Against the Protestants More asserted both the existence of Purgatory and the doctrine that we may help the Holy Souls by prayer and acts of atonement. He proves this from the doctrine of the Communion of Saints and from the fact that the sufferings of Christ benefit all mankind. He also argues from St Paul's practice of praying for others and of requesting that they should pray for him. Similarly, the whole Church prayed for the deliverance of St Peter from prison (Acts 12:5). If then God hears the prayers of others for someone suffering 'a little pain or imprisonment in the world', *a fortiori* He will listen to men's 'humble and hearty prayer' for those suffering in the 'hot fire of purgatory'.[104]

More also defends Catholic belief concerning miracles. He teaches that they are quite reasonable: even the Utopians believed in them, prayed for them to happen and quite often were blessed with them.[105] To the objection that people sometimes allege false miracles, More replies that God is always faithful to His people, and in His providence will see to it false miracles are exposed, just as He did in the Old Testament when He 'brought to light the false fained miracle of the priests of the idol Bell in the old time, as appeareth in the fourteenth chapter of the prophet Daniel'.[106] In the case of the alleged miracles of the Nun of Kent, More counselled Fr Rich not 'to wed' himself to them lest they be afterwards proved false.[107] More himself found so much to wonder about in nature that he found it easy to accept miracles. He tells beautifully a 'merry tale' of a young couple, still 'quick and quething', who courted, married and were finally left alone on their wedding night. When the Messenger impatiently tells More to finish the story, he goes on to tell how 'the seed of them

102. *EW* 656; *Resp.* 201; *CWR* 221.
103. *EW* 384–5.
104. *EW* 326–7.
105. *Ut.* 225.
106. *EW 1931* II, 45–6.
107. *SL* 200.

twain turned in the woman's body, first into blood, and after into shape of a man-child, and then waxed quick, and she great therewith, and was within the year delivered of a fair boy . . . And methinketh that this is as great a miracle as the raising of a dead man'. The frequent occurrence of such marvels should not blind us to the miracles which continually happen around us. [108]

According to More the Church's authority is necessary for a preacher to proclaim the Word of God. Those who are silenced by their superiors should obey. Yet Protestants were maintaining that 'they were by God bounden to preach, and that no man nor no law that was made or could be made had any authority to forbid them'. As if God would send them to 'preach heresies and sow sedition among Christian men!' [109]

More foresaw that once the authority of the Church was ignored, ever worse heresies would spring up. It had already occurred to some extent: infant baptism had been rejected by some; lawful authority, both religious and civil, had been denied by others; marriage was being undermined, the Divinity of Christ rejected. In the end, the principles of the Protestants would lead to the very denial of God, the devil and the immortality of the human soul. They would end up 'thus reckoning upon nothing but only for the body'. [110]

On the other hand, heresy has been allowed by God for a purpose. Heretics are 'God's scourge' which He allows to afflict the Church for a while. But in His mercy He will in time bring an end to the punishment of the Church, convert those who have been deceived by error, and those who are incurable He will cast into hell: 'as an old naughty rod, before the face of His faithful children of His Catholic Church, when He hath beaten and corrected them therewith, so as a tender mother doth, break the rod in pieces and cast it in the fire.' [111] Heresy then is allowed by God as a punishment for the sins of His Catholic children, but when it has served its purpose it will be destroyed.

The above summary of More's apologetic doctrine shows how much loyalty played a part in his theological thinking: first, his own loyalty to Catholic doctrine – a loyalty based on intelligent conviction; secondly, his unshakable trust in the loyalty of a provident Father and of a Christ faithful to his promise to leave his Spirit of truth forever in his Church. This is why More was loyal to the Catholic faith: the true Church will never be overcome – [112]

> For as the sea shall never surround and overwhelm all the land, and yet hath it eaten many places in, and swallowed whole countries up, and many places now sea that sometime were well-inhabited lands, and hath lost part of his own possession in other parts again; so the faith of Christ shall never be overflowen with heresies, nor the gates of hell prevail against Christ's Church, yet as in some places it winneth

108. *EW* 131–2.
109. *EW 1931* I, 81.
110. *EW* 656–7.
111. *EW* 630.
112. *Apol.* 180.

in new people, so may there in some places by negligence be lost the old.

5. More's Defence of Catholic Customs

Seeing that the Reformers called into question many Catholic customs and pious practices, More felt called upon to defend them. In doing so he exercised that restraint and balance which we have seen before. His loyal defence of Catholic practices did not blind him to the truth that in some quarters they were abused. On the other hand abuse does not take away the proper use of a thing: an argument which More repeated insistently. More himself had attacked the stupidity of some customs and the motives with which some people practised them. So did Erasmus: it seems that he wrote *The Praise of Folly* in More's house and with his encouragement. But More was more restrained than Erasmus. He distinguished more carefully between legitimate use and abuse, whereas the remarks of Erasmus are almost universally derisive.[113]

Clerical celibacy was one of the issues raised by Luther and the other Reformers. The laxity of many clerics was a source of scandal which stimulated thoughts on measures for reform. More himself had touched on the subject in *Utopia*, in which celibacy was optional for the clergy. What was More's point in writing such a thing? Was it merely a reminder that the priesthood and celibacy do not necessarily go together? Was it a tentative suggestion as a means for remedying a widespread problem? This is just one of the tantalizing queries which arise from *Utopia*.[114] Against the Reformers, More admitted that the legislation requiring priestly celibacy was not of divine origin as is seen in the New Testament. But chastity was highly recommended by Christ if practised for his sake. It is indeed, said More, a great gift; it is even a 'seldom gift' in that it is practised by a number relatively smaller than those who do not practise it. But this does not mean it is a 'rare gift' when considering the whole of Christendom. More argued that even among the Jews, 'who most magnified generation', chastity was highly regarded, especially being recommended to priests when they served in the temple. How much more then should it be practised by the priests of Christ, who was born of a virgin, and lived and died a virgin, and who counselled virginity. Granted it is a counsel of perfection which may be freely followed or not, it surely is fitting that the Church allow only the celibate to enter Christ's temple 'to serve about the Sacrament'.[115]

The question of vows was also very much to the fore in the Reformers' programme. This was a matter which roused More to an angry retort. By conviction and temperament he considered that a man should stand to his promises and to his commitments.[116] At the end of his *Responsio* he violently takes Luther to task for violating his vows and encouraging others to do like-

113. EDWARD L. SURTZ S.J., *The Praise of Wisdom*, Chicago, 1957, 181–2.
114. *Ut.* 227.
115. *EW* 227–231.
116. CHAMBERS, 86.

wise: 'And the pledge and promise which, if made to men, only a wicked man would violate, they do not scruple to violate when made to God.'[117] More asked his opponents to find patristic support for their interpretation of Scripture to allow 'for wedding of monks, friars and nuns, which the whole Catholic Church all these fifteen hundred year, before these late lewd heresies began, have ever more abhorred and holden for abominable'. If they could find, he continues, one of the Fathers who says that breach of vows is no sin, he will concede them everything, so certain is he that unanimous tradition is 'against these vow-breaking brethren'.[118]

The practice of self-denial also came under fire from the Reformers. The attack sprang from their notion of good works. More gives a vivid account of a sermon by one of the new preachers who appeals to the people to 'leave these inventions of men, your foolish lenten fasts and your peevish penance, and minish never Christ's thank'. This particular preacher believed that it takes away from the value of Christ's passion if we believe our own penance is also necessary.[119] Others conceded that 'fasting serveth but for the temperance of the flesh'. But this is not sufficient either, says More, because not only did holy men like Moses, Elias, Paul and others fast, but even Christ himself did so, and he had no need to tame the flesh. The value of our practices is bound up with the mystery of our incorporation into Christ. Of themselves they have no value, but united with the Passion and death of our Head they become meritorious, because 'His pleasure is, that we shall also take pain our own self with Him, and therefore He biddeth all that be His disciples take their crosses on their backs as He did, and with their crosses follow Him.'[120] It may strike us as strange to find More using an argument which is not very theological, but which would appeal to the 'common man', in support of belief in the efficacy of self-denial for oneself and the souls in Purgatory: if a man prays and gives alms for the Holy Souls, he cannot lose, because if his belief in Purgatory is not true, he will still receive reward for his good faith. On the other hand, if another man does not believe in Purgatory and does no good works, and if he is wrong and there is ('as indeed there is') a Purgatory, he loses because he has made no satisfaction, has no friends whom he has helped from Purgatory, and will have more to answer for because, not fearing Purgatory, he will be inclined to sin more. To illustrate More tells a story of a 'lewd gallant and a friar'. The gallant asked the friar why he was walking barefoot in frost and snow thereby causing himself great pain. The friar answered that the pain was small if a man remember hell. 'But what if there be no hell', said the gallant, 'then art thou a great fool.' The friar replied: 'Yea, master, but what if there be a hell, then is your mastership a much greater fool.'[121]

117. *Resp.* 260; *CWR* 689.
118. *Apol.* 31.
119. *Dial. of Comf.* 193.
120. Ibid. 194.
121. *EW* 329; I have changed the wording slightly.

More also defended the use of images. In the first place they are useful, even for those who are accustomed to meditation on the subjects depicted: even a contemplative 'findeth himself more moved to pity and compassion upon the beholding of the holy crucifix than when he lacketh it'. There is little danger of idolatry, because even a dog can see the difference between an image and the real object: 'for no dog is so mad but he knoweth a very coney from a coney carved and painted.'[122] The lawfulness of images is shown from the fact that they are only signs. Other signs are in continual use, words, for example, even the holy name of Our Lord, 'which name is but an image representing His person to man's mind and imagination'.[123]

The veneration of relics led to some curious abuses that earned the contempt of the Protestants. Again keeping the matter in perspective, More could see its humourous side as is evident from the words he puts into the mouth of the Messenger: some saints seem not to have had bodies because they have no shrines, but 'to recompense that withal, there be some again that have two bodies to lend one to some good fellow that lacketh'. He is alluding to the fact that different shrines and monks had conflicting claims as to the possession of certain relics: 'For both places plainly affirm that it lieth there. And at either place they show the shrine. And in the shrine they show a body, which, they say, is *the* body and boldly bide thereby that it is, alleging old writing and miracles also, for the proof.' Either the miracles are false or the saint had two bodies which would be the 'greatest miracle of them all'. How does all this fuss over a man's bones, and setting his carcase in a gay shrine, and then kissing his bare scalp, make a man a saint? Moreover, some things pointed out as relics are undoubtedly false, and, as Chaucer says, a bone worshipped for a relic could easily be a bone 'of some holy Jew's sheep'.[124] More simply replies that the abuse of a thing does not take away the use: in some countries they hunt on Good Friday morning which does not mean we should do away with Good Friday.[125] Moreover, just because the bodies of some saints cannot be found, one may not conclude, as the Messenger had implied, that such saints never existed. For example no one doubts that Our Lady or St John the Evangelist existed even though their bodies have not been found. And if they were, no one would neglect to enshrine them.[126]

To the Reformers' complaint that the Church would not allow vernacular editions of the Scriptures, More came out definitely in favour of such translations. He knew of no good reasons why they should not be put into English: 'all those reasons, seemed they never so gay and glorious at the first sight, yet when they were well examined they might in effect . . . as well be laid against the holy writers that wrote the Scripture in the Hebrew tongue . . . in Greek, and

122. *EW* 121; CAMPBELL, 148; 'coney', i.e. a rabbit.
123. *EW* 114.
124. *EW* 190.
125. *EW 1931* II, 167.
126. Ibid. II, 156.

against all those in likewise that translated it out of every of those tongues into Latin.' But if the Bishops thought some restriction was needed, they could impose some limitation, as a father will discretely keep a knife away from a child who may cut his finger. If regulations were considered necessary, More would offer these suggestions: the first three gospels might be allowed to some people and the fourth forbidden; some might be allowed to read the Acts, but not the Apocalypse; the Ephesians, but not the Romans. He would prefer the whole Bible to be allowed to all men and women, but if that were unacceptable to the Bishops, it would be better to allow them some of the Bible rather than none 'according to the moderation as I speak of, or some such other as wiser men can better devise'. [127]

6. Defence of the Morals of Catholics

One of the principal causes of the Reformation was the unworthiness of many Catholics, especially clergy and religious. More could not but admit that some complaints were based on fact. On the other hand, he replied that some charges were based on rumour, some were too sweeping, some were completely false and some were followed by conclusions which did not logically follow. Throughout the *Apology* he roundly slates the anonymous writer (St German) for basing his evidence on what 'some say'. In the *Supplication* he rejects as false the figures upon which Fish had computed the income of the clergy throughout England. [128] In his book against Luther More had savagely rebuked him for attributing the faults of individual Popes to the Papacy itself. [129]

Some of Christopher St German's remarks were so general that they must be true in some cases: some 'serve not God as they should do, but some of them love authority and some love their ease, and some serve God of vain glory for laud and praise of men'. If this is the case, says More, the trouble is not of recent origin but was always present and always will be 'as long as the world lasteth' because of human nature and free will. [130] In dealing with the more specific allegations against Dr Horsey and his assistants, More puts on record a brief eye-witness summary of the Hunne case. [131]

Much of the criticism of the clergy, said More, sprang from a hypocritical righteousness on the part of the critics, indeed from an ever present trait in human nature that no matter what our superiors do, we are never satisfied: 'in reproach of them neither good nor bad passeth unreproved'; whether they be familiar or solitary, sad or merry, we criticize them; if they keep few servants they are niggards, if they keep many they are pompous; 'if a lewd priest do a lewd deed, then we say, "lo see what sample they show us!"' But we fare as do the ravens and the carrion crows, that never meddle with any quick flesh, but

127. *EW* 243–6.
128. *EW* 293–5; TAFT's introduction to *Apol.* xxvi.
129. *Resp.* 129–130; *CWR* 81.
130. *Apol.* 78.
131. Ibid. xxvi.

where they find a dead dog in a ditch, thereto they flee and thereon they feed apace.' If a good man preaches, a short sermon will do, and even then we regard neither his words nor his example. 'But let a lewd friar be taken with a wench, we will jest and rail upon the whole order the year after and say, "Lo what sample they give us"!'[132]

It is easy for an outsider to say that the clergy and religious have an easy life, that they are wealthy and secure in their cloisters. But if such a person were himself asked to make a decision to give up his freedom and possessions and enter a monastery, if he faced up squarely to the sacrifice involved in vowing chastity, he would still prefer his present way of life: 'if that easy life and wealthy that is in religion were offered to us, as weary as we be of wedding, we would rather abide all our old pain abroad, than in a cloister take a religious man's life for ease.'[133] Against the charge that the 'spirituality' do not appear to give alms, More replies that this proves nothing, as Our Lord counselled that sometimes we ought to give in secret; if we give openly, it should not be from motives of vainglory, but from the desire of giving good example. More testifies that the 'spirituality' in general fulfil the duty of almsgiving both openly and secretly.[134]

In general More was prepared to defend both the learning and goodness of the clergy of England, specially the secular clergy, in comparison with the spirituality of any other country. He admits 'therein many lewd and naught', but in such a multitude, without a miracle, it could scarcely be otherwise. The same complaint could be made against any large body, and indeed against the 'temporality', the laity, too: 'all be bad enough: God make us all better.'[135] Moreover, there will always be a direct proportion of goodness between the laity and the clergy, because the clergy come from the laity.

Summary: In the foregoing sections we have attempted to show how the loyalty of St Thomas More for the Church was shown in his defence of its doctrine, customs and members by rational methods which had regard for truth and justice.

ARTICLE III

DUTIES TO THE STATE

A The Individual's Duty to serve the Commonwealth

A person of such outstanding character and genius as Thomas More will frequently have difficulty in deciding where he can best use his talents, or indeed,

132. *EW* 225.
133. *Apol.* 93.
134. Ibid. 116.
135. *EW* 225.

which of his many talents he should specially cultivate. In his early life, he was torn between the conflicting attractions of law and orders. Having chosen the former, he was later faced with the decision whether to carry on his profession as his own master, devoting himself in his leisure time to literary pursuits, or whether he should accept the ever more pressing invitations of the King to enter his service. This latter problem is thrashed out in the first book of *Utopia*, where Raphael Hythlodaeus takes the negative view, viz. that a wise man should not become a courtier, and More the affirmative view that it is his duty to do so. Really, however, the dialogue is More's own debate with himself as he weighs the advantages and disadvantages of entering the King's service. More had undoubtedly discussed the matter with his friends, including Erasmus, whose point of view is unmistakably evident in the words of Hythlodaeus. Hythlodaeus argues that when a philosopher enters the service of a prince, he loses his liberty and is tempted to betray his ideals and integrity. He is clearly disillusioned at the avarice of kings and courtiers: he believes that they are not really concerned with truth and justice, but only seek advice which coincides with their own policies and interests. A philosopher therefore is wasting his time trying to influence kings for the better. More replies that a truly generous and philosophic spirit will apply talents and industry to the public interest, even at the cost of personal disadvantage. Nor should the difficulties of public service discourage one from making his contribution to the common good: 'You must not abandon the ship in a storm because you cannot control the winds . . . What you cannot turn to good you must make as little bad as you can.'[136] The dialogue shows that More was well aware of the troubles ahead when he entered public life. But in the end he decided it was the way by which he could best benefit the commonwealth and also render his own condition more prosperous.[137] The Utopians considered it their second obligation after loving God to seek a happy life for themselves and for others. As long as the laws of the country are not broken, 'it is prudence to look after your own interests, and to look after those of the public in addition is a mark of devotion'.[138]

We have already seen that More considered that the king exists for the people, not the people for the king. The common good was always uppermost in More's mind. But the common good is often achieved, not according to the ideas of any one citizen, but by the interplay of opinions, by the resolution of varying and sometimes opposing tendencies. More was a man who realized the importance of team-work. As an individual in the machinery of the state, he had a limited role to play, and it would be to the interests of the common

---

136. *Ut.* 55, 101; for Erasmus' opinion see REYNOLDS, *Thomas More and Erasmus* 117, 131, 217.
137. *Ut.* 55; *SL* 94, letter to Fisher: 'Much against my will did I come to Court (as everybody knows and as the King himself in joke sometimes likes to reproach me).'
138. *Ut.* 165.

good to limit his vision to the interests he represented, since it was the duty of other people to represent other interests. For example, as Burgess of Parliament in 1504 during the reign of Henry VII he was a representative of the people. More used his great persuasive powers in Parliament to oppose the King's request for a huge taxation levy. On the other hand, as Speaker of the House in 1523, he strongly recommended that Parliament grant Henry VIII's request for a similarly great sum of money. On the first occasion he spoke for the interests of the people: on the second he was the House's representative to the King but also the King's spokesman in the House, so he dutifully passed on the King's demand. At the same time he restrained Cardinal Wolsey from violating 'the ancient privileges of the House'. In his opening speech in Parliament More had pleaded for the right of 'every man to discharge his conscience without fear of the King's dreadful displeasure'. Such freedom of speech in Parliament would profit both the King and his realm. [139] Another example of his duty to a section of the community was his refusal to accept a pension from the King as a reward for his work on the legation to Flanders because the citizens of London would distrust his loyalty to them in the event of his representing them in litigation against the King. [140] On two occasions More made speeches in Parliament which have caused surprise to commentators. The speeches are partially explainable when it is realized that he was speaking on behalf of the King. One was the condemnation of Wolsey after More himself had been appointed Lord Chancellor. [141] The other was his announcement of the doubts on the validity of the King's marriage: '. . . you well know that the King our sovereign lord hath married his brother's wife, for she was both wedded and bedded with his brother Prince Arthur . . . if this marriage be good or no, many clerks do doubt.' [142] In neither case did More compromise the truth. He was merely presenting cases which had been judged or were to be judged by the competent authorities: in the circumstances, his own personal opinion was not relevant.

B More's Practice of Law

Under this heading, we consider More's contribution to the welfare of his country under the three aspects of lawyer, judge and officer of the law.

As a lawyer More soon proved himself the most capable in England. [143] According to Stapleton his brilliance was matched by his honesty, as he would never accept a case unless, after a thorough examination of the issues, he was completely satisfied of its justice. If he were not satisfied, he would ask his client to give up the case, or else seek the advice of another lawyer. This is probably a

139. CHAMBERS, 87, 200–218.
140. SL 70.
141. CHAMBERS, 240 ff.
142. REYNOLDS, 203, quoting HALL, Henry VIII, 1904, II, 185–194.
143. ALLEN, IV, no. 999.

pious exaggeration on the part of Stapleton.[144] When he became a judge, More soon acquired the reputation for honesty and impartiality. Roper reports him as saying: '. . . son, I assure thee on my faith, that if the parties will at my hands call for justice, then, all were it my father stood on the one side, and the devil on the other, his cause being good, the devil should have right.' Something of the sort apparently happened when More ruled against his son-in-law, Giles Heron.[145] On becoming Lord Chancellor, More was charged 'uprightly to minister indifferent justice to the people, without corruption or affection'. In reply, More said that 'if they saw him, at any time, in anything digress from any part of his duty in that honourable office, even as they would discharge their own duty and fidelity to God and the King, so they should not fail to disclose it to His Grace'.[146] More discharged his high office very meritoriously according to his biographers. He made himself available so that suits might more easily be brought before him; he refused to sign *sub poenas* unless they were absolutely necessary; he dealt with cases rapidly so that justice would not be delayed: indeed so quickly did he handle cases that there came a day when 'no more suits did remain'.[147] Erasmus may have been a biased witness, but in this matter his opinion was shared widely: 'The King could not have chosen a first magistrate more just or more incorruptible.'[148] More's contribution to English law is not found in any leading judgments 'but in the tradition he established of evenhanded and speedy justice' and thereby 'the strengthening of public confidence in the law'.[149]

As a law-officer, More tried to quell the Evil May Day riots (4 May, 1517). The part he played was preserved in the London tradition and recorded in the Elizabethan play, *The Play of Thomas More*.[150] But the chief matter to concern us will be More's administration of the heresy laws. The play just mentioned does not make the slightest suggestion that More was remembered as a great persecutor, and this fact was used by Professor Chambers to show that the London tradition did not regard him as such.[151] Erasmus wrote that under More no one in England suffered the death penalty for heresy. He was mistaken,

---

144. STAPLETON 17. We have just seen that More was prepared to act in cases in which he did not believe. It was for the judge to decide where justice lay. See also *Moreana* no. 2, Feb. 1964, notes, p. 115, where Professor ALBERT GARRETSON is quoted as concluding 'that More was a great lawyer in just this quality of being able to represent a case completely, though not himself persuaded.' (Ref. *The New York University Law Review*, Nov. 1963, 820.)
145. HARPSFIELD, 53, following ROPER; CHAMBERS, 268–9.
146. ROPER, 39.
147. CHAMBERS, 274.
148. REYNOLDS, *Thomas More and Erasmus*, 217.
149. REYNOLDS, 189; for probable influence of More on English ligislation regarding public hygiene, distinctions in cases of homicide, and special treatment of minors in larceny cases, see RICHARD O'SULLIVAN, 'Sir Thomas More the Lawyer' in *The Spirit of the Common Law*, Tenbury Wells, 1965, 29.
150. CHAMBERS, 45, 147.
151. Ibid. 46; 278–9.

but it shows that More had no international reputation as a heretic-hunter. After More's death it appears that his enemies tried to undermine his reputation by spreading false stories about his dealings with Reformers to counteract the universal condemnation of his execution. Such rumours were started even in his life-time by some of the less scrupulous Reformers. More deals with these charges in his *Apology* where he flatly denies them. We must leave it to the historian to estimate the evidence. Our task will be to compare some of the verdicts to get an idea of how More acted, and then to see how his actions accord with his theory and the virtue of loyalty in the Christian life.

Father Bridgett investigated the charges made against More and concluded that he certainly was not guilty of injustice as regards the civil law. Nor was More 'the reluctant administrator of laws, the existence of which he regretted'. He approved of the heresy laws but maintained they had been administered with utmost leniency and indeed with dangerous laxity.[152] Taft went into great detail on this question: he gave More's own words concerning the charges which were made during his life-time. More claimed that no heretic had ever had 'so much as a fillip on the forehead' whilst in his custody.[153] Again he challenged the 'Pacifier', who had alleged widespread injustice in the treatment of Reformers, to prove his claim in a single case from those which had taken place in London.[154] Professor Chambers, a non-Catholic and great admirer of More, examined the evidence and concluded that from 1519 to February 1531 no death sentence was passed on a heretic in the diocese of London; (local law-officers would have dealt with them in other dioceses). The fires of Smithfield recommenced only after More had fallen from favour and effective power in February 1531.[155] In August of that year, Bilney was burnt at Norwich; Tewksbury and Bayfield perished in December. More resigned from office on 16 May 1532. Foxe, the Protestant martyrologist, mistakenly made More responsible for the arrest and execution of John Frith, but these events took place after More's resignation. Recently another writer summarised the position: '. . . as chief officer of that government, he did see that the Bishops' burning edicts were carried out. The result was four burnings during More's administration: Bilney, Bayfield, Tewksbury and Bainham.'[156] Chambers

---

152. BRIDGETT, 255.
153. *Apol.* 133; for further details of other cases see text and notes, lxxxiii ff; 99; 126 ff.; 315; 321 ff.
154. Ibid. 129.
155. For these cases see CHAMBERS, 274–282; CAMPBELL op. cit. 199; *Encyclopedia Britannica*, London, 1960, vol. 9, p. 855.
156. L. MILES, op. cit., note 21, 176–7. This author's comparison of Colet's and More's attitudes to clerical shortcomings and heretics does not show that Colet was a Reformer at heart as he claims. Colet preached to the clergy concentrating on their failings: More was defending them from outsiders; Colet was a priest and a pastor: More was a law-officer with administrative duties. Colet, like Erasmus, wanted to reform the Church from within. A less odious comparison from More's point of view would be between his actions and the dealings of other law-officers with religious non-conformists, either before or after the Reformation.

maintained that the reason for the increase in heresy cases was not the fact that More was Lord Chancellor (which he had been since October 1529), but the replacement of Tunstall by Stokesley as Bishop of London. Tunstall and More had combatted heresy by trying to prevent the import of books, by countering with apologetic writings, and isolating by imprisonment those who attempted to spread their teachings. After their submission to Henry's Supremacy (January 1531), some of the clergy tried to reassert their orthodoxy by taking more severe measures against heresy. The author just cited, Miles, goes on: 'It is unfortunate that Catholic apologists have sought to exonerate More from these burnings on the grounds that he was merely doing what he was required by law to do. Had More conscientiously opposed such burnings, he could have refused to carry out the bishop's sentences, and if necessary, could have resigned his office.' We do not know of any Catholic apologists who have tried to excuse More on this pretext. Bridgett explicitly rejected such an excuse seventy years ago. Taft and Hollis clearly show that More approved of the heresy legislation. [157] Miles agrees that More did not have heretics flogged – and this is some advance in More's vindication – but he alleges he inflicted other indignities. Whatever he may mean by this, we may accept More's affirmation that he acted only within the powers allowed him by law.

In his Epitaph More wrote that he was 'a source of trouble to thieves, murderers and heretics' with the comment in his letter to Erasmus: 'I wrote that just to be smart.' [158] We should not put too much emphasis on this statement: as a humanist he realized the legitimacy of hyperbole; as a controversialist he was making a parting shot at his greatest opponents. We have seen that he pointed to his unimpeachable record in the specific charges made against him during his life-time: he even claimed that the Reformers were all treated with justice and charity. He defended the Church for its part in the punishment of heresy, saying that the Bishops merely pronounced a person guilty and then left him to the civil authorities for measures which were entirely in their domain. More could not very well explain his own practical policy without involving the policy of other law-officers. But it seems from Chambers' investigations, that while it was left to More to take the initiative in putting the machinery of the law into action, convicted persons were treated with leniency rather than severity. In the case of Frith, it was the King who instigated the procedure, and it is not unlikely that he was responsible with Stokesley for the change in policy in the last ten months of More's Chancellorship. Was the King trying to prove his orthodoxy so as to obtain more easily from Parliament the title of the Supremacy? As Taft points out, this explanation fits More's character: 'Is there a real paradox in his character? Did the man whose nature was so full of tender pity and charity harden himself to steel when a heretic faced him? Or was the infinite rigour his theory, and the infinite

157. CHRISTOPHER HOLLIS, *St Thomas More*, London, revised edition 1961, 132.
158. *SL* 180–1.

pity his practice?'[159] More was not by nature harsh, cruel or vindictive. He occupied an office which he had reluctantly accepted out of loyalty to the King. He then found himself called upon to do an unpleasant, though morally defensible task. Our particular interest in this question is to see how a spiritual man will react under such circumstances. In the first place we see that More courageously faced up to the distasteful consequences which followed convictions he had worked out according to objective norms. But we also find him on guard lest in the exercise of his duty he should succumb to righteous sadism:[160]

> But verily thus will I say, that I will give counsel to every good friend
> of mine, but if he be put in such room, as to punish an evil man lieth in
> his charge, by reason of his office, else leave the desire of punishing
> unto God and unto such other folk as are so grown dead in charity,
> and so far cleave to God, that no secret shrewd affection, under the
> cloak of a just and virtuous zeal, can creep in and undermine them.
> But let us that are no better than men of a mean sort, ever pray for
> such merciful amendments in other folk, as our own conscience
> showeth us that we have need in ourself.

Anyone in authority should be on guard lest a perverted desire for cruelty creep into his motives. Let him leave punishment to God, or if immediate action is required let him make use of those who are 'grown dead in charity' who probably will not become any worse by the penalties they inflict. The more spiritual man should remember his own sins and pray for the amendment of transgressors.

Summary: All historians seem now agreed that More did not go beyond the law in dealing with heretics. More himself claimed he did not subject them to (non-capital) corporal punishment, but that they were treated with justice and charity. As to the death penalty, it seems that More was satisfied if heretics were simply imprisoned. The executions which took place during the last ten months of his Chancellorship were possibly due to the insistence of Stokesley and perhaps Henry.[161] It seems improbable that More took the initiative in ordering these executions, but he carried them out. In doing so he acted as his conscience dictated, as we have seen in Chapter I.

C Loyalty to the Crown

By the term 'Crown' we include members of the royal family, principally of course the King, as personifying the whole nation. We have seen how the common good and the will of the people were basic criteria in More's political

---

159. *Apol.* lxxxiii. This opinion has its attraction but does it not contain an inherent accusation of duplicity on More's part? I have discussed this point briefly in *Moreana* no. 15, Nov. 1967, 247.
160. *EW* 1405 (misprinted 1421 in *EW*).
161. Henry's reign is notorious for the big number of executions of criminal, political and religious offenders. For Stokesley's record as a persecutor see CHAMBERS, 208.

creed. But these things were concentrated in the head of state so long as the people did not withdraw their mandate. On the accession of Henry VIII and Queen Catherine, More presented some verses praising them in anticipation of a blessed reign, and incidentally, reflecting adversely on Henry VII. About 1519 More showed sensitivity for national prestige in his controversy with the French scholar Germain de Brie who rather cleverly replied by questioning More's loyalty, pointing out his earlier implied criticism of Henry VII. [162] But there was no doubting his loyalty to Henry VIII. Once he agreed to enter Henry's service after his brilliant defence in the case of the Pope's ship, [163] More proved a reliable and conscientious counsellor and official. His correspondence shows a discreet silence on matters of state. Henry was satisfied with More's service until the question of the marriage arose. This is shown for example by the fact that he granted Wolsey's request of a monetary reward for the 'faithful diligence' More had exercised as Speaker, because, as Wolsey said 'no man could better deserve the same than he hath done', and 'he is not the most ready to speak and solicit his own cause'. [164] After his appointment as Lord Chancellor, More replied to the King's praise by saying that 'he had done no more than was his duty'. [165] More's devotion to Queen Catherine is testified to by Chapuys in his letter to Emperor Charles: 'he is an upright and learned man, and a good servant of the Queen.' [166] More always spoke highly of the King's virtues and would not allow even oblique criticism of Henry's piety as is shown in this incident from Roper: the Duke of Norfolk discovered More singing in the parish choir dressed in a surplice, whereupon he said:

> 'God body, God body, my Lord Chancellor, a parish clerk, a parish clerk! You dishonour the King and his office.' 'Nay', quoth Sir Thomas More, smiling upon the Duke, 'Your Grace may not think that the King, your master and mine, will with me, for serving of God, his Master, be offended, or thereby count his office dishonoured.'

Roper is also the authority for the words spoken by More to Cromwell:

> 'Master Cromwell', quoth he, 'you are now entered into the service of a most noble, wise and liberal prince. If you will follow my poor advice, you shall, in your counsel-giving unto his grace, ever tell him what he ought to do, but never what he is able to do. So shall you

162. CHAMBERS, 190–191; SL 74.
163. ROPER, 9–10: 'Now happened there after this, a great ship of his that then was Pope to arrive at Southampton, which the King claiming for a forfeiture, the Pope's Ambassador, by suit unto His Grace, obtained that he might for his master the Pope have counsel learned in the laws of this realm and the matter in his own presence (being himself a singular civilian) in some public place to be openly heard and discussed. At which time there could none of our law be found so meet to be of counsel with this Ambassador as Sir Thomas More . . .' This incident has not been corroborated from any other source. There seems to be no evidence in the Public Records Office, London, and I was unable to find any record in the Vatican and State Archives, Rome.
164. CHAMBERS, 207.
165. ROPER, 39.
166. CHAMBERS, 239; see also SL 2; 162.

show yourself a true faithful servant and a right worthy counsellor. For if a lion knew his own strength, hard were it for any man to rule him.' [167]

More's letters are frequently studded by the praises of Henry or affirmations of loyalty to him, and occasional references to Queen Catherine. [168] In another section we will see how More tried to exercise this loyalty until his final words on the scaffold.

D More's Supra-National Outlook

In his life of More Chambers set out to show that the key to More's consistency is to be found in his concept of Christendom as a unity. I have already shown that this unity was the cause for which he endured martyrdom. It was an ideal which More had worked for all his life. Roper records a conversation with his father-in-law in which More said he would gladly be put into a sack and thrown into the Thames if thereby three great things could be accomplished: 'The first is, that where the most part of Christian princes be at mortal war, they were all at an universal peace. The second, that where the Church of Christ is at this present sore afflicted with many errors and heresies, it were settled in a perfect uniformity of religion. The third, that where the King's matter of his marriage is now come in question, it were to the glory of God and quietness of all parties brought to a good conclusion ... otherwise it would be a disturbance to a great part of Christendom.' [169]

The senselessness of war was a frequent subject among the humanists: More's Utopians consider war 'as an activity fit only for beasts'; they feel sorry for the enemy soldiers because 'they know that the common folk do not go to war of their own accord but are driven to it by the madness of kings'. [170] More regarded as confidential his advice to the King when he spoke to him as counsellor, but we can be sure he tried to restrain Henry from war whenever possible. Especially would he have regarded war against the Emperor as war upon the secular head of Christendom in its struggle against the Turk. [171] More spoke with evident pleasure of the part he played as ambassador at Cambrai in the inscription for his tomb: 'In that place he witnessed to his great joy, the renewal of a peace treaty between the supreme monarchs of Christendom and the restoration of a long-desired peace for the world.' [172] Much of *Utopia* is an indictment of war because of the many social evils to which it gives rise. The humanist William Budé regarded Utopia as a great gift by More to the inter-

---

167. ROPER, 51; 56.
168. *SL* 2; 94; 102; 172; 178; 180; 191; 192.
169. CHAMBERS, 231
170. *Ut.* 118–122.
171. CHAMBERS, 231.
172. *SL* 181.

national community: 'Thomas More . . . has made known to the world in this our age the pattern of a happy life and a perfect rule of good behaviour. Our age and future ages will have this history as a precious source of noble and useful laws which each one may take and adapt to the use of his own state.'[173]

ARTICLE IV

RESPONSIBILITIES TO INDIVIDUALS

A Duties to his Father

There is no doubting the influence John More had on the life and character of his son, nor the filial affection he commanded in return. John More was very anxious for his son to follow him in the practice of law, and it is certain this was one of the main elements which decided More's choice. Erasmus tells how the father tried to discourage his son's classical studies, thinking they would distract him from law, and how he even cut off his supplies to get obedience.[174] According to More himself his upbringing was quite strict. On the other hand his father had a sense of humour which was inherited by Thomas. Perhaps too the influence of the father can be seen in More's rather hasty second marriage: for John More married four times.[175] Apart from the period in More's youth when he was tempted first by the classics, then by the religious life – during which period there may have been some friction – More's relations with his father were exemplary. Roper tells us of his 'natural affection for his father':

> Whensoever he passed through Westminster Hall to his place in the Chancery by the court of the King's bench, if his father, one of the judges thereof, had been sat ere he came, he would go into the same court, and there reverently kneeling down in the sight of them all, duly ask his father's blessing.

Roper then goes on to describe More's care for his father on his death-bed.[176] More paid his final tribute to his father in the inscription on his tomb:[177]

> His father, John More, was a knight and chosen by the King as member of the group of judges known as the King's Bench; he was an affable man, charming, irreproachable, gentle, sympathetic, honest, and upright; though venerable in age, he was vigorous for a man of his years; after he had lived to see the day when his son was Chancellor of England, he deemed his sojourn upon earth complete and

173. STAPLETON, 32.
174. ALLEN, IV, no. 999.
175. CHAMBERS, 54.
176. ROPER, 43.
177. *SL* 181–2.

100

gladly departed for heaven. The son . . . young More . . . now felt the loss of his father. . .

B Duties to his Wives

Little is known of More's first wife Jane. According to Erasmus he chose her for his wife when she was very young. We feel very much inclined to doubt the story told by Roper that More felt more attracted to Jane's younger sister, but married Jane out of pity to save her from grief and shame. It is hard to imagine More telling of such a thing, even if it were true, as he would have been merely praising himself and it would have been disloyal to his wife. A recent biographer doubts the story and suggests Erasmus as the originator. [178] It may also have been a dim memory in Roper's mind (and his memory did play an occasional trick) of one of More's merry tales, or even one of his father's, possibly at the expense of Alice, More's second wife, whom he laughingly described to Erasmus as 'nec bella admodum, nec puella'. [179] She was older than More, being forty and he thirty-two at the time of their marriage. This was certainly a union in which sentiment took second place to reason. Erasmus speaks of his love for Jane (even though she found him a little demanding at first), and tells how he educated her so that she would have been the ideal companion for the rest of his life. [180] In his epitaph More speaks loyally of both his wives, of Jane, his *uxorcula*, the wife of his youth and mother of his children, and of Alice who was more devoted to those children than are many mothers to their own. He tactfully says: 'I cannot decide whether I did love the one or do love the other more. O, how happily we could have lived all three together if fate and morality permitted. Well, I pray that the grave, that heaven, will bring us together.' [181]

More's second marriage, we have said, was one of convenience rather than romance. Alice ,as Erasmus says, was 'a shrewd and watchful housewife', and More succeeded in getting her to join in the family recreations such as music, but apparently not in the study of the classics. More loved Alice with a deliberate, personal love, rather than with a youthful, sentimental love. Erasmus testifies that he lived 'on as sweet and pleasant terms as if she were both young and lovely'. In a letter to Faber in 1532, he wrote: 'he loves and cherishes her although she is sterile, although advanced in age, not otherwise than if she were a girl of fifteen years.' [182] So his love was genuine even though there was no suggestion of romance. Fr Basset suggests that there is some likelihood that this second marriage was pre-arranged as a celibate union. [183]

---

178. Basset, 84. For an explanation similar to mine see Hollis, op. cit. 31.
179. Allen IV, no. 999.
180. Ibid.
181. *SL* 182. Note that Rogers uses the translation 'morality' where the original has *religio*. It is not certain that simultaneous bigamy is contrary to *natural* morality.
182. Surtz, op. cit. 234.
183. Basset, 101.

Alice was often the centre of More's banter about women, but only in a good-natured way. One story tells of a man who noticed his wife causing herself pain in order to beautify herself 'for the pride of a little foolish praise' by binding up her hair and bracing in her middle. Finally he said to her: 'Forsooth, madam, if God give you not hell, He shall do you great wrong!' [184] In the *Supplication*, More describes certain souls looking out from Purgatory and listening to the conversations of their widows with their new husbands: one such woman says: 'God have mercy on my first husband's soul, for he was a wise and honest man, far unlike you.' The souls comment: 'And then marvel we much when we hear them say so well of us, for they were ever wont to tell us far otherwise.' [185] There is also the story about Alice who one day came home from confession and said to her husband: 'You can be merry for I have finished with my past nagging and now intend to start afresh.' [186] These stories indicate the good-natured banter which went on between More and Alice.

But there are also indications of differences of opinion. When Alice learnt that More was using a hair-shirt, she tried to persuade his confessor to forbid him to continue with it. [187] The story in the *Dialogue of Comfort* of the husband sitting by the fire making goslings in the ashes with a stick is perhaps a hint that Alice did not appreciate or understand his plight of conscience: 'Go forward with the first', she urges him, 'for as my mother was wont to say, God have mercy on her soul, it is ever better to rule than be ruled.' The husband replies: 'In this I dare say you say the truth, for I never found you willing to be ruled yet.' [188] It seems that More regretted her lack of understanding during those last years of his life. He appears not to have written to her, though he mentions her in a good-humoured way in his letters to Margaret as 'your father's shrewd wife' and 'my good bedfellow'. But she is not mentioned in his last letter which he wrote to his daughter Margaret on the eve of his beheading, even though he mentions all the other members of his family. Perhaps the omission was an oversight or perhaps it was a silent complaint.

C Duties to his Children

Erasmus described the More family circle in his oft-quoted letter to von Hutten: 'With . . . kindness he rules his whole household, in which there are no tragic incidents and no quarrels. Indeed his house seemed to have a sort of heavenly felicity about it.' [189] More's devotion to his children is abundantly illustrated by his correspondence as well as by his biographers. Stapleton tells that ·More

---

184. STAPLETON, 126; *EW* 1203.
185. E. E. REYNOLDS, *Sir Thomas More*, London, 1965, 24.
186. BASSET, 94 quoting HARPSFIELD, *The Lives of Saint Thomas More*, WILLIAM ROPER and NICHOLAS HARPSFIELD, Everyman's Library, No. 19, London, 1963, 106.
187. CHAMBERS, 109.
188. *Dial. of Comf.* 285; 'goslings', i.e. drawings, designs.
189. ALLEN, IV, no. 999.

would administer reproof with such gentleness that afterwards the offender would love him all the more. Margaret Giggs who ... was almost from her infancy brought up with More's daughters, used to relate how sometimes she would deliberately commit some fault that she might enjoy More's sweet and loving reproof. Twice only in his life was he ever known to be angry.' [190] More's own words in a poem-letter to his children, bear out the same tenderness to them: [191]

> ... Nature in her wisdom has attached the parent to the child and bound them spiritually together with a Herculean knot. This tie is the source of my consideration for your immature minds, a consideration which causes me to take you often into my arms. This tie is the reason why I regularly fed you cake and gave you ripe apples and fancy pears. This tie is the reason why I used to dress you in silken garments and why I never could endure to hear you cry. You know, for example, how often I kissed you, how seldom I whipped you. My whip was invariably a peacock's tail. Even this I wielded hesitantly and gently so that sorry welts might not disfigure your tender seats.

Erasmus tells us that he got a better response from his family by coaxing and banter than do others by severe commands. [192] With a letter to Margaret, More sent money she had asked for, saying he would have sent more 'except that as I am eager to give, so I like to be asked and coaxed by my daughter, especially by you, whom virtue and learning have made so dear to my heart'. [193]

More's concern for the education of his children in virtue and learning is the subject of his famous letter to Gonnell where he gives his ideas on education. 'I prefer learning joined with virtue to all the treasures of kings', he declares. He touches on the danger of pride, haughtiness and avarice. He wants them to be taught 'piety towards God, charity to all, and modesty and Christian humility in themselves'. He specially advocates the higher education of women and girls, in which he was one of the pioneers in England. He quotes the example of Jerome and Augustine in recommending the study by women especially of the Scriptures. [194] In another letter to Margaret, More says: 'I assure you that, rather than allow my children to be idle and slothful, I would make a sacrifice of wealth, and bid adieu to other cares and business, to attend to my children and my family.' [195] He had them taught the classics, astronomy and general science. Again to Margaret he wrote: 'I earnestly hope that you will devote the rest of your life to medical science and sacred literature, so that you may be well furnished for the whole scope of human life, which is to have

---

190. STAPLETON, 96. In fact More is known to have been angry on several occasions as I mention elsewhere in this book.
191. *Epig.* no. 248, p. 230.
192. ALLEN, IV, no. 999.
193. *SL* 109–110.
194. *SL* 103 ff.
195. *SL* 109.

a sound mind in a sound body.'[196] Though the correspondence with his young children smacks of grammatical exercises, More's human interest makes many appearances, as when he specially praises John for his great efforts and his polished style, but above all for his wit in turning jokes against his father, which he does well but with moderation so that he preserves his respect towards his parent.[197]

Throughout More's correspondence, the ideas of virtue and learning are inseparable twins: in his letters to his children, to Gonnell their tutor, to his fellow humanists and especially in the letter to Oxford University, one is not mentioned without the other. It was in this last letter that More enlarged on the connection between them.[198] He severely reprimanded a preacher who had attacked 'the new learning' at the university, then went on to explain the utility of humanistic, secular studies. It is true that such studies are not necessary for salvation, he admitted, but even secular education does train the soul in virtue. Such study is almost the sole reason why students come to Oxford University. Even those who go there to learn theology need to start by studying the human sciences, so that they will know something about the workings of human nature, and something about human expression. These things can be learnt from the poets, orators and historians of classical literature. A theologian without this background may be able to converse with fellow academics, but he certainly would be incapable of preaching a sermon which would reach the common man. He goes on to explain how the liberal arts and philosophy are a path to theology. A knowledge of Hebrew, Greek and Latin is indispensable for a knowledge of theology, 'that august queen of heaven' who dwells in Scripture and pursues her pilgrim way through the cells of the Holy Fathers. The principles enunciated in this letter are ideas which had been evolving in More's mind, especially as a result of his contact with the humanists. The letter to the university was simply the occasion for him to publicize his matured convictions. His desire to apply these ideals to his own children is shown by the fact that he shortly afterwards outlined a similar policy in a letter to their tutor, Gonnell.

More himself took a very positive part in the spiritual training of his family. He led the family prayers and had the Scripture read at meals. Appropriate selections from the Bible were read on the greater feasts. It is probable that he wrote both *The Four Last Things* and the *Dialogue of Comfort* primarily for the spiritual welfare of his own family. Roper tells how he often warned his children that the time could possibly come when they would see virtue punished and vice rewarded: 'if you will then stand fast and firmly stick to God, . . . though you be but half good, God will allow you for whole good.' In fact Our Lord went to heaven 'with great pain and tribulation', so 'we may not look at

196. *SL* 149.
197. *SL* 150.
198. *SL* 99.

104

our pleasure to go to Heaven in feather beds'.[199] The Utopians had the custom of family confessions, the wives confessing to their husbands, the children to their parents. They admitted their faults and begged pardon.[200] More would have taught his children to apologize for their faults. Erasmus tells us that there were no 'tragic incidents nor quarrels' in the More household. Concerning the Holbein family drawing, Erasmus wrote to Margaret: 'I seem to behold through all your beautiful household a soul shining forth still more beautiful. I felicitate you all on that family happiness, but most of all your excellent father.'[201]

In a letter to Peter Giles introducing *Utopia*, More speaks of his busy life in the legal profession, and regrets that he has no leisure time for study. When he comes home from business he feels it is his duty to converse with his wife, children and servants, otherwise he would be a stranger in his own home. One has a duty to be agreeable towards those whom nature or fortune has made one's companions in life. On the other hand, he adds in passing, you should not spoil those of whom you have charge, otherwise they will become your masters.[202] More saw the care of his dependants as a duty, as is shown by his comment on Scripture in the *Dialogue of Comfort:* 'Saint Paul saith ... He that provideth not for those that are his, is worse than an infidel. Those are ours that are belonging to our charge, either by nature or by law, or any commandment of God. By nature, as our children, by law, as our servants in our household.'[203]

In a letter to Erasmus More complained of having to spend so much time away from his family while he was engaged on official tasks. Even when he was absent for only a short time, he said, his heart went back to his wife and children. He then adds another complaint that the King, although he gave a liberal allowance for More's retinue, made no consideration for his household in London: 'And although I am, as you know, a kindly husband and an indulgent father and a gentle master, still I have never had the least success in persuading the members of my family to do without food, for my sake, until I came home.'[204] More abandoned a lucrative practice when he entered the King's service: Erasmus wrote to von Hutten that even when he was not spending all his time in the practice of law, he was making more income than any other lawyer. However, as Erasmus also tells, he spent his money with generosity, he often remitted fees and he was 'the general patron of all poor people'. The Elizabethan play referred to above calls him 'the best friend the poor e'er had'.[205] When More fell from favour he became a relatively poor man,

199. CHAMBERS, 189.
200. *Ut*. 233.
201. ALLEN, VIII, p. 2212.
202. *Ut*. 41.
203. *Dial. of Comf.* 256.
204. *SL* 69–70.
205. CHAMBERS, 47.

but by this time his children were adults and in good positions. He tried to make provision for his property so that his family would not lose more than necessary because of his refusal to take the oath. [206]

More's care for his children was particularly evident at times of illness. Roper tells the story of how Margaret's 'miraculous' recovery from the sweating sickness was attributed to More's prayers. [207] He also prayed for the women of the household when they were expecting babies: a letter to Margaret bears this out: [208]

> In your letter you speak of your imminent confinement. We pray most earnestly that all may go happily and successfully with you. May God and our Blessed Lady grant you happily and safely to increase your family by a little one like to his mother in everything except sex. Yet let it by all means be a girl, if only she will make up for the inferiority of her sex by her zeal to imitate her mother's virtue and learning. Such a girl I should prefer to three boys.

The stilted classical Latin of the earlier letters gave place to equally beautiful, but more natural English in the correspondence from the Tower. In these letters More continually reassures his family of his prayers for them, and asks them to remember him in return. At various stages he was deprived even of writing material but still he contrived ways of communicating with his family: [209]

> And such things as I somewhat longed to talk with you all, concerning the world to come, our Lord put them into your minds, as I trust He doth, and better, too by His Holy Spirit, who bless you and preserve you all. Written with a coal by your tender loving father, who in his poor prayers forgetteth none of you all, nor your babes, nor your nurses, nor your good husbands, nor your good husbands' shrewd wives, nor your father's good wife neither, nor our other friends. And thus fare you heartily well for lack of paper.

Shortly after this letter he was able to write at greater length in reply to one from Margaret, in which she had 'in a vehement piteous manner' tried to persuade him to take the oath. Roper, her husband, maintained that this was merely a ruse on Margaret's part in order to gain admittance to see her father. However, in her letter to Alice Alington, she gives the details of a long discussion with her father in which he defends his position. It is possible that even this letter, in the familiar dialogue form, was 'staged' to give More the opportunity of replying to the objections people were making against his 'scruple' of conscience.

That More had some success in the spiritual formation of his children

---

206. DERRETT, 'More's Conveyance of his Lands and the Law of "Fraud"' in *Moreana* no. 5, Feb. 1965, 18–25; 'More's Attainder and Dame Alice's Predicament', *ibid.* no. 6, May 1965, 9–17.
207. CHAMBERS, 183.
208. *SL* 155.
209. *SL* 223.

appears from their later record. All the men were imprisoned after More's execution, the women were harassed, some of them imprisoned; many of them were forced into exile; Giles Heron, Cecily's husband, was executed in 1540 with three monks and a friar for treason, possibly because of his loyalty to More.[210] More wrote of them with affection and gratitude in his last letter: he mentions by name his children, foster-children and children-in-law. To Margaret he said: 'I never liked your manner toward me better than when you kissed me last for I love when daughterly love and dear charity hath no leisure to look to worldly courtesy.' He was alluding to her action after his trial when she publicly embraced him as he was escorted back to the Tower to await execution. Similarly he spoke proudly of John: '... recommend me to my good son John More. I liked well his natural fashion. Our Lord bless him.'[211]

D Duties to Others

1. Servants and Neighbours

'The charity of More was without bounds', wrote Stapleton. He then goes on to give details of the great generosity of More to the poor, especially those of his own district.[212] His solicitude for his employees and neighbours is again evident in his letter to his wife Alice after he had heard the news of the burning of his barn which caused damage to his neighbours' property and also threatened his own people with unemployment. He instructed Alice to make compensation to his neighbours, 'for an I should not leave myself a spoon there shall no poor neighbour of mine bear no loss by any chance happened in my house'. Similarly, if the accident has taken work from his employees, they are not to be dismissed unless other masters can be found for them.[213]

More also took care about the morals of his servants. He made sure that 'his man-servants and maid-servants should sleep in separate parts of the building, and should rarely meet together'.[214]

2. Friends

Stapleton gives in his fifth chapter of More's life a list of the English and foreign humanist friends with whom he corresponded; it is a formidable list of some of the foremost men of the age. These were his natural friends, though he had many others even among the common folk whom he invited to meals in his house.[215] The first amongst More's friends to come to the minds of most people would be Erasmus.' There is one craving for glory which I cannot shake

---

210. See *Corr.* 78, footnote; REYNOLDS, 341; for Margaret Gigg's heroic service of the Carthusians, CHAMBERS, 331.
211. *SL* 257.
212. See HOLLIS, op. cit. 38 ff.
213. *SL* 171.
214. Cf. SURTZ, op. cit. 255.
215. Quoted HOLLIS, op. cit. 39.

off . . . that I shall be commended to the most distant ages by the friendship, the letters the books, the pictures of Erasmus.'[216] The letters between these two men are full of mutual praise, rather overdone to modern tastes, but for all that obviously genuine. More did much for Erasmus: he gave him board in his own house, he obtained patrons for him, he looked after monetary matters in his absence. With his pen he defended Erasmus against the attacks of Dorp and the Monk, justifying his study of the Greek New Testament and also such writings as *The Praise of Folly*. More was even prepared to end his quarrel with de Brie because, as he said, 'the fact that de Brie is your friend shall weigh more with me than that he is my enemy.'[217] He urged Erasmus to revise his works before republishing because his enemies were looking for an opportunity to embarrass him: 'Out of my loyalty and anxiety for you, I urge you and I beg you to do at least this much.'[218] He continually congratulated Erasmus on his great literary achievements, and urged him to take up the pen against the Reformers: 'I would eventually like to see a treatise on our faith flow from that heart of yours.'[219] There is a great deal in common between More and Erasmus as regards spiritual theory: both built their spiritual lives on the Scriptures, the Fathers and inward conviction. In practice there was more of the ascetic in More: he was martyr material, whereas Erasmus was destined to die a holy death in his bed: 'Let others affect martyrdom. I do not think myself worthy of such an honour'; but he also wrote: 'I am ready to be a martyr for Christ if He will give me strength to be so . . .'[220] The importance of More's friendship to Erasmus is outside our scope, but it may be gauged from what has already been quoted and by Erasmus' testimony after More's death. Although in his first anguish at the sad news he expressed the wish that More had kept out of the whole controversy, his calmer thoughts were of admiration: 'Thomas More, Lord Chancellor of England, whose soul was more pure than any snow, whose genius was such as England never had – yea and never shall again, mother of good wits though England be.'[221]

Throughout his books and correspondence More continually heaps praises upon his friends. In *Utopia*, he expresses his admiration for Cardinal Morton, the former Lord Chancellor, in whose household More served as a boy. In the same place he lauds the loyal friendship of Peter Giles.[222] In a letter to Erasmus he speaks of the culture, asceticism and the pleasantness of Tunstall.[223] In the letter to the Monk, he mentions the virtue and learning of Fisher, and points to Colet, his early spiritual director, as 'the equal of any of our countrymen in

216. Quoted BRIDGETT, 110.
217. Quoted STAPLETON, 62.
218. *SL* 79.
219. *SL* 164.
220. REYNOLDS, *Thomas More and Erasmus*, 228–9.
221. CHAMBERS, 73.
222. *Ut*. 49; 59.
223. *SL* 70.

108

scholarliness and in holiness of life for many, many centuries'.[224] He wrote to
Dorp to commend his sincerity and truthfulness which he had demonstrated in
his public recantation of his attacks on Erasmus.[225] We must pass over many
other examples and come to his second-last letter, which he wrote shortly
before his death to a friend of forty years standing, the Italian merchant,
Antonio Bonvisi. It is a remarkable letter concerning the beauty of friendship.
He expresses regret that, after receiving such great hospitality, 'not as a guest,
but a continual nursling' in his house, he has been a 'barren lover', because he
has neglected 'his duty' of doing something in return. He goes on to attribute
the gift of such a friendship to the grace of God: 'For the felicity of so faithful
and constant friendship in the storms of fortune (which is seldom seen) is
doubtless a high and noble gift proceeding of a certain singular benignity of
God.' All he can do now for his friend is pray for him: 'I therefore my dear
friend and of all mortal men to me most dearest do (which now only am I
able to do) earnestly pray to Almighty God' to reward such kindness by
granting the fruition of the most Holy Trinity. He concludes: 'Thus of all
friends most trusty, and to me most beloved, and as I was wont to call you the
apple of mine eye, right heartily fare ye well.'[226]

3. Opponents
I use the term 'opponents' in a broad sense of anyone with a difference of
opinion. Such people fall into various categories, some of which we have
already examined. We have seen the principles which he used in criticising the
ignorant or lax churchmen of his day, in his treatment of the Reformers both
as a controversialist and as a law-officer. He endeavoured to give these people
a fair and just judgment according to his objectively formed conscience. During
the difficulties concerning the marriage of Henry and the Act of Supremacy,
More refused to condemn those who adopted different courses. Before the
matter reached danger point he warned the Bishops of the consequences of
supporting Henry's divorce by telling some of them privately the parable of
the offending virgin. Giving in to Henry would not necessarily save the Church:
'when they have deflowered you, then will they not fail soon after to devour
you.'[227] While matters were open to free discussion, some of the 'best learned'
had, 'after great diligence' come to the same conclusion as More, yet when the
matter became law with a penalty attached, they had taken the oath. More
knew of no new evidence which could have made them change their minds;
nevertheless, he refused to judge them, and would not entertain the possibility
of unworthy motives such as fear of Henry.[228] Right to the end, he refused to
criticize the King, Queen Anne, his judges, or any who brought about his

224. *SL* 125.
225. *SL* 112.
226. *SL* 254–7.
227. ROPER, 58.
228. *Corr.* 527.

downfall, except Rich, whom he accused of perjury – an action he considered necessary for his defence. The case of Rich is a typical example of More giving vent to anger against an opponent. Other instances have already been mentioned: the speech against Wolsey, his writings and actions against the Reformers, and his condemnation of Elizabeth Barton. But the passions, including anger, are a part of human nature, and so long as they are exercised in accord with reason they are not morally wrong. Our Lord was angry with the money-changers in the temple. These cases, especially the castigation of Rich, were ones in which More thought that his indignation was legitimate and that he was justified in quashing such people. [229]

We may fittingly conclude this section with More's own advice on the practice of charity to friends and opponents. We should not hate any living man, says More, be he good or bad. If we hate a good man, we are bad ourselves. If the man we hate is bad, he may amend, die well and go to God, and if we get to heaven too, that man will love us and we shall love him forever: 'And why should I now then hate one for this while which shall hereafter love me for evermore? And why should I be now then enemy to him with whom I shall in time coming, be coupled in eternal friendship?' On the other hand, if such a man does not repent and is damned to 'outrageous eternal sorrow'. it would be cruel to hate him now: rather we should pity his plight. [230]

ARTICLE V

DUTIES TO HIMSELF

A Temporal Welfare

Erasmus has already testified to us that More, as a lawyer, soon became a wealthy man. This prosperity continued for the greater part of his life and even at the time of his imprisonment he owned valuable property. He considered it his duty to provide a standard of living in keeping with his profession and office. Personally he exercised great moderation in the matter of clothes, food and comfort, but he tried to observe the dictates of reason in a balanced diet and proper care of the body: 'mens sana in corpore sano' was his advice to his children. More appreciated the beauty of nature and kept a small zoo as well as a collection of rare insect specimens. He was not adverse to building up wealth, but he had a carefully considered policy for its proper use. In the *Dialogue of Comfort* he discusses at length the attitude a Christian should have to worldly goods. [231] Erasmus in the letter to von Hutten describes More's

229. Cf. RICHARD C. MARIUS, 'What kind of Man was Thomas More?', *Moreana* no. 4, Nov. 1964, 115–7.
230. *EW* 1405 (misprinted 1421.)
231. *Dial. of Comf.* 178; 248 ff.

liberality in spending money and in giving it to the poor. More himself as a youth wrote verses introducing the *Book of Fortune* in which he advocated a policy concerning 'the gifts of Fortune'. If you must 'meddle with her treasure', he says, 'trust not therein, and spend it liberally'. Money came easily to More, but he parted with it just as easily, for [232]

Remember, Nature sent thee hither bare;
The gifts of Fortune – count them borrowed ware.

More also enjoyed good literature and music as well as debate and witty conversation. He touches the subject from a spiritual angle in several places: it is a case where his theory was rather more severe than his practice: '. . . as for sleep and gaming (if any gaming be good in this vale of misery in this time of tears) it must serve but for a refreshing of the weary and forewatched body, to renew it unto watch and labour again.' [233] In the *Dialogue of Comfort* he states that God allows us rest and recreation because of our imperfection: they are like sauce which is allowed us as a 'small moderate refreshing of the mind against heavy discomfortable dullness'. God can also use worldly things to draw us to things spiritual. God promised prosperity to the Israelites to entice them to follow Him, because of their spiritual immaturity: the promise was made 'to draw them to God with gay things and pleasant, as men to make children learn give them cake-bread and butter'. [234] He quotes Solomon and St Thomas Aquinas in support of 'proper pleasant talking' but then puts into the mouth of Anthony a slight reprimand for the excessive readiness of men to indulge in 'wanton idle tales'; however, he confesses: 'myself am of nature even half a gigglot and more. I would I could as easily mend my fault as I well know it; but scant can I refrain it, as old a fool as I am.' [235]

It is also interesting to note More's concern for his good reputation. When he resigned the Chancellorship, rumours were started that he had been forced to do so by the King. He resented such implications and took pains to see that the truth was publicised. All his life he had looked forward to the time when he could retire in order to devote himself to spiritual matters. Years before he had written a letter to Archbishop Warham congratulating him on his wise retirement from the office of Lord Chancellor; this letter is a perfect summary of More's own motives. More countered the rumours of the 'chatterboxes' by having engraved on the inscription for his tomb the statement that he had resigned because of bad health and with the King's approval. He sent a copy of this inscription to Erasmus with a letter in which he encouraged Erasmus to publish the truth. He commented that he took these steps because he considered it his duty to protect his reputation. [236]

---

232. CHAMBERS, 157.
233. Quoted by CLAUDE SHEBBEARE, *Sir Thomas More – A Leader of English Renaissance*, London, 1929, 32, from More's *Answer to the First Part of a Poisoned Book*.
234. *Dial. of Comf.* 174–5.
235. Ibid. 185.
236. *SL* to Warham, 88; to Erasmus, 180.

B Spiritual Welfare

1. Choice of Vocation

We are told by Erasmus and by More's biographers that in his youth he gave serious thought to the possibility of entering a religious order. Many answers have been given to the question as to why he decided on a life in the world. Erasmus tells us he could not shake off the desire for marriage: 'Maluit igitur maritus esse castus quam sacerdos impurus.'[237] Stapleton follows a similar explanation: 'he feared, even with the help of his practices of penance, that he would not be able to conquer the temptations of the flesh.'[238]

The same author suggests as a possibility that the laxity of the monasteries dissuaded him. Seebohm expresses it more strongly: 'But that . . . he did turn in disgust from the impurity of the cloister to the better chances which, he thought, the world offered of living a chaste and useful life, we know from Erasmus.'[239] In a conversation with Mr E. E. Reynolds, I asked him for his opinion. He replied that what Erasmus said was probably the nearest we can get to the truth. Erasmus was an intimate of More, and his statement is the closest thing we have to an explanation by More himself.

Further investigations will be in the realm of hypothesis, but, granted this, we may be allowed to offer suggestions on the probability of already suggested opinions. Mr Reynolds suggests that More's letter to Colet, the Dean of St Paul's and his spiritual director, in October 1504, contains an allusion to the help Colet gave him in making an important decision: 'By following your footsteps', wrote More, 'I had escaped almost from the very gates of hell.'[240] Since More's marriage followed shortly afterwards (between one and three months) there may have been a connection. It seems however that there are some difficulties. More would hardly allude to the contemplative life as 'the very gates of hell.' Again, More described himself as having escaped by following Colet's footsteps: this would not be in reference to a decision to enter the state of matrimony. Again, More goes on to describe himself as 'falling back again into gruesome darkness . . . I am sinking because you do not look back at me.' More feels himself sinking under the difficulty he is experiencing because of Colet's absence, so it seems it was not a question of guidance that had proved decisive. The letter deals with Colet's good influence on More by his preaching, example, and advice, as against the bad influence of the world as represented by the city whose vices More describes. It seems to me then that this letter was later than his decision to remain a layman, and that it dealt with the temptations typical of many young men: the temptation to laxity, indifference, medio-

---

237. ALLEN, IV, no. 999.
238. STAPLETON, 9–10.
239. Op. cit. 151; BRIDGETT's comment: 'Erasmus has not a word of More's turning in disgust from anything, but on the contrary, he implies that he turned with regret from a state which he loved and reverenced, but to which he feared to aspire.' Pp. 23–4.
240. SL 4; REYNOLDS, *Thomas More and Erasmus*, 38 ff.

112

crity or even complete immorality. Perhaps it was the ordinary struggle of youth with the virtue of chastity. As regards More's choice of vocation Fr Basset suggests it is 'very likely that Colet decided for the younger man'. [241] I am more inclined to think More made such a vital decision for himself. Certainly later in life he would not hazard his soul on another man's judgment, nor indeed expect another man to bear such a burden, as he said to Margaret in the Tower: 'I never intend (God being my good Lord) to pin my soul at another man's back, not even the best man that I know this day living.' [242] Moreover, if what Fr Surtz says about Colet's views on celibacy and marriage are true, Colet would have been expected to encourage a good man like More into the priesthood rather than marriage. [243]

Another possible factor in More's decision not to become a contemplative is suggested by Fr Basset. Commenting on a sentence from the *Dialogue of Comfort*, he says that in More's case (given his character etc.) the urge to live in the cloister may have been a form of escape. This may have been true during More's family life: several times he said that he would have retired to contemplation but for his family. [244] But it was not true when as a young man he was as yet uncommitted. He had the true, balanced view of the monastic ideal which he cherished till the end of his days: he regarded it as a state of perfection. Fr Basset claims that More was temperamentally unfit for the contemplative life because of fear, diffidence and scruples. We submit however that this is an erroneous assessment of More's character. Like any normal man, when faced with difficult decisions he had moments of doubts, indecision, fear and anxiety: but this was because of the problems themselves, not because of any defect of character. He was humble but he was not neurotically diffident; he had a well informed conscience which was morally discerning in the greatest detail, but he was not scrupulous. [245]

Why then did More decide to marry rather than enter a monastery or become a priest? I think we should look for the answer in More's efforts to discern objectively the will of God from the concrete circumstances of his life and the particular talents and qualities with which he found himself endowed under the providence of God. There were several factors to be considered. Perhaps none of them individually was sufficiently strong to be taken alone as the decisive element. But the overall effect of these factors was to direct More to the law and to marriage. One of these factors was doubtless the wish of his father. We have already seen how much John More wanted his son to follow him into the legal profession. He was also evidently a keen advocate of married life – he himself married four times. The virtue of *pietas* was strong in More: he would have at least looked for an indication of the will of God in the

241. BASSET, 74.
242. *Corr.* 516.
243. SURTZ, op. cit. 229.
244. CHAMBERS, 307.
245. Cf. *SL* 65, concerning 'white lies'.

authority of his father. More also realized that he was gifted with brilliant legal talent; being a pragmatic Englishman, he would have taken this as an indication that God wished him to invest this talent in a utilitarian career. Again, he delighted in female company; as Erasmus tells us, he loved joking with them, and his writings contain many jokes about them.[246] He experienced first-love at the age of sixteen when he met a girl named Elizabeth who was fourteen. When he met her again later in life, he wrote a poem to her to remind her of their youthful romance.[247] Erasmus comments on the modesty of More's early conduct with girls: 'Cum aetas ferret, non abhorruit a puellarum amoribus, sed citra infamiam, et sic ut oblatis magis frueratur, quam captatis: et animo mutuo caperetur potius quam coitu.'[248] His attraction to mixed society is also evidenced by his insistence on the education of his wives and daughters. It is at least possible he understood this facility with women to have been given him by God for a purpose. As to Erasmus' remark quoted above: it is difficult to think of More as a 'licentious priest'. That he did not enter the Charterhouse was no reflection on it: indeed the community there was above reproach. Thirty years later it yielded the first fruits of Henry's persecution. But there were plenty of unworthy priests and monks with whom More had come into contact. In his humility he may have been influenced by this fact, as he thought of himself as being weaker than others.[249] It was probably a consideration of this sort to which Erasmus referred.

To summarize: More's considered opinion was that God's will for him was to be a lawyer and a married man. This was indicated to him by a balanced and objective view of the circumstances, which would have included: the wish of his father; his obvious legal ability; his enjoyment of female company; his estimation that celibacy would be a risk to him in view of the failure of others. This is an application of More's belief in the providence of God as manifested in the concrete circumstances of life.[250]

2. The Salvation of his Soul

As we have already remarked, in More's spirituality the concepts of obedience, duty and obligation greatly outweigh considerations of counsel and supererogation. Throughout his spiritual writings, there is much more stress put onto the saving of one's soul than onto the effort to reach higher grades of holiness. The treatise on *The Four Last Things* is an indication of this mentality. It appears again in his most spiritual works, such as *A Treatise to Receive the Blessed Body of Our Lord*, where he spends considerable space speaking of

---

246. Again we differ from Fr Basset's assessment: 'He loved her [Jane] with an ardour which was tongue-tied, inhibited, donnish, and, superficially, pedantic...', BASSET, 85.
247. Ibid. 20.
248. ALLEN, IV, no. 999. Both ALLEN and CHAMBERS mistranslated 'citra infamiam' as meaning that More's youth was not above reproach; see SURTZ, op. cit. 255.
249. E.g. *Corr.* 527.
250. Cf. *Ut.* 217; *SL* to Alice, 169 ff.

unworthy communions. This is not to say that More did not know love as a motive: we have seen the opposite is true when we considered motives in the first chapter. In his inscription for his tomb he asks the reader to pray for him while he lives that he may not shudder at the thought of death, but that, because of longing for Christ, death may be for him the gateway to a happier life.[251]

The love of God for His own sake and the desire to save one's soul are not mutually exclusive: in fact, as far as concrete duty is concerned, the two things coincide. In facing death More was motivated by the perfect love required for martyrdom, but he was also very conscious of the peril to his soul if he took the oath of Succession; more than that: he considered it would be a sin of temerity if he put himself forward for martyrdom by speaking out against the oath. Because of such presumption God could justly withhold the grace to endure martyrdom and he would lose his soul.[252] Hence More realized that the duty he owed to himself of saving his souls was also a duty he owed to God. The way in which he combined this duty of personal salvation with his duties to others will be best illustrated in the matter to be considered in the next chapter.

CONCLUSION TO CHAPTER II

Human life is a complexity of duties: to God, Church, State, neighbour and oneself. More was acutely aware of his various duties and assiduously tried to fulfil them. Fidelity to duty is thus a marked aspect of his spirituality. Moreover our saint trusted implicitly in God's fidelity to man, especially as regards his promise to His Church. More also admired and appreciated the loyalty he found in others, especially his friends.

251. *SL* 182.
252. *SL* 253.

CHAPTER III

LOYALTY IN THE CONFLICT
OF LAWS AND DUTIES

Hitherto we have been examining materials which made up an important part in the life of St Thomas More, viz. law and duty. The law, in the wide sense we saw in chapter one, was for More the general framework which creates an order conducive to the attainment of man's immediate and final ends, considered from both the individual and collective points of view. Duty comprises the more detailed requirements of conscience and therefore gives man specific guidance in the fulfilment of his concrete commitments. For most of his life More was able to practise his theory because the same belief was shared pacifically by the society in which he lived. But at the end of his life his hierarchy of authority was subjected to attack from without and from the society which he had been able to serve conscientiously up to that time. It is now our intention to discover how he resolved this conflict. The practical course upon which he decided brought him to prison and the scaffold. His trial is of interest for many reasons: it is of great historical importance; from the legal aspect it must rank as one of the most fascinating in history with the unique situation of England's greatest lawyer and ex-Chancellor using his great knowledge and experience of law in his efforts to save himself. But it was above all a religious event: it involved the laws of marriage established by God; it involved the Supremacy of the Church; it involved an oath, which is an act of religion; it was above all a case of conscience, and its outcome was martyrdom, the apex of a Christian's conformity to Christ.

Our treatment pre-supposes a knowledge of this part of More's life and will be an attempt at a theological evaluation of his actions. First we will try to define the issues in conflict. Then we will examine how More reacted to the new situation, and how he contrived to carry on his duties despite the conflict.

ARTICLE I

THE ISSUES IN CONFLICT

A The Question of the King's Marriage

In 1501 the 'beautiful' and 'charming' Catherine of Aragon entered London 'amid a tremendous ovation' and 'thrilled the hearts of everyone' as the bride of Prince Arthur, elder brother of Henry.[1] The union ended tragically with the death of the Prince but in order to perpetuate the alliance with Spain, Catherine was given in marriage to Henry with the necessary papal dispensation from the impediment of affinity. Later, from motives outside the scope of this essay, Henry conceived a 'scruple' concerning the validity of this union, and directed his advisors, including More, to investigate the matter. More himself describes how the King approached him: '[he] showed me', writes More, 'that it is now perceived, that his marriage was not only against the positive laws of the Church and the written law of God, but also in such wise against the law of nature, that it could in no wise by the Church be dispensable.'[2] This was the first time More had heard the argument about the marriage being against the natural law: he was familiar with the objection that it was against the positive law of God as expressed in the 'Law Levitical', but the 'Law Deuteronomical' seemed to More to allow a precedent which would indicate the Pope could dispense.[3] The first tension arose for More when he could not see how the natural law was so involved a dispensation was impossible. A conflict of loyalties was also immediately created by the fact that in giving legal advice to Henry he would be acting against the interests of Catherine and her daughter, Mary, to both of whom More had been very devoted. More's advice to Henry was that he would have a better chance of success if he concentrated on another line which had already been proposed, viz. the dispensation itself was not in accord with the requirements of canon law.[4]

In 1528 Clement VII set up a Legatine Court in England to enquire into the charge that the King was living in unlawful and invalid wedlock. Since Henry did not appear as petitioner Catherine was deprived of a *locus standi*.[5] The main charge was that the marriage was invalid because of the natural law prohibition as expressed in *Leviticus* especially in view of the consummation of the first marriage of Catherine; an alternative case was advanced against the validity of the Papal Bull of dispensation on the grounds it was granted for reasons which were false and insufficient. The case was eventually recalled to Rome where it dragged on for several years. Because of the delay Henry decided to settle the question in England and accepted the declaration of annulment given by Archbishop Cranmer in May 1533. For More this brought further issues into conflict: the disregard for the instructions of the Roman Pontiff, the recognition of Anne Boleyn as Queen and of her offspring as heirs to the throne.

B The Affair of the Nun of Kent

In February 1534 More's name was included in a Bill of Attainder which was

1. *SL* 2–3.
2. Ibid. 207; *Corr.* 493; ROPER, 37.
3. See Lev. 20 : 21; Deut. 25 : 5 ff.
4. *SL* 207.
5. PHILIP INGRESS BELL, 'The Trial of Thomas More', in *The Month*, vol. 23, 1960, 326.

introduced into Parliament. He was charged with misprision of treason because of his dealings with the Nun of Kent, Elizabeth Barton.[6] She had claimed visions and made prophecies concerning the King which were not verified within the time predicted by her. She and her accomplices were subsequently executed for treason at Tyburn.[7] More was charged with having known of these treasonable activities and with not having denounced them. More's answer to the charges is contained in letters to the King and Cromwell.[8]

C The Oath of Succession

Having succeeded in getting his name removed from the above mentioned Bill of Attainder, More was immediately faced with a further decision. Parliament had passed the First Act of Succession which required an oath from all subjects stating that they acknowledged the succession to the throne by the children of Henry and Anne. But the form of oath actually proposed contained other elements which were unacceptable to More. In the first place, the oath was not in agreement with the statute passed by Parliament, and therefore the Commissioners had no right to exact it. This legal objection was not unimportant to More. Also the additional content of the oath was contrary to what More believed: viz. that the King's first marriage was against the natural law and invalid; that this union with Anne Boleyn was valid and lawful; and that not even the Pope may dispense from certain impediments.[9] Except for the first legal objection, which he apparently revealed to Margaret,[10] More kept the reasons for his refusal secret, with the comment that people would be surprised if they knew them.[11] Fr Bridgett mentions the possibility that these less obvious reasons could have been due to his knowledge of further impediments to the marriage of Henry and Anne: 'Anne Boleyn's affinity to Henry, her pre-contract of marriage with Percy, or some other impediment still more secret we cannot now discover, any more than we can know the grounds on which Cranmer pronounced that Anne's marriage with Henry had been null from the beginning.'[12]

D The King's Supremacy of the Church of England

Henry VIII gained control of the English Church by a series of manoeuvres

6. 'Misprision of treason', i.e. an offence akin to treason but involving a lesser degree of guilt and not liable to capital punishment. The term was attached to concealment of treason but in this case it was used for the obstinate refusal to take the oath. See Roper, Glossary, p. 130.
7. Chambers, 279.
8. *SL* nos. 47, 50–53.
9. Geoffrey de C. Parmiter, 'St Thomas More and the Oath', *Downside Review*, vol. 78, 1960, 1–13; specially p. 8.
10. Roper, 78.
11. *SL* 232, letter to Wilson: More describes his reasons as 'some other peradventure, than those that other men would ween.'
12. Bridgett, 382–3; Henry's relations with Mary Boleyn are mentioned by Chambers, 225.

beginning in January 1531 with the Convocations of the Clergy, and culminating (as far as we are concerned) with the Acts of Supremacy and Treasons in November-December 1534. It became high treason to deprive the King of his title of Supreme Head on earth of the Church of England. More had already stated his belief that the Pope is the Head of the Church on earth, his primacy is of divine origin, and only a General Council may depose him or alter his decisions. The conflict was heightened for More when he was officially commanded by the King's Commissioners, and with royal backing, to express his opinion on the statute of Supremacy. So his belief in the teachings of Christ came into conflict with the declaration of Parliament; the King's command to express his opinion was in conflict with his duty to save his life. He doubtless also balanced his duty to preserve himself against his duty to speak out for the benefit of other people, especially any who sought guidance, such as Dr Wilson had done earlier with regard to the oath of Succession. [13]

ARTICLE II

MORE'S RESOLUTION OF THE CONFLICT

A The Marriage Question

1. Duties to God and the Church

We have seen in a previous section that More believed the Catholic Church to be God's authoritative representative on earth in matters of faith, and in particular, in the doctrine of marriage, which she teaches to be, by divine institution, a sacramental and indissoluble union. More's resistance to the repudiation of the Pope's jurisdiction was founded on his adhesion to the Catholic Church, and ultimately on his confidence in God's fidelity to His promise to be with His Church till the end of time. The Marriage Question was therefore a matter of ecclesiastical jurisdiction, and More was prepared to assist in the examination of the matter so long as the usual processes of law were adhered to. Thus he praised the King for submitting his case to the authority of the Church: 'he did well and virtuously for the acquieting of his conscience to sue and procure to have his doubt decided by judgment of the Church.' [14] More's duty to God assumed priority over his other duties in so far as he refused to assist the King in proving the invalidity of the Marriage on the grounds that it was prohibited by natural law, because he believed that such a reason was not true. His duty to the Catholic Church, as represented by the Roman Pontiff, obtained precedence over the national bodies who decided the case in England in Henry's favour.

13. *SL* nos. 58–9.
14. *SL* 208.

2. Duties to King and Parliament

Even though it was against his inclinations, More acceded to the King's request to investigate the validity of his marriage to Catherine. As we have seen, More could not agree that the Scriptures forbade the dispensation. Hence he excused himself from further cooperation, saying it was a matter 'for an ordinary process of the spiritual law, whereof I could little skill'. The King agreed to use More only on other matters, but asked him to study the question further in the company of members of the clergy. More dutifully gave full attention to the case 'with a mind as toward and as conformable as reason could in a matter disputable require', but since he could not agree, the King again promised to use him only in matters where his conscience was at ease. More, on his part, undertook not to assist the opposite view by writing, or even by reading books in support of the validity of the marriage. He even burnt one book which he happened to have in his possession. He told Cromwell, in the letter from which these facts are taken, that he did not consider himself such 'to take upon him the determination or decision of such a weighty matter, not boldly to affirm this thing nor that therein'. [15] It appears then, that, since he could not serve the King positively, he decided to act passively on the whole question by not expressing an opinion and by disowning any right or ability to do so.

More considered it his duty to take up the Chancellorship at the King's request, even though he seems to have realized that it was possibly a bait to entice him to the King's side on the divorce question. He stayed in office as long as he conscientiously could, but once the English Church unilaterally declared itself independent of Rome, he saw that he must resign. He did so on the day after the submission of the clergy, but in a way which would not appear disloyal to the King: he pleaded bad health. This was not a figment. In his letters to Erasmus he gives details of a chest ailment for which he had consulted physicians who had pronounced it dangerous. [16] It was a case where More had a valid excuse for acting in the way he wanted to. Before he resigned, however, he carried out his duties on the King's behalf, going so far as to announce in Parliament the results of an opinion poll concerning the validity of the marriage which had been conducted in the Universities and which generally favoured the King, but without revealing his own opinion.

In his retirement More repeatedly expressed loyalty to Henry, and continued to accept the authority of Parliament in recognizing Anne Boleyn as Queen, ('this noble woman really annointed Queen') and in accepting the succession of her offspring. It is true he refused to attend her coronation as it could have been interpreted as a public act of approval. Otherwise, he would neither dispute nor murmur, and was even prepared to equivocate concerning 'His Highness being

15. *SL* 208–11.
16. *SL* 172; to Cochlaeus, 177; cf. Inscription, ibid. 182.

in possession of his marriage'. [17] This was consistent with his life-long policy of not causing public embarrassment to lawful authority, and of not disturbing the peace. So long as the people did not withdraw their mandate, it was the duty of King and Parliament to administer the country, and it was the duty of subjects loyally to abide by their decisions up to the point where obedience could stand with salvation. After this point one could change the law by discussion in the proper circles, or by passivity, but he should try not to disturb peace and order. More rigidly adhered to this policy: for example, he refused to accept a letter from the Emperor Charles through his Ambassador Chapuys unless it was also shown to Henry. He had rightly guessed that the letter contained a suggestion he should compromise his loyalty to the King. [18]

3. Duties to Others

Among those who were most affected by the Marriage Question were Queen Catherine and Princess Mary. It was well known that More's sympathies lay with them, but there was little he could do for their cause because of his prior duty to Henry. At best he could help them by the negative policy of not condoning the divorce. That More's protest by silence was not ineffective is shown by the lengths to which his opponents went to destroy him. More knew that if he were brought to trial and condemned he would receive an opportunity of speaking out concerning the marriage. When the time came, he did so. [19]

4. Duties to Himself

Restricting ourselves for the moment to the Marriage Question, we can see that what was uppermost in More's mind, coupled with his concern for God's laws, was his concern for his own spiritual welfare. He diligently informed his conscience on the marriage, and adhered to his opinion because he considered it true. To betray the truth would have been to jeopardize his salvation. Though he protested publicly and frequently that he had resigned because of ill-health and with the King's approval, nevertheless the timing of his resignation makes one think that his health was not the only reason, nor even the main reason, for requesting release from office at that particular juncture. More did his best to keep on good terms with the King, and in a letter to Cromwell asserted that he was prepared to forgo all he owned in this world except only his soul rather 'than abide of his Highness one heavy displeasant look'. [20]

That More was also concerned for his material well-being is shown by his efforts to convince Henry and Cromwell of his innocence from the charge of positively opposing the divorce. [21] His refusal to receive the letter from Chapuys was also a measure to protect himself from the charge of disloyalty.

17. *SL* 211.
18. Cf. CHAMBERS, 250.
19. Ibid. 341.
20. *SL* 215.
21. *SL* 206–11.

B The Case of the Nun of Kent

1. Duties to the King

When More heard that his name had been included in a Bill of Attainder because of his alleged knowledge of the treason of Elizabeth Barton, the 'Nun of Kent', he indignantly wrote to the King and to Cromwell, giving a detailed account of his dealings with the Nun, and enclosing a letter he had written to her as further evidence of his innocence. He had warned the Nun that he would not hear anything from her concerning 'other men's matters, and least of all any matter of princes or of the realm'.[22] He declared himself shocked that anyone should suggest he could be so disloyal and ungrateful to the King as to enter into such a conspiracy: 'if any of them, or any man else, report of me as I trust verily no man will, and I wot well truly no man can, any word or deed by me spoken or done, touching any breach of my loyal troth and duty toward my most redoubted sovereign and natural liege lord, I will come to mine answer, and make it good in such wise as becometh a poor true man to do: that whosoever any such thing shall say, shall therein say untrue.' His loyalty to the law-court made him alter his own opinion of the Nun. He accepted its findings that she was guilty of 'detestable hypocrisy', that she was inspired by the evil spirit, that she was a 'false deceiving hypocrite', and that by her own confession 'she was proved naught'. In a passage reminiscent of St Paul he asserts: 'neither good man nor bad, neither monk, friar nor nun, nor other man or woman in this world shall make me digress from my troth and faith, either toward God, or toward my natural prince, by the grace of Almighty God.'[23] More's violent assertion of loyalty was successful in getting his name removed from the Bill of Attainder.[24]

2. Duties to the Nun

We mentioned above that More changed his opinion about the Nun's character. Was he being fair to her in so doing? His letter to her shows that he spoke to her with the greatest respect, and it was surely for her good, as well as his own, and the King's honour, that he warned her of the danger of getting mixed up in politics. We may note how he used the law, not to trap a victim, but to put her on guard against making herself liable to severe penalties. This policy was in harmony with his earlier thoughts on the purpose of law, its use and abuse.[25] It is also in contrast to the use made of law by Cromwell and his associates as a means to trap and destroy their adversaries, such as More and Fisher. More's conversations with the Nun were carried out in a purely private capacity. He was not 'set to search and examine the truth upon likelihood of some cloaked

22. *SL* 184.
23. *SL* 199–201.
24. Abbé GIBAUD has drawn my attention to the fact that the House of Lords three times refused to pass the Bill of Attainder while More's name was on it.
25. See above, p. 33

evil' as Cromwell was afterwards commissioned to do. So More gave her the benefit of good repute. Having warned her not to speak about the King's affairs, he spoke with her about non-political matters and was rather impressed by her meekness. In his conversation with Father Rich, the Nun's accomplice, he warned him not to speak about any revelations which she claimed to have had concerning the King. Until it was proved otherwise More considered the Nun to be a good woman: even if she were very bad, as long as she appeared good, he would account her for good.[26] However after her trial and confession, More accepted the verdict and heartily condemned her malice and treason. He considered that the circumstances warranted this apparently cruel action. She had, after all, disregarded his advice, brought about her own destruction and that of others, and involved More himself and Fisher in the business so that they came into considerable danger. He doubtless felt anger towards her for her rashness and irresponsibility.

3. Duties to Himself

More's warnings to the Nun contained an element of self-interest. If he had listened to her prophecies about Henry, he would have been faced with the unpleasant alternatives of denouncing her or of coming under the Treasons Act (1352) himself. Later when he actually did come into danger he wrote his letters to the King and Cromwell to defend himself from the charges on which his name was included on the Bill of Attainder. Again he felt justified in condemning the Nun after her execution so that no one could suspect he had any sympathy for her. His outburst against her may have been due to anger, but he thought it justified as a means of saving his own liberty. He undoubtedly accepted the findings of the court as true, and considered it allowable to endorse the legal verdict in his own interests.

C The Oath of Succession

1. Priority of Laws

It will be convenient for our purposes to consider the succession issue at the point when More refused the oath put to him by the King's Commissioners in April 1534. The problem was a real one before that time, but the oath is a handy resumé of the whole question. The actual wording of the oath as put to More has not been preserved, but we may be fairly certain that it was similar to the form in which the oath was put to the members of both Houses of Parliament.[27]

When he was asked to take the oath, More requested a copy of the statute, made a comparison, then refused to take the oath. He refused to tell the Commissioners or anyone else why he refused,[28] with the exception that, according

26. *SL* 199.
27. PARMITER, op. cit. 2.
28. *SL* 220.

to Roper, he spoke to Margaret of the discrepancy between the oath and the statute. By refraining from drawing attention to the discrepancy, More shrewdly provided for his legal defence, since, if he had been brought to trial, he would have been able to demonstrate that the Commissioners were acting *ultra vires* because the oath they offered was illegal. It may have been only a temporary protection for More, (as he said, *'quod differtur non aufertur'*), but it would have discredited and embarrassed his persecutors. If the oath was illegal, it follows that More's imprisonment was also illegal. The insufficiency of the oath was eventually noticed and a second Act of Succession ratified it retroactively. More was not brought to trial on the issue of the oath, but his imprisonment was convalidated by an Act of Attainder in November, 1534.

In what way did the oath disagree with the statute? It required the swearing of statements in no way justified by the statute; e.g. it forbade any allegiance to any person other than the King, within or without the realm; it required the repudiation of any oath already taken to anyone except the King; it required all subjects to 'observe, keep, maintain, and defend this Act above specified, *and all other acts and statutes made since the beginning of the present parliament in confirmation or for due execution of the same.*' The words in italics cannot be justified by the statute. These discrepancies would have made it illegal for More to take the oath according to the laws of the realm. [29]

However More's objections on these purely legal grounds were accidental, because he would still not have been able to take the oath even if it had been in agreement with the statute. More did not believe that the marriage between Henry and Catherine was against the law of nature, even on purely Scriptural authority. This is a matter to which he had given a great deal of study and discussion, but he could not agree with the King. We may assume he adopted his stand also on ecclesiastical authority. The fact he urged Henry to follow a different line suggests that in More's opinion to question the competence of the supreme ecclesiastical authority would tend to undermine this authority. Especially in the Church, the supreme authority must be able to define its own competence. It can be argued that the very use of authority in a given matter established the existence of such competence (in the case of the *supreme* authority), at least when there is a series of acts. But even in an individual case, such as the dispensation given for the marriage of Henry and Catherine, the very exercise of jurisdiction creates the strong presumption that the authority (supreme in its own order) is competent to exercise power according to the axiom *fecit ergo potuit*. This explains More's reluctance to advise Henry to pursue this line, and his suggestion that a more likely approach would be to try to establish falsehood or insufficiency in the petition for the dispensation from the impediment of affinity. This had already been investigated by Henry's advisors. It was used as an alternative case, but was rejected by the Legatine court on the production of conclusive evidence to the contrary. [30] The case

29. PARMITER, op. cit. 10.
30. *SL* 232, note 42.

had been recalled to Rome and no decision had been reached when Cranmer declared Henry's marriage with Catherine invalid and his union with Anne valid. More would not have accepted the competency of Cranmer's court to decide the issue, involving as it did a repudiation of the Pope's jurisdiction. When the Pope eventually decided that Henry's first marriage was valid (23 March, 1534) More's stand was vindicated. It was a preference of divine and ecclesiastical law over declarations issuing from Cranmer's court and the Act of Succession as passed by the English Parliament. It follows that More rejected the validity of the new union because of its being prohibited by divine law (Matt. 19:4) and perhaps by other impediments of purely ecclesiastical law.[31]

More did not however reject the oath and the statute on which it was based *in toto*. He accepted Parliament's competency to determine the succession to the throne and he was prepared to swear an oath framed in such a manner as might stand with his conscience.[32] So long as the King and the Parliament kept within matters of their proper jurisdiction, More remained loyal to them, as is borne out by his acceptance of the succession and his many affirmations of devotion to the King and to the realm during his imprisonment, during his trial and at his execution.

2. Fulfilment of Duties

a. Duties to God

We have just seen how More resolved the conflict of laws brought about by the Oath of Succession. His refusal to take the oath was based on a conscientious objection. He had formed his conscience 'neither suddenly nor slightly but by long leisure and diligent search for the matter', and since the oath conflicted with 'the general council of Christendom',[33] it was his duty before God not to take it.

b. Duties to the King and Parliament

As he regarded the succession to be within the competence of Parliament, More advised the King's Councillors that he was prepared to swear the oath if he could see it framed according to his conscience. He would not declare the reasons for not accepting the proffered oath, because, as he said, he did not wish to exasperate his Highness further. He also pleaded that he was carrying out his duty to the King by not discouraging others from taking the oath: 'as touching the whole oath, I never withdrew any man from it, nor never advised any to refuse it, nor never put, nor will, any scruple in any man's head, but leave every man to his own conscience.'[34]

In his conversation with Margaret in the Tower, More summed up the difficulty of doing his duty to the King: 'in this matter if it were possible for me to do the thing that might content the King's Grace, and God therewith not

31. See above, p. 119.
32. *SL* 222.
33. *SL* 221–2.
34. *SL* 220–3.

offended, there hath no man taken this oath already more gladly than I would.'[35] He repeated a similar thought in a letter to Master Leder: 'I beseech our Lord that all may prove as true faithful subjects to the King that have sworn as I am in my mind very sure that they be, which have refused to swear.'[36]

c. Duties to Others

Dr Nicholas Wilson. Dr Wilson was asked to take the oath on the same day as More: he likewise refused and was imprisoned in the Tower. More was led to believe some time later that Wilson had changed his mind and had taken the oath. He wrote to him wishing him 'thereof good luck'. He went on to say he would not reveal his own mind nor know 'no man's else'. He shrewdly stated however that for himself to swear would be to endanger his soul.[37] This may have encouraged Wilson to resist again (unless the previous information given to More was false), for we find that Wilson wrote to More to ask for guidance. This letter put More in a difficult position. It could have been a trap. If he broke silence he could have endangered his life. Yet, on the other hand, he was under an obligation to help Wilson who had appealed to his charity in his spiritual necessity. More's letter in reply is a masterpiece of simplicity and cunning. He begins by expressing his sorrow at Wilson's troubled conscience, but then states that he is even more sorry he cannot give him the help for which he had asked. However the rest of the letter is an attempt to give such assistance. More was on dangerous ground, so he took the precaution of writing in such a way that if the letter fell into Cromwell's hands he would find nothing in it which could incriminate him. More's advice to Wilson amounted to a reminder of the investigations they had carried out together on the marriage question. He briefly recalled the places in the Scriptures, 'the old holy Doctors', and 'the councils and laws on either side'. More reminded Wilson that he had told him everything he could on the subject when they were both 'indifferently' considering the matter at the King's command. He now had nothing new to add: 'though I had all the points as ripe in mind now as I had then and had still all the books about me that I then had, and were as willing to meddle in the matter as any man could be, yet could you now no new thing hear of me, more than you have, I wyn, heard often before, nor I wyn I of you neither.'[38] As regards the oath, More adopts the same procedure: he will not meddle with other people's conscience. But he does nonetheless remind Wilson in general terms that certain things bind under 'peril of damnation' – what they are More does not say. The rest of the letter is a spiritual discourse in which he expresses 'trust in God and in the merits of his bitter passion', confidence in the help of God, and prayer for Wilson himself, his friends and enemies ('if I have any'). He asks Wilson to send the letter back to him: he does not wish it to be discovered as it might compromise the servant who would perhaps be punished

35. CHAMBERS, 309, quoting letter of Margaret to Alice Alington.
36. *SL* 244.
37. *SL* 227–8.
38. *SL* 231: 'wyn', i.e. suppose.

for carrying letters between the prisoners. (It may also have been a device to test Wilson's sincerity, or a precaution against a trap: if the letter did not come back he could suspect a plot; if it did he could use it in his defence against any possible charge that he had encouraged Wilson's resistance.) The sum effect of the letter was to assist Wilson by a general reminder of their studies and by the statement that he can still see no reason to alter the conclusion to which they had come. The spiritual encouragement contained in the letter would only have meaning on the assumption that Wilson would persevere in his resolve not to take the oath. It appears he held out for several years.[39]

His Family. Did More have a duty to his family to guide them in what would have been for them also a spiritual crisis? We should remember they were all adults by this time; they had enjoyed the benefit of a good moral and religious education. Just as More refused 'to pin his soul at another man's back', so he would not take the burden of another's salvation onto himself. He probably had discussed the issues with them before the law forbade it. His opinion on the oath was made sufficiently clear by his refusal to take it. It appears his family took the oath with a mental reservation. But More's main discussion of the issues for the benefit of his family is contained in the dialogue related by Margaret in her letter to Alice Alington. Margaret puts up one objection after another to her father: that he would lose his friends at court; that he was blindly following Bishop Fisher; that he could take the oath with a mental reservation; that nearly everyone else had taken it; that he was bound to follow the law of Parliament. More answered the objections patiently and assured Margaret he had given the matter long and serious thought. He was not a simpleton, but an educated and judicious man whose duty it was to follow reason. Such was More's way of giving spiritual direction to his family in the crisis. To have been more explicit would have been unnecessary, and because of his duties to himself and the realm, to go beyond what was sufficient would have been wrong.

d. Duties to Himself

More declared frequently that he could not take the oath because it would endanger his salvation. After refusing the oath for the first time at Lambeth, he wrote to Margaret to tell her of the interview. He had told the Commissioners: 'unto the oath that was offered me I could not swear, without the iubarding of my soul to perpetual damnation.'[40] He suffered the penalties for misprision of treason rather than do so. His refusal to give his reasons for not taking the oath was partly due to his fear of falling into the sin of presumption and thereby losing his soul.[41]

It is interesting to see the devices which More used in an effort to save his

---

39. CHAMBERS, 318.
40. *SL* 217; 'iubarding', i.e. jeoparding, imperilling.
41. *SL* 253.

life. As we said above, his desire to save his life was intimately bound up with his eternal salvation. This being understood, let us examine these efforts. When he first refused the oath of Succession, seeing the Commissioners were displeased, he offered to take an oath saying that his objections were purely spiritual and conscientious: and if they would not take his word on that oath, why should they accept it for their oath?[42] They refused this and charged More with obstinacy. More's next move was to promise to reveal his objections in writing on 'the King's gracious licence or rather his such commandment' that such a declaration would neither offend the King nor bring More 'in danger of any of his statutes'. They answered that though the King may give his licence under letters patent,[43] it would not save him from the penalties of the statute. More said he would accept such a licence from the King and would trust to his honour that he would not suffer the penalties. (Apparently More's offer was not acceptable to the King.) More's comment on the refusal to safeguard him against the statutes was that, if he would be punished for revealing his reasons, it was not obstinacy for him to remain silent.

Cranmer then put the argument to More that, since he would not condemn others he must be doubtful. But his duty to the King was certain. Therefore he must obey the King. More answered nothing to this, but thought to himself (as he later wrote to Margaret) that he could not accept the argument: his refusal to condemn others did not imply his own conscience was not certain: 'in my conscience the truth seemed on the other side.'[44] The Abbot of Westminster then said that More had reason to fear his conscience was erroneous because the whole of the Parliament was of the opposite opinion. More's reply was that the general Council of Christendom was on his side. Finally More agreed to swear to the succession if he could see an oath so framed it could stand with his conscience. This offer was also unacceptable to them. These counter-moves were More's effort to avoid misprision of treason with its harsh penalties and also to demonstrate that he was not acting from mere obstinacy.

D. The Supremacy of the Church of England

1. Priority of Laws

Henry VIII obtained the title of Head of the Church of England for the first time when the Convocations of Canterbury and York recognized him as 'their only and supreme Head'. A saving clause, which vaguely acknowledged that the King's Headship was subject to the Law of Christ, had been inserted at the suggestion of Bishop Fisher. On 15 May, 1532, the clergy made their complete submission to the Crown. The next day More resigned as Lord Chancellor on the excuse of failing health. In 1533 the Act of Restraint of Appeals to Rome was passed through Parliament. In November 1534 the Act of Supremacy was

42. *SL* 217–8.
43. 'Letters patent', i.e. official letter giving royal protection.
44. *SL* 221.

passed, then an Act of Treason by which it became an offence to deprive the King of his title. There was no oath attached to these two statutes. They became operative on 1 February, 1535.[45]

More had escaped the charge of treason and the death penalty by refusing to give his reasons for not taking the oath of Succession. But by not taking the oath, he was liable to the charge of misprision of treason. It was for this refusal that he was held in the Tower, without trial from 17 April, 1534, and by Act of Attainder from November, 1534. It was thought the new legislation (the Acts of Supremacy and Treason) would either force him to submit or bring him to execution, but for a time such efforts were again thwarted, for More again had recourse to silence, for which no penalty existed. Even his earlier device of not commenting on the oath had caused Cromwell to consider the possibility of legislation to force an answer. This is probably what More is alluding to in his letter to Margaret from the Tower:[46]

Now have I heard since that some say that this obstinate manner of mine in still refusing the oath shall peradventure force and drive the King's Grace to make a further law for me. I cannot let such a law to be made. But I am very sure that if I died by such a law, I should die for that point innocent afore God.

Such legislation, wrote More, would be an 'unlawful law', and his death would come about 'without law, or by colour of a law'. On 30 April, 1535, Cromwell asked More whether the King could exact of him 'such things as are contained in the statutes'. More shrewdly replied, 'I would not say the contrary', which was quite a non-committal answer. Cromwell then asked his opinion on other statutes. This could have been a trap as the oath (which had been ratified by Parliament) also covered other statutes connected with the Act of Succession. Again More offered no comment.[47] On 3 June the King's Council visited More, 'to drive me', he wrote, 'to say precisely the one way, or else precisely the other' concerning the Supremacy. When More again refused an answer, Cromwell suggested that the King might make laws to force a plain answer. More replied that he would not question the King's authority, but he thought it hard a man should be forced to say one thing to the loss of his body, or the opposite to the loss of his soul. Cromwell replied that he (More), 'or at the least wise Bishops', used to force an answer from heretics about the primacy of the Pope.[48] We will see More's answer later. The incident shows how Cromwell's mind was working to find a way to close the loophole in the laws which More's silence had exposed. This was achieved two years later when refusal to answer interrogations about the King's titles became treason.[49]

More considered that the Act of Supremacy was directly repugnant to the

45. REYNOLDS, *The Trial*, 54 ff.
46. *SL* 237.
47. *SL* 247–8.
48. *SL* 251–2.
49. BELL, op. cit. 331.

law of Christ (divine positive law), and therefore not binding in conscience. We have already seen More's account of the development of his thought on the Pope's primacy. More was so certain of its divine origin that it would be to the peril of his soul to believe otherwise. However, as it was not defined, he did not wish to impose his opinion on others. So he based his stand on the Law of Christendom, the teaching of the universal Church:[50]

> ... for that primacy is at leastwise instituted by the corps of Christendom and for a great urgent cause in avoiding of schisms and corroborate by continual succession more than the space of a thousand year at the least ...
> And therefore sith all Christendom is one corps, I cannot perceive how any member thereof may without the common assent of the body depart from the common head. I cannot perceive (but if the thing were a treating in a general council) what the question could avail whether the primacy were instituted by God or ordained by the Church.

After the Act of Succession More refused to state his opinion about the King's title except to refer Cromwell to the letter from which the above extract is taken. 'And now I neither will dispute King's titles or Pope's ... and otherwise ... I never intend to meddle.'[51] However, when he was asked why he could not be pressed for a precise answer whereas the Bishops had extracted answers concerning the Pope from heretics, he replied that the cases were different, because in the latter case the Bishops were demanding that heretics assert their belief concerning a doctrine held 'through the corps of Christendom'; in his own case, he was being asked to assert something affirmed in England but denied by other realms:[52]

> thereto I answered that sith in this case a man is not by a law of one realm so bound in his conscience, where there is a law of the whole corps of Christendom to the contrary in matter touching belief, as he is by a law of the whole corps though there hap to be made in some place a law local to the contrary, the reasonableness or the unreasonableness in binding a man to precise answer standeth not in respect or difference between heading or burning, but because of the difference between heading and hell.

He had used a similar argument to the Abbot of Westminster when he first refused the oath saying, 'I am not bounden to change my conscience, and confirm it to the council of one realm, against the general council of Christendom.' He used identical words after the verdict at his trial.[53] But both these statements were outside the critical period between 1 February and the trial. The discussion of the case with Cromwell is more carefully worded: he simply pointed out that there was a difference between the two cases.

50. *SL* 212–3.
51. *SL* 246.
52. *SL* 251–2.
53. *SL* 222; CHAMBERS, 341.

It appears from these instances that for the most part More preferred to base his stand on the common belief of Christendom, 'the law of Christendom', trusting that this would be more likely to gain admission, especially in court, than the theological arguments of which he was certain, but which others, including Catholics, still disputed. If More's speech after the verdict was really an arrest of judgment, it would seem that he was urging an outside law, or a higher law (the law of Christendom and the law of Christ) as a test of the validity of the statutes of the English Parliament.[54] More's idea of Christendom as a corporate, and even as a juridical unity, was also at the basis of his part in the conversation with Sir Richard Rich in the Tower, which we have analysed more fully in another place.[55]

2. Fulfilment of Duties
a. Duties to God and the Church

By his death as a martyr, St Thomas More testified to his belief in the Roman unity of Europe and his loyalty to ancient Christianity.[56] He refused to separate himself from the Catholic Church, or recognize the national schism implied in the royal Supremacy. To do so would have been to sin against the teachings of Christ. He was executed for denying the royal Supremacy. So his death was martyrdom in the theological sense of the word. 'He did not die for a legal quibble.'[57]

For a number of years More had foreseen the possibility of a violent death at the hands of the executioner because of the trends in Henry's policies. He had psychologically prepared himself for such an eventuality by meditation on the Passion of Christ and his martyrs. His strong faith in God and the future life gave him strength to overcome the barriers which were put in the path he had conscientiously chosen. Although he used every device he knew to avoid death, he realized his danger, as is evidenced by the discussion of persecution and martyrdom which is the subject of the *Dialogue of Comfort*.[58] His resignation to God's will is brought out by his recognition of divine providence in his being allowed to spend his last days in the seclusion of a cell so that he could prepare himself for death as he had always wished. Again he trusted in God's help if martyrdom were the only alternative: 'Howbeit, if God draw me to Himself, then trust I in His great mercy, that He shall not fail to give me grace and strength.'[59] He ended his short speech on the scaffold saying that he died

---

54. J. DUNCAN M. DERRETT, 'The Trial of Thomas More', *EHR*, vol. LXXIX, no. 312, July 1964, 449 ff. Also REYNOLDS, *The Trial*, 53, describes 'the law of Christendom' as the test invoked by More.
55. See Appendix with its note 21.
56. Cf. Chesterton's remark quoted by REYNOLDS, *The Trial*, xiv.: 'He saw . . . . that the real hopes of learning and liberty lay in preserving the Roman unity of Europe and the ancient Christian loyalty for which he died.'
57. REYNOLDS, *The Trial*, xiv.
58. Cf. LELAND MILES, 'Patristic Comforters in More's *Dialogue of Comfort*', *Moreana* no. 8, Nov. 1965, 9–20.
59. *SL* 253.

primarily as God's good servant:[60]

> ... he was beheaded in the great square in front of the Tower, and said little before execution only that the people there should pray God for him and he would pray for them. Afterwards, he exhorted them and earnestly beseeched them to pray God for the King, so that He would give him good counsel, protesting that he died his good servant and God's first.

b. Duties to King and Country

The King. The most remarkable, and the most ironical thing about the downfall of More was that, though he was to die a traitor, he retained his personal loyalty to Henry to the very end and to the highest degree compatible with his duty to God, the Church and himself. Having refused to repeat his views on the Supremacy, he immediately professed himself to be faithful to the King: 'the King's true faithful subject I am and will be, and daily I pray for him and for all his, and for all you that are of his honourable Council, and for all the realm ... I am the King's daily bedesman.'[61] He declared himself 'very heavy' because the King thought he had 'an obstinate mind and evil toward him'. 'Yet have I', he went on to say, 'no remedy to help it, but only to comfort myself with this consideration that I know very well that the time shall come, when God shall declare my truth toward his Grace before him and all the world.' He reminded the King again (through Cromwell) of the lesson which his Highness taught him at his 'first coming to his noble service, the most virtuous lesson that ever prince taught his servant', *viz.* 'to looking first upon God and next upon the King'. Even the element of flattery in More's remarks about the King (which were more natural then than they would be today) is the best type of flattery: he speaks about the King's goodness, virtue, generosity etc. in a way calculated to bring out the best in the King's nature. Again at his trial, according to the most trustworthy accounts, he avoided anything which would appear to slight the person of the King in any way. His final words to his judges were: 'I desire Almighty God to preserve and defend the King's Majesty and to send him good counsel.'[62] Even on the scaffold he was obedient to the King's last command not to speak much. He simply protested that he died the King's good servant as well as God's: 'Qu'il mouroit son bon serviteur *et* de Dieu premierement.'[63]

Duties to the Realm. We may have expected that More, as a public figure, would have tried to give some guidance to his country in this critical period of its history. Actually a careful examination of the case reveals that More contrived to counsel the government as best he could under the circumstances. From the study of his letters, his conversations, his very silence,

---

60. REYNOLDS, *The Trial*, 151.
61. Ibid. 246–7.
62. HARPSFIELD, 197.
63. Ibid. 266. More's subtle choice of the word 'and' instead of 'but' brings out the whole point of his position: true service of God and King are not opposed but complementary.

his trial, his speeches in court and on the scaffold, there clearly emerges a firm anti-schism policy. From the start he based his stand on the authority of the community of Christendom. The universal belief in the Papacy was the reason why Bishops could demand a positive answer about it from heretics, while the isolated belief of the English could not justify the Commissioners' interrogation concerning the Supremacy of the King. Before the Act of Supremacy, More had written to Cromwell giving his opinion concerning the Papacy. After the Act he referred Cromwell to that letter. If he had failed to guide the government then, he had no reason to believe that he would be able to succeed now. At his trial, he again gave an outline of his thought on the subject. But his appeal was not directly to the theological arguments for the Papacy, but to the general witness of Christendom. His practical admission of the superiority of a Council over the Pope must be seen in the light of his anti-schism policy. If Henry would not submit to the Pope with regard to his marriage problem, at least he might accept the ruling of a General Council. He had used the same argument of the unity of Christendom to the Commissioners at Lambeth Palace when he first refused the oath. It was again the first argument in his speech after the verdict. But there he went further, and showed by theological reasoning from Scripture and Tradition that Christ had willed the papal primacy as a safeguard to that unity. He argued that 'this realm, being but one member and small part of the Church, might not make a particular law disagreeable with the general law of Christ's Universal Catholic Church, no more than the City of London, being but one poor member in respect of the whole Realm, might make a law against an Act of Parliament to bind the whole Realm'.[64] He appealed to the tradition of England itself, including the laws and statutes, and the Magna Charta: 'Quod Anglicana ecclesia libera sit et habeat jura sua integra et libertates suas illaesas.' He pointed to the oath taken by the King and all Christian Princes to the Holy See. He appealed to the loyalty of Englishmen to that See which had begotten them in Christ when St Gregory sent St Augustine to their shores.

It was not always possible for More to use these explicit arguments. For many months his silence was his loudest advice to his countrymen. This had some effect because Cromwell reported to him in prison that it was unsettling the realm: the King 'thought that by my demeanour I had been occasion of much grudge and harm in the realm'. But surely too More's preference of death was made in the hope that the kingdom would realize what was happening. He was prepared to accept death if it would benefit the King: 'would God my death might do him good.'[65] At the end of his trial he recalled that St Stephen's prayer had brought about the conversion of Paul, who was consenting to his death, and hoped that similarly he would meet his judges again in heaven.[66]

---

64. REYNOLDS, *The Trial*, 121; DERRETT, 'Thomas More and the Legislation of the Corporation of London', reprinted from *The Guildhall Miscellany*, vol. II, no. 5, Oct. 1963, n.p.
65. *SL* 248–9.
66. J. R. CAVANAUGH, 'The St Stephen motif in More's Thought', *Moreana* no. 8, Nov. 1965, 59 ff.

It would surely be permissible piously to believe that More offered his life for the spiritual welfare of his country.

c. Duties to Others

St John Fisher. Bishop Fisher, also imprisoned for refusing to take the oath of Succession, sent notes to More asking for legal advice to help him escape the Treasons Act. Possibly he felt that, as a Bishop, he had a stronger obligation to speak out against the statute. More replied that he must ultimately decide for himself. He intimated that he could escape the death penalty by silence and advised him not to rely on the insertion in the statute of the qualifying word 'maliciously' as a protection in law, if he contemplated speaking out on the subject. Fisher availed himself of this advice. However he was eventually tricked by someone, presumably Rich, into saying that the King was not the Supreme Head. He claimed at his trial that his assertion was not malicious because he was giving his opinion for the spiritual guidance of the King, as his interrogator had claimed that he was seeking the Bishop's real opinion on behalf of the King. As More had predicted his plea that he had not spoken 'maliciously' did not save him. More's own use of the term 'maliciously' in his own defence was a somewhat different matter.[67] Unfortunately the correspondence between the two saints had to be destroyed.

His Family. As no oath was required under the new statute, More's family was not subject to further crisis, so long as they did not deny the King's Supremacy. More evidently tried to protect his property for his family in the event of his death.[68] His writings in the Tower and his last letters to his family show how he tried to prepare them spiritually for his death.[69]

Sir Richard Rich. At a crucial point in his trial, More accused the key witness, Richard Rich, the Solicitor-General, of perjury. He then proceeded to discredit Rich as a witness by recalling his reputation in the parish wherein they had both lived: 'you were esteemed very light of your tongue, a common liar, a great dicer and of no commendable fame.'[70] This denunciation was certainly a legitimate legal device, but only on the assumption that it was basically true. The same must be said of the allegation by More of perjury on the part of Rich. Such a strongly worded denial of Rich's testimony would be most unethical if his evidence were true. We adhere to the opinion that his evidence was in fact false. Therefore More was excused from his duty of charity because Rich had forfeited his reputation by his false allegations and because another duty had a prior claim, *viz.* the duty to himself.

67. See below, p. 141
68. DERRETT, 'More's Conveyance of his Land and the Law of "Frauds",' *Moreana*, no. 5, 18 ff. There is no question of moral fraud.
69. Cf. *SL* 245 for concern for family.
70. HARPSFIELD, 189.

d. Duties to Himself

The 'via media' of silence which More decided to follow when faced with the Act of Supremacy appeared to him as a definite duty, not as a course which he could freely choose or reject. In the first place, it seemed to him at this stage of his history that his foremost duty was the salvation of his own soul. Other duties were to be fulfilled only in so far as they did not conflict with this one. To accept the King as Supreme Head of the English Church would have imperilled his salvation. On the other hand, he considered himself not only excused from speaking out, but even bound not to speak out against the statute (until the end of his trial), first because of the spiritual obligation on himself to avoid the sin of presumption; second, because of his duty to preserve his life with the legal ability with which Providence had endowed him. After the verdict at his trial the situation was changed. He had been found guilty of treason and the death penalty was to be imposed. Now his duty demanded that he discharge his conscience. He delivered a carefully prepared oration concerning the Primacy of the Roman Pontiff as proved from the Gospel account of the giving of the keys to St Peter, and as upheld by all the Fathers, Councils and Saints for over a thousand years.

More's Pre-Trial Strategy. More was interviewed by Cromwell and the Council on 30 April 1535. Cromwell told him that it was the King's pleasure to know his mind on the Act of Supremacy. More replied that he had already discharged his duty in his earlier conversations with the King and in his letter to Cromwell himself (both before the Act was passed). At the King's offer to let him go 'abroad in the world again' if he conformed, More replied, 'I would never meddle in the world again to have the world given me . . . but my whole study should be upon the passion of Christ and mine own passage out of this world.' More was unmoved by Cromwell's further efforts to frighten him: his pleasure was 'to mind only the weal of my soul, with little regard of my body'.[71]

On 3 June the Council again approached More for a definite answer, and commanded him on his allegiance to the King either to confess the Act lawful or else declare his malignity. 'Whereto I answered that I had no malignity and therefore I could none utter.' He denied having an evil mind towards the King. He could do nothing in the circumstances to put the King's mind at rest, but the time would come when God would declare his truth to the King. 'I thanked God that my case was such in this matter through the clearness of mine own conscience that though I might have pain I could not have harm.'[72] Then came the discussion of the Bishops' authority to force an answer from heretics, in which More again brought out that the difference between the cases appeared to him, not between beheading and burning, but between beheading and hell.

More easily evaded Cromwell's next move to try and get him to accept an

71. *SL* 245–8.
72. *SL* 249–50.

136

oath obliging him to answer an interrogatory of questions which would be asked on the King's behalf, according to the procedure used in the Star Chamber. More anticipated the nature of the questions correctly and refused the oath. The Counsellors then marvelled that More persisted in his stand, seeing that he was not sure of his opinion. 'Whereto I said that I was very sure that mine own conscience so informed as it is by such diligence as I have so long taken therein may stand with mine own salvation.' Then they taunted him that if he was so ready to die as he had maintained, why did he not speak out clearly against the statute: 'It appeared well I was not content to die though I said so. Whereto I answered as the truth is, that I have not been a man of such holy living as I might be bold to offer myself to death, lest God for my presumption might suffer me to fall back. Howbeit, if God draw me to it Himself, then trust I in His great mercy, that he shall not fail to give me grace and strength.'[73]

On 7 May Fisher had been tricked into a denial of the Supremacy. He was again interviewed on 12 June and on the same day Sir Richard Rich with four other men visited More's cell to take away his books and writing materials. Rich used the occasion in another attempt to extract a denial of the Supremacy from More. We have no record of this conversation directly from More himself since he was no longer allowed pen and paper. Our sources for it are: 1. a document discovered by E. E. Reynolds in the London Records' Office which appears to be a report upon which the Indictment against More is based; 2. the fourth count of More's Indictment itself; 3. Roper's account of More's defence at his trial against this part of the charge.[74] If we correlate these sources we can get an idea of what took place.

Whilst the others were trussing up More's books, Rich again urged More to conform his mind to the statute and again More declined, saying, 'Your conscience shall save you and my conscience shall save me.' Rich then proposed a case for More's consideration: if he, Rich, were made King by an Act of Parliament, would not More be bound in conscience to accept him as such? More replied that he would offend if he refused because he would be bound by the Act since he could (conscientiously) give his consent. But that was a simple case.

At this point there is a vital discrepancy between our sources. According to the Indictment and the document discovered by Reynolds, More put the next case: suppose Parliament passed an Act that God be not God, and that it be treason to deny that Act; if Rich agreed with this statute, would he not offend? Rich agreed that he would offend because it is not possible to make God not God. Then, according to the same sources, Rich put the third case: the King has been made Head on earth of the Church of England so why ought not More accept him as such just as in the first case he would accept Rich as King. More is alleged to have replied, 'Those cases are not like because a king can be made

73. *SL* 252–3.
74. For an analysis of these sources see Appendix.

by Parliament and can be deprived by Parliament, to which act any subject . . . may give his consent, but to the case of a primacy the subject cannot be bound because he cannot give his consent . . . and although the King were accepted as such in England, yet most outer parts [i.e. foreign countries] do not affirm the same.' Reynold's document gives Rich's concluding words to More: 'Well, Sir, God comfort you, for I see your mind will not change which I fear will be very dangerous to you for I suppose your concealment to the question that hath been asked of you is as high offence as other that hath denied it. And so Jesu send you better grace.' The 'other' who is referred to as having positively denied the Supremacy was undoubtedly Fisher.

While Roper's account agrees with the Indictment on the first case it then diverges somewhat. According to Roper when More had answered the first case (that Rich were made King) Rich immediately followed with a second: suppose Parliament enacted that Rich should be Pope? More countered this, saying 'To make answer to your . . . case: Suppose Parliament made a law that God should not be God?' Rich agreed that such a law would be null. The *logical* conclusion should have been: just as such a law would not bind because it is beyond Parliament's competence so a law making Rich Pope would not be binding. But *in fact* Roper's account concludes: '"No more", said Sir Thomas More, as Master Rich reported of him, "could the Parliament make the King Supreme Head of the Church".'

The discrepancy between the two accounts is important. One account (the report and the Indictment) is evidently Rich's version of what was said, whilst the other is More's, except for the conclusion which is a *non sequitur* in so far as it speaks of the *King* since the case under discussion was that *Rich* had been made Pope. Whatever may be said of the criminality of Rich's version, More's account contains nothing treasonable since it was not forbidden to deny that the Parliament of England could elect the Supreme Head of the Church, i.e. Pope. Which account is to be accepted? Leaving aside for the time being the arguments More himself used at his trial, I submit that a careful scrutiny of the report and the Indictment reveals evidence that More's words did refer to the primacy of the universal Church and not to the Supremacy of the King in England.

I put forward the following arguments for this position: first, the fact that the allegedly treasonable words in the fourth count are reported in Latin whereas in the previous counts they are quoted in English leads one to suspect that an effort was being made to gloss over the changes which had been made in the report of the conversation. Rich, it should be remembered, was hoping for the support of witnesses. Secondly, the Indictment, following the report, speaks of 'the case of a *primacy*'. The word *primacy* was used of the office of the Pope, but not of the Supremacy of the King. Thirdly, the words attributed in the Indictment to More, *viz.* 'although the King were accepted as such in England, yet most outer parts do not affirm the same', fit better into More's account than into Rich's. The simple non-affirmation by foreign countries of a primacy bestowed by the English Parliament is a conclusive argument that the Parliament cannot elect a Pope but it is not a valid argument against the competence of the English Parliament to elect a head of the Church in England – which, it could be argued, is a matter for the English alone and its non-recognition by outsiders is irrelevant. Fourthly, as Reynolds has argued, Rich's concluding words which are recorded in the report but are omitted from the Indictment, state that More has *concealed* his mind on the Supremacy, which implies that More had pursued his resolve not to discuss the matter, as he had stated when Rich first entered.

It is the present writer's opinion then that More's account of the interview is true and Rich's false. I believe also that Rich deliberately contrived his cases with a view to obtaining a statement such as is reported in Roper, 'No more could the Parliament make the King Supreme Head of the Church.' If the phrase, 'Supreme Head of the Church', referred to the papacy the words were certainly not treasonable because Parliament never pretended that it could elect a Pope.[75] But Rich changed the context by altering his case in the report from one about the primacy to one about the supremacy. Hence he merited the castigation which was dealt out to him by More at the trial.

More's Defence at his Trial. On 1 July 1535 Sir Thomas More was brought to trial on the charge of falsely, traitorously, and maliciously depriving the King of his title of Supreme Head on earth of the Church of England. There were four articles or counts in the Indictment, which More heard for the first time when it was read in court. Before the trial itself started More was offered an opportunity of freeing himself of the charge by acknowledging the Supremacy of the King. Having refused, he set about a defence against the charge. His aim was to use every ounce of legal skill to save himself from execution by proving his innocence. In dealing with the first three counts, he admitted the substance of the allegations, but denied that they incriminated him. But concerning the fourth count, he denied the evidence upon which it was based.

The first count was that he had kept silence when asked by Cromwell to give his opinion on the King's title on 7 May. This date, which is given in the Indictment, appears to be an error. Had More realized this and challenged it, the Indictment would have been disallowed as invalid.[76] More's defence against the count was: 'touching I say, this challenge and accusation, I answer that, for this my taciturnity and silence, neither your law nor any law in the world is able justly and rightly to punish me, unless you may besides lay to my charge either some word or some fact in deed.' The King's Attorney then

---

75. It therefore becomes purely theoretical to ask if they were treasonable even in the case of their referring to the King's Supremacy. The Supremacy was not *based* on the statute but on the King's right which existed before the statute. It was treason to deny the King's title, but not to deny Parliament's competence to confer it, since it did not claim to confer it, but merely declared that it existed.
76. REYNOLDS, *The Trial*, 86–7.

objected that a loyal subject will give his opinion when asked. More gave a double answer. The first was to invoke the maxim of law, *qui tacet consentire videtur*; the second was a real answer: 'in things touching conscience, every true subject is more bound to have respect to his said conscience and to his soul than to any other thing in the world'; moreover, he had given 'no occasion of slander, of tumult and sedition against his Prince'.

The second count alleged that More had written to Fisher in the Tower urging him 'in no wise to agree and condescend to the said statute'. The letters between the two prisoners could not be produced because they had been destroyed. More explained: Fisher had asked him what he had said to the Commissioners, and he had replied: 'I had informed and settled my conscience, and . . . he should inform and settle his.'

The third count was similar: it alleged collusion between More and Fisher because both when interviewed had used the same words: 'the statute was like a two-edged sword' which would destroy either body or soul. It was alleged that the words themselves were treasonable as was also the agreement between the prisoners. More's reply was that he had made the remark only conditionally: *if* 'the Statute were like to be a double-edged sword, he could not tell in the world how a man should demean and order himself but that he should fall into one of the dangers.' As to conspiracy, More replied that the similarity of comments was due to 'the correspondence and conformity of our wits, learning and study, not that any such thing was purposely concluded upon and accorded betwixt us'.[77]

Some historians of More's trial consider that the court accepted More's explanation of the first three counts, and so proceeded immediately to the fourth, on which alone he was apparently convicted.[78] This count causes some difficulty. It was omitted altogether from the earliest accounts of the trial, i.e. the *Paris News Letter* and the *Expositio*, but was supplied by Roper in a manner that is somewhat puzzling. The wording of the Indictment is also clumsy. This has led to differing explanations of the veracity of the evidence given by Sir Richard Rich. Apparently the allegation was that in a conversation with Rich More had denied the competence of Parliament to enact that the King should be Supreme Head on earth of the Church of England. This denial followed after the discussion of other cases concerning the powers of Parliament and their limits. It was alleged that the denial of competence implied a denial of the Supremacy, and so More was guilty of treason.

At this stage More's defence took a rather violent turn. He flatly denied having said that the Parliament could not make the King or declare him to be Supreme Head of the Church of England. He called Rich a perjurer, and endeavoured to demolish his testimony by undermining his repute. He then gave

---

77. HARPSFIELD, 185–8.
78. REYNOLDS, *The Trial*, 105; DERRETT, 'The Trial of Sir Thomas More', *EHR*, vol. LXXIX, no. 312, July 1964, 450.

his version of the conversation: he and Rich had not been discussing the Supremacy of the Church of England, but that of the whole Church. Rich had asked More if Parliament could declare him to be Pope, and More had replied with another case: can Parliament declare that God should not be God? More's case had brought out that there are limits to the powers of Parliament. If he applied the principle to Rich's case it would be simply to show that the English Parliament could not elect the Supreme Head of the Church i.e. the Pope. If it did it would be an empty title because other countries would not recognize it. This was evidently a different account from what Rich had given and did not constitute treason because the English Parliament had never pretended that it could do such a thing. More attempted to persuade the court that his account was true, first by arguing from the fact that he would be unlikely to declare his mind to Rich when he had steadfastly refused to do so even at the repeated demands of the King and the Council. Then he declared on a self-imposed oath (not recognized legally by the court) that Rich was lying: he argued from this that if he were a person who would make a false oath, he would not at that moment be on trial for his life. Rich called upon two witnesses to support his evidence, but they declined to do so, saying that they had not listened to the conversation. However More knew that the court could legally accept Rich's evidence as at that time the testimony of one witness was sufficient. [79] So as an alternative defence, which would in no way weaken his main argument, More submitted that the discussion of cases is not malicious because the position a person espouses for the sake of debate is not necessarily his true position. Such conversations were common among lawyers. Cases were suggested by one to another, not as a serious belief to which the author committed himself, but simply to see how his companion would retort. If it were shown to be untenable, he would abandon the standpoint. Such, said More, was the nature of his conversation with Rich. Therefore it was not malicious and did not contravene the statute.

It seems that the last count was the only one accepted by the court and the one upon which the jury found More guilty. The position I have adopted in this section leads me to conclude that the court's judgment was erroneous because it was based on the perjured evidence of Rich, and that More should have been discharged as innocent of the crime of treason.

After the verdict More spoke against the legality of the statute, contending that it was contrary to the law of Christendom. If this was really a stay of judgment, as the question of Audley to Lord Fitz James and the rather strange reply seem to suggest, [80] More was going to the extreme length of attacking the validity of the statute itself in order to save himself. The court overruled his motion and the death penalty was passed.

79. See above, p. 58. More himself had defended the acceptance of the testimony of one witness in certain cases, including heresy and treason.
80. HARPSFIELD, 196–7.

Considering the great disadvantages under which More defended himself, we cannot but admire the brilliant skill which he displayed throughout his trial. My point is that, even though he realized he was fighting a lost cause and that his chances of acquittal were virtually nil, he fought the fight in a fair but tough professional manner with the object of fulfilling a duty: that of trying to save his own life.

CONCLUSION TO CHAPTER III:
RESOLUTION OF THE CONFLICT

Priority of Laws in Conflict

Thomas More was obedient to the laws of the English Parliament right up to, but not beyond, the point where they conflicted with the law of Christ and the law of Christendom in spiritual matters. He was prepared to accept the Succession as determined by Parliament; he did not speak, write or act against the Act of Succession but kept silence on his reasons for objecting to it. He did not infringe the Act of Supremacy by speaking, writing, or acting against it, but remained silent on the issue. He also showed his duty to Parliament by refusing the Oath of Succession in so far as it was not justified by the statute (i.e. between the first and second Acts of Succession). On the other hand, he obeyed the laws of Christ and Christendom, and disobeyed the law of Parliament by refusing to take the oath of Succession in so far as it contained matter repugnant to divine and ecclesiastical law. By not affirming the Supremacy of the King he acted in conformity with the law of Christ.

Priority of Duties in Conflict

Just as More worked out a priority among the laws which were in conflict, so we can detect a hierarchy of loyalties in the fulfilment of duties. Uppermost were his duties to God and the spiritual duty of saving his soul. But in putting these above everything else, More did not abandon his other duties, but skilfully endeavoured to carry out lesser ones as far as he was able and so long as they did not prevent him adhering to his principal obligations. His success in fulfilling so many of his duties during the conflict demonstrates his ingenuity and sincerity. His achievement of a delicate balance of duties in the crisis was unique. He tried to live by the rule of law till the very end, showing thereby his patriotism and his belief in the value of his country's institutions. But his unyielding devotion to the Universal Church because of its foundation by Christ as a unity bespeaks supernatural fortitude and loyalty.

CONCLUSION

In the following pages an attempt will be made to trace the derived and original elements in St Thomas More's thought, particularly in regard to the theme of this thesis, viz. loyalty in his spirituality. Then we will make some judgments regarding his contribution to spiritual doctrine, especially with the object of determining whether his thought assists the evolution of modern spiritual theology. Finally, some suggestions will be offered for future studies in More's thought.

1. DERIVED ELEMENTS IN MORE'S THOUGHT

The roots of More's doctrine spread deep and wide. It would be both impossible and unnecessary to trace them all in any but the most general terms: impossible in a short space, because the subject is almost as vast as classical and Christian literature combined; unnecessary, because, as any of the modern commentaries on the works of More show, much work has already been done.[1] More himself did not always give references to his sources, so certainty of influence is not always possible. In this connexion we regret the loss of More's library: it would have provided a valuable key to the question of much of More's thinking. Nevertheless, we can discover the broad outlines of his education. Having attempted this general description, we will then concentrate more attentively on his spirituality.

The Holy Scriptures were undoubtedly our saint's principal source.[2] According to More, theology, the queen of the sciences, resides first and foremost in the Bible. We have seen that he made extensive use of the Scriptures in his apologetical works, quoting from many parts of both Testaments, and indeed selecting passages not commonly used. Even more pronounced is the impact of Scripture on his spiritual works, some of which (e.g. *The History of the Passion*) are continuous commentaries. Many of the elements in More's spirituality are derived ultimately from Scripture, e.g. the doctrine of the Mystical Body, the interiority of prayer etc., but the selection of them for emphasis is due to intermediate influences. We have seen that the reading of the Bible was carried out

---

1. E.g. the Yale edition of *The Complete Works of St Thomas More*.
2. Abbé GERMAIN MARC'HADOUR, *Thomas More et la Bible*, Paris, and its English counterpart, *The Bible in the Works of Thomas More*, Nieuwkoop (Holland), both 1969–.

in More's household regularly; we have also pointed out More's advocacy of vernacular translations as well as his encouragement of projects involving the critical study and reconstruction of original texts – suggestions which were viewed with considerable suspicion in some quarters.

The Scriptures were for More the end for which other studies were the means. The pagan classics were important to him because they prepare one to study the Scriptures and help one to express the wisdom which is found in them. To support his contention of the value of a liberal education as an introduction to divinity he quotes the authority of the Fathers.[3] The chief value in the study of the 'old holy doctors' themselves is that they serve as guides in the interpretation of the Bible. For More then, the Scriptures were the most weighty authority and a most nutritious food in the spiritual life.

Various editors of More's works, especially the *Utopia*, have pointed out his familiarity with the principal Greek and Latin thinkers and writers. A list would include Homer, Isocrates, Xenophon, Socrates, Plato, Aristotle, Aesop, Plutarch, Tacitus, Sallust, Suetonius, Diogenes Laertius, Cicero, Cato, Seneca, Lucian, Vergil, Terence; he also drew upon Stoic and Epicurean philosophy in *Utopia*. From the pagan classics More learnt something of the philosophy of law, especially in relation to what we would now call social justice and the common good; he derived an appreciation of the drama of history; he built up from them a store of anecdotes; his early satirical humour was modelled on the classics.

In the course of his writings, More displayed a very wide knowledge of Christian literature.[4] He seems to have read, at least in part Ignatius, Polycarp, Irenaeus, Origen, Cyprian, Augustine, Jerome, Chrysostom, Basil, Gregory of Nyssa, Gregory Nazianzen, Lactantius, Eusebius, Ambrose, Arnobius, Hilary, Cassian, Theodoret, Boethius, Gregory the Great, Bernard, Peter Lombard, Albert, Thomas Aquinas, Duns Scotus, Gerson, Chaucer, to name some of them.

It seems that More was particularly struck by St Augustine and the fact that as a young man he publicly lectured on *The City of God* has instigated many comments on the dependence of More on the great Bishop of Hippo. Later in life, however, More derived a great deal from St Jerome: from him More's conviction of the all importance of the Scriptures was reinforced; from him he learned the value of the critical study of the original texts, of vernacular translation, and of new and better translations; he noticed Jerome's appreciation of the classics; from Jerome he probably derived encouragement in his pioneering of the education of women;[5] from him he learnt how to despise humbug and how to insult his opponents.

3. *EW 1931* II, 83.
4. LELAND MILES, 'Patristic Comforters in More's *Dialogue of Comfort*', *Moreana*, no. 8, Nov. 1965, 9–20.
5. For an early connection between Margaret More and the women of Jerome's school, see HARPSFIELD, 80–1.

St Cyprian too influenced More, especially in his concept of the unity of the Church (cf. Cyprian's *De unitate catholicae ecclesiae*), and also provided More with accounts of the sufferings of the martyrs which he used as material for meditation in his preparation for execution.

Boethius may also be singled out for special mention as there are similarities which are not usually referred to. That he was one of More's models is shown by the references to him in More's letters.[6] In the background of Holbein's painting of More's family there is depicted an open volume of Boethius. Both More and Boethius were philosophers and theologians, both humanists with a penchant for style; both of them were married and had children; they were both statesmen; both suffered imprisonment and martyrdom (at least probable in Boethius' case); both wrote dialogues concerning consolation while awaiting death. Boethius had been popular throughout the Middle Ages and so it is not surprising that he should also be admired by More.

It is difficult to trace precisely the English ancestry of More's spirituality. Various authors have detected Benedictine, Franciscan, and Carthusian influences. There is certainly much of mediaeval spirituality in More: the great importance he placed on the Four Last Things, asceticism, preparation for death, the Communion of Saints, the Passion of Christ etc. It is impossible to assert any definite dependence on individual authors, as More did not always give his sources, especially when the matter was more or less commonplace, but there is a similarity of approach between More and some of the earlier English mystics, e.g. Walter Hilton (+ 1395) and Richard Rolle (+ 1349).[7] It was characteristic of these mystics to speak of contemplation, not as the prerogative of a few select souls, but as the normal development of the Christian life; they were suspicious of extraordinary phenomena because of the danger of illusions;[8] the contemplative must not lose contact with the rest of existence, but should absorb his milieu in his ascent towards God, his sole end. These mystics concentrated on giving simple, practical, common-sense advice concerning the ordinary crises of soul, such as temptations and illusions, and their remedies. Now there is much of this in More's *Dialogue of Comfort*, where he deals with concrete problems, and gives some very discreet advice: he discusses mainly the problem of a Christian faced with persecution, but he brings in also such things as scruples, the temptation to commit suicide, the proper use of wealth and many other similar questions. He is not so interested in systems as in individual cases, and in this too he resembles his countrymen.

Of his contemporaries, the most dominant influence during More's formative years was probably John Colet, the Dean of St Paul's. He was More's spiritual director and guided his friendships and his reading. More was above all

---

6. *SL* 146; letter from Margaret to Alice Alington relating a verbal reference of her father to Boethius while More was in the Tower; see REYNOLDS, *Margaret Roper*, London, 1960, 82.
7. FELIX VERNET, 'Anglaise . . . (Spiritualité)', in *DSAM*, tome I, coll. 625–59.
8. Cf. More's advice to Elizabeth Barton, *SL* 196–8.

impressed by Colet's own uprightness of life and estimated him as one of the holiest men that England had produced for centuries. Naturally the young More was influenced by the opinions of Colet, particularly those expressed from the pulpit. Actually Colet was not a great scholar or a balanced thinker: he was essentially a moralizer, and a similar trait is detectable in his protege. Colet's forthright condemnation of unworthy churchmen as the greatest threat to the Church was echoed in many of More's writings. Colet was severe on hypocrisy, superstition, subtle speculation and the minimalism of contemporary theologians, all of which are deplored in the works of More. We know that Colet brought the writings of Pico della Mirandola (+ 1494) before the notice of Erasmus. It is not too improbable therefore that he (Colet) was also the one who brought Pico to the attention of More. More translated the life and a selection of the writings of this Italian nobleman. Authors are somewhat divided in determining the exact direction in which Pico influenced More: Stapleton thought that Pico was a model layman upon whom More patterned his life after deciding to leave the monastery. Later biographers have suggested that the opposite is true: that he influenced him towards the religious life. The argument is that Pico had intended to join the Dominicans, and according to Savonarola, suffered in Purgatory for delaying entry (as may be read in More's translation of the *Life* of Pico). Secondly, the translation by More is dedicated to a nun, Joyeuce Leigh. Moreover, most of the writings of Pico which More selected to translate inculcate the theory of sanctification by detachment. On the other hand there is the fact that Pico spent his life in the world as a very active humanist. Again, his writings contain the germ of an 'involvement' theory of holiness: he discusses the Martha and Mary theme (found also several times in More) and comes to a compromise: 'And I desire you not so to embrace Martha that ye should utterly forsake Mary. Love them and use them both, as well study as worldly occupation.'[9] More also noted the fact that Pico was 'always merry'. It seems that Pico himself was drawn in two directions, between the use of his great abilities in the world and the exploitation of his charming personality in society, on the one hand, and on the other, the traditional theory that man should despise the present things and long for his eternal home. Perhaps the problem had not crystallized in Pico's mind, as it did not in More's, but in both cases it is represented by the opposition between their active lives and their desire to enter monasteries. The direction in which Pico influenced More could be determined if we knew exactly when he made his translation, but as we do not know, we cannot be apodictic. There are similarities of which we can be certain, e.g.: devotion to the Passion, mortification, abstinence from lawful pleasures,[10] a merry disposition and attachment to humanist ideals.

Colet was also the centre of a group of English humanists that included Lily,

---

9. More's translation, *EW 1931*, I, 369. In the context the words are spoken *to* Pico, who comments that he will not 'gainsay' the opinion.
10. Ibid. 379.

Linacre, Grocyn, Fisher and others, all of whom would have contributed to the intellectual atmosphere in which More matured. Into this circle stepped Erasmus of Rotterdam. Colet was responsible for an important development in the whole humanist movement when he channelled the genius of Erasmus into the study of the Bible and the Fathers.

What impact did Erasmus have on his younger friend? As we would expect, it was enormous. In the monastery at Steyn, Erasmus had imbibed, perhaps in spite of himself, something of the spirituality of the inmates, the spirit of *Devotio Moderna*. Strange to say, it was there also that he was introduced to humanism and also to St Jerome. The foundations were laid for the Erasmian spirituality: a simple, biblical, Christocentric approach with stress on the interior nature of prayer. This subjective approach led Erasmus into psychological descriptions of the role of the passions in the interior life. *Devotio Moderna* had already affected English spirituality, but Erasmus was for More his most direct contact with it. More was impressed by the great decisions and the great undertakings of Erasmus: his decision to tackle Greek and translate the New Testament, his writing of the *Folly*, but especially the editions of the Fathers. We can be sure that More patronised Erasmus and that his library contained the Erasmian editions of 'the old holy doctors' whom More so loved and so often quoted. Erasmus then influenced More, as he did so many others, through the authors whom he made available. Erasmus enjoyed More's hospitality and conversation, and doubtless much of the interaction between their minds took place in these discussions. As we have seen, for example, authors detect the opinion of Erasmus on avoiding civil service in the position adopted by Hythlodaeus in *Utopia*. Erasmus developed a theory of spirituality which contained many elements that are found in More's practice. It is said that Erasmus himself never experienced the devotional warmth and joy which appears in More, but this is not to deny that he sincerely believed and tried to practise what he preached.

More corresponded with a number of other continental humanists but none of them seem to have had any noteworthy impact in the realm of doctrine. The Reformers caused More to react somewhat. To some extent they dictated the subjects of debate in his controversial works.

Like other men of the time, More drew from nature. The Utopians considered the investigation of nature to be an act of homage pleasing to the Creator. More himself had a collection of unusual animals and specimens of insects; he had his children instructed in the science of astronomy so they could admire the 'sublime wonders of the Eternal Workman'; he encouraged Margaret towards the study of medical science and sacred literature so that she would have 'a healthy soul in a healthy body'. We saw earlier how he was impressed by the great miracle of the conception and birth of an infant.

John More, the saint's father, was one of the main factors in deciding his son's character and career. From him Thomas inherited a ready wit and a store of anecdotes. John was a great believer in married life, and married altogether four times. One wonders whether he persuaded his son to give up the idea of a religious life and whether he guided his son into a second marriage so soon after the death of Jane. We do know for certain that there was a conflict of wills when young More first became interested in literature. His father took umbrage because he thought it would interrupt his legal studies. So it seems that John was determined his son should follow in his legal footsteps, and he was eventually successful in bringing this about. The law was John More's most significant legacy to his son.

After years of the study and practice of law, it is not surprising that More's thinking was very coloured by it. When he discussed law in his writings, it was the concept of English law that was uppermost. He was familiar with the methods and distinctions of Canon Law and scholastic notional categories, but his own mind worked along the lines of the Common Law. For example there is his use of precedent as instanced in his allowing exceptions to the fifth commandment, 'Thou shalt not kill', if God himself has allowed or commanded death for certain crimes; also if Christ, St Paul and Polycarp insulted their wicked opponents it was permissible for him to do so; and if Jerome could revise the New Testament, so could Erasmus. Again More is much more at home discussing individual cases, or the merits of individual laws rather than systems of law, or law in the abstract. We have seen that he preferred historical categories (primitive law, Mosaic law etc.). From the courts he learned the value in debate of the *argumentum ad hominem*, as well as the forensic style he used in his controversies. But above all, More's practice of law gave him a realistic conviction of the necessity of law in human society – a conviction that was in marked opposition to the theories arrived at by Luther in academic surroundings. He developed a strong sense of justice, especially of community justice as appears particularly in *Utopia*. His sense of justice extended to his controversies when he allowed his opponents a fair opportunity to express their positions. For More law was necessary for order, and order was necessary for man fo fulfil his duties to God, country and family. This leads us to the idea of loyalty. The fact that treason laws became so strict during Henry's reign is explained mainly by the growing absolutism in England. But it was partly due to the strong sense of loyalty which Englishmen of the period felt to the Crown as representing their national aspirations. We have seen something of More's theory that the King was the shepherd of the people and that he derives his power and authority from them. So long as they did not withdraw their mandate through Parliament, the subject was bound to obey him. More's own devotion to Henry went much further than obedience.

Parallel with this development of the idea of national loyalty, More developed a similar regard for the spiritual and supranational society of Christendom. Basically More's attachment to the Church was due to his conviction that Christ would be loyal to his Church, that he would be faithful to his promise to be always with the Church particularly through the operation in her of the Holy Spirit. It followed for More that the Christian must be loyal to Christ by

148

living according to the Church's doctrine. More drew inspiration and encouragement from the loyalty shown in their passions by Christ and his martyrs. Besides the *History of the Passion,* there are copious references to the Passion of Christ throughout More's writings and in the early biographies. He prepared for his own martyrdom by meditating on the Passion of Christ and his own passage out of this world. He saw the value of martyrdom as a good work because the martyr, united in the Mystical Body with Christ the Head, shares in his merit. Devotion to the martyrs is correlative with devotion to the Passion. As the end drew near we find references, by word and deed, to John the Baptist, [11] Stephen, [12] Cyprian, Ignatius, Boethius. He imitated them by praying for his judges and by giving a gift to his executioner. The example of Christ and the martyrs was doubtless a major influence on More.

All the Christian influences on More came together in his understanding of the corps of Christendom, the Mystical Body, in which are linked together, not only the Church's members in many countries, but also the saints of the past who are now in heaven, as well as the souls in Purgatory, all of whom look to Christ the Head. Christ's Vicar on earth is the Pope. The Church militant is united by the ever present Spirit of Truth; the badge of Christians is 'love and charity'. [13] The ultimate objective norm for the guidance of conscience is the universal belief of Christians, especially as propounded in a General Council. More appealed to the practice of Christendom and the prescription of a General Council to justify his prosecution of heretics, and later to explain his own stand when the English Church accepted Henry as its head.

II. ORIGINAL ELEMENTS IN MORE'S THOUGHT

As the previous section illustrates, St Thomas More was an unashamed eclectic. Yet he was a discriminating connoisseur who chose his material with the perspicacity and independence of an expert. He had a huge stockpile of wise sayings, historical incidents, cases and anecdotes, where he could always find

---

11. *Dial. of Comf.* 327; REYNOLDS, 263; cf. 'Rastell Fragments' in HARPSFIELD, 242; 'Ordo Condemnationis', in HENRY DE VOCHT, *Acta Thomae Mori,* Louvain, 1947; the authenticity of this mention of the Baptist by More at his trial is dubious: see REYNOLDS, *The Trial,* 130, and review in *Moreana,* no. 2, Feb. 1964, 96. The *Ordo* describes More as comparing Henry to Herod, but there is no mention of it in the other accounts of the trial. It would have been offensive and disloyal to Henry, and therfore contrary to More's policy, and it would have been a weak argument as it was open to the obvious rejoinder that the cases were different as Henry was *putting aside* his brother's wife, the very opposite to what Herod did. The phrase in the *Ordo,* 'marito superstite', does not help because it could be argued that the impediment would still exist even if the brother had died. However, the reference shows that people were thinking of the similarities of the cases. See also ESTRADA, op. cit., 36.
12. JOHN R. CAVANAUGH O.S.B., 'The Stephen Motif in More's Thought', *Moreana* no. 8, Nov. 1965, 59–66.
13. *EW* 314.

something apt for the subject with which he was dealing. But his originality went beyond wisdom of choice and intelligent use. Where exactly does this originality lie? According to Fr Surtz, the novelty of *Utopia* lies not in the details, but in the 'incomparable design', in the ensemble. The same author gets closer to the mark when he attributes the success of *Utopia* to the fact that 'More asks the right questions'.[14] Certainly More arranged his material well, but his design was not that of a scientific treatise, divided up neatly into divisions and subdivisions. His usual framework was that of dialogue. His approach was therefore exploratory, experimental, inductive. He sought to provoke thought, to stir up discussion, to lead the reader to form the right conclusion rather than to propound a definitive doctrine. The dialogue form, which he so frequently adopted, suited his temperament and his purpose. It allowed him to express both sides of a debate, it gave him freedom to digress, to relieve concentration at times with a 'merry tale'. On the other hand, these written conversations were not aimless: they were purposefully planned to cover a certain area. Sometimes instead of dialogue, he adopted a homiletic style of commentary, as for example in the *History of the Passion*, but the development of thought is again not deductive but rather existential.

More was not anxious to tie himself to a particular system of thought, or to become the disciple of any one thinker. He wrote to Dorp: 'Now I come to Aristotle, whom I love above many, but still along with many.'[15] Even individual Fathers, being human, could err: e.g. he wrote of Augustine: 'I trust him in most things, as much as I do anybody; but I don't trust any one man in all things.'[16] We saw how he retained his independence of conscience in the matter of the oath: 'I never intend . . . to pin my soul at another man's back, not even the best man that I know this day living: for I know not whither he may hap to carry it.'[17] He quietly dissociated himself from the extreme positions of some of his most influential friends: the fact that Erasmus was his 'darling' did not mean he subscribed to all his opinions. In fact, the Englishman was more just and more balanced than Erasmus in denouncing unworthiness among churchmen. On the other hand, he was much more aggressive than Erasmus in his controversies with the Reformers. Although More admired Colet, he did not go to the lengths that Colet did in attacking scholastic theologians, and especially was able to appreciate the genius of St Thomas Aquinas, whom the Dean lumped together with later thinkers in the period of decline. Again More continually refused to be drawn into seeking for solutions to problems in abstract speculation: he did not try to probe the mystery of predestination; in the question of the Presence of Christ in the Eucharist he stopped at the edge of the mystery and left the explanation in the omnipotence of God: God

14. Introduction to his small edition of *Utopia*, New Haven and London, 1964, xiii, xxvi.
15. *SL* 52.
16. *SL* 37; *Corr.* 83, 1. 203 ff.
17. *Corr.* 516.

can cause Christ's Body to be present in many places and further inquiry is beyond our finite minds. These examples give sufficient proof of More's independence of mind. He was willing to draw arguments from anywhere if he judged them true, but he followed no one blindly. He considered doctrines and arguments individually and made no apparent effort to find an all embracing system or to create one of his own. Thus he felt free of *a priori* assumptions and in a position to assess each situation on its merits. Nevertheless there is a consistency in his approach and thought.

In the sphere of spirituality, More again showed creative ability, not only in assembling borrowed material, but in bringing new ideas into the field. We have seen that, like Erasmus, he described subjective reactions in the spiritual life. But in some respects at least, he was in a better position to do so than Erasmus, because of his own personal experience in dealing with men as a lawyer, judge, advisor, and as father and spiritual guide to the members of his household. But the most outstanding example of subjective description by More is his treatment of the psychological states of a person faced with martyrdom. Nothing comparable to the *Dialogue of Comfort* in intensity of feeling had been written since the age of the martyrs. Even the *Consolations of Philosophy* of Boethius differed in that it did not bring in the greatest motives of all – the Christian ones. More's *Dialogue of Comfort*, his writings on the Passion, the prayers and letters he composed in the Tower, are unique first-hand evidence of the conflict of fear and joy, of the tensions of nature and grace, the choice of heaven and hell, of the anguish of moral isolation, of a desire to serve both God and King. Many treatises have been written on the theology of martyrdom, and many books have described the sufferings of martyrs. But rarely do we have at first hand a description by the martyr himself of his spiritual reactions as he deliberately elects a path which he knows will inevitably bing him to a barbaric death.[18] The field was won in More's mind and will before it was won in prison and on the block. The record of this battle is to be found in these writings of More: they constitute a unique source for the study of the conscious experience of a martyr.

More was endowed with a remarkable imagination and the gift of vivid description. He used these abilities in his treatment of such matters as scruples, the temptation to suicide, the part played by the imagination in temptations against chastity, the influence of latent motives. Again we have an effort at a psychological analysis of states of mind in the spiritual life.

It is uncommon to find in spiritual authors the use of humour that we find in More. In his humanistic writings and in the *Responsio ad Lutherum* he used the satirical, sarcastic, at times insulting style that he had learnt from Lucian and Erasmus. But later his 'merry tales' become more mellow, kinder and more

---

18. More was conscious of the possibility of torture. He aslo realized that the penalty for treason was execution by being hanged, drawn and quartered. In fact he was not tortured, and the King commuted his sentence to simple beheading.

subtle. His sense of humour helped him to see human weakness and such things as the abuse of relics in perspective. He made use of these tales, not only in his apologetic works, but also in his ascetical ones. Only once does he come close to putting these jokes on a doctrinal basis, but he shows himself somewhat reluctant to encourage them because people do not usually need to be persuaded to be merry: rather most people need to restrain themselves and be somewhat more serious. He even suggests that his sense of humour is one of his weaknesses: 'Myself am even half a gigglot'; then he tells his story from Cassian of the preacher who found his congregation dozing while he was speaking of heaven: so he announced that he was going to tell a merry story, but when they sat up to listen to it, he went on with his instruction about heaven. [19] The moral of course is that we do not need any encouragement to interest ourselves in earthly amusement, but it takes an effort to interest ourselves in the future life. This explanation provides a key to the understanding of More's downgrading of such things as sex. Even though he regarded marriage as a sacred institution and the reproduction of children as bordering on the miraculous, there are at times signs of what one might suspect to be a Manichaean or puritanical attitude: he suggests that the sex act is something filthy. [20] Is there an opposition in these two attitudes? Is there a contradiction between More's own life and this second depreciatory aspect? The answer is that he adopted the stricter view for pedagogic reasons: he knew such things did not need any positive encouragement or justification. People were sufficiently prone to them without describing their attractions.

Comparing the life of More with his ascetical writings, we cannot but notice a dichotomy between them. He led a holy life in the world, as a married man, as a lawyer, judge and statesman; as a humanist he boldly asserted the benefits of a liberal education. Yet when he wrote in an ascetic mood, the traditional spirituality is uppermost. He longed for the opportunity to spend his last days in a monastery to prepare himself for death, and he considered himself the object of God's special care when he was given his wish of solitude in a cell of the Tower. In spite of the wholeheartedness with which More gave himself to his life's work, there remained the attitude that this world is a passing shadow and that the only reality is in the next life. More's practice was sanctification by involvement in the world, but his written, *ex professo* theory was that holiness is found in detachment, in retirement from the world. Does this mean that there was a contradiction in More's spirituality?

Before answering this question, it may be permitted to make some observations about the Christian life in general. It is proposed in some quarters today that the so called 'monastic' spirituality, with its self-denial, detachment, and

---

19. *Dial. of Comf.* 185.
20. Ibid. 346: 'Now tell some carnal minded man ... that man and woman shall there [in heaven] live together as angels without any manner, mind or motion, unto the carnal act of generation, and that he shall thereby not use his old filthy voluptuous fashion; he will say he is better at ease already, and would not give this world for that.'

flight from the world is unsuitable for Christians living in the world; that the concepts of sanctification by detachment and sanctification by involvement are mutually exclusive. But is the humanist spirituality a completely different way from monastic spirituality? Is there an adequate distinction between the contemplative life and the apostolic?

In the state of pilgrimage every Christian undergoes a process which associates him with the redemptive acts of Christ. It is a process which inserts him into Christ dying but rising again. This process then has a double aspect: the actions of dying and rising are concurrent. The Christian begins to die at his baptism and continues to do so till the general resurrection. Similarly, when the waters of baptism roll from his forehead, he begins to rise in glory – again a process that goes on until its climax in the Parousia. There is then a double polarity in the Christian life: death and glory. Suspended between the two, the Christian will be influenced by both; both must play a part in his life. The Church teaches Christ crucified and risen again, she teaches self-denial and joy. There are in the Church individuals and institutions whose special mission is to remind the world of both cross and resurrection.

To the man in the world, the religious life will appear as specially suited to bear witness to the passion and death of Christ, and thereby to the necessity of mortification.[21] The voluntary poverty, chastity and obedience of the religious are a graphic reminder to the world of the death of the Saviour: by his poverty the religious bespeaks the naked poverty of Christ on the cross; by his chastity he signifies the virginity of the dying Christ; by his obedience he reminds us that Christ was obedient to death, even to the death of the cross. The renunciation of his rights is like martyrdom, except that the heroic element is voluntarily pursued. So the religious state is one of perfection because it designates a complete subjective response to Christ's invitation to take up the cross.

On the other hand, testimony to the glorified Christ, and of the Kingdom to come, is given by the married Christian. Like all the sacraments, marriage signifies the redemptive acts of Christ – his Passion, death and resurrection, and is a pledge of the future happiness of the Christian himself. But of all the sacraments, marriage especially attests the risen, glorified Christ. Christ rose a King enriched with a Kingdom; he rose wedded to an immaculate spouse – the Church, the new Eve and Mother of all the living – who had been born from him as he slept in death; he rose no longer under obedience, but as the Head of all creatures. The state of the majority of Christians testifies to the glorious Christ: their possessions foretell the hundredfold that Christ has won; their marriage bliss prefigures the eternal nuptials of the Church with God; their freedom proclaims the glorious freedom of the sons of God.

---

21. This does not exclude the eschatological signification of the religious life, viz., that the religious by his renunciation shows his absolute preference of spiritual goods over temporal goods, and thereby gives witness to the Kingdom of God. The sacramental signification of the married state, which we outline here, points to the future life by analogy: temporal happiness is a foretaste of the future life of union with God.

What has been said applies to *states* of life and the testimony they bear to the world. The effectiveness of this testimony will depend on the fidelity of the individual to his calling. Moreover the state a person chooses does not exclude the development of the characteristics of the opposite state because every Christian must die to sin and live to grace personally. The ecclesial states of religion and marriage serve to remind us of this: so the religious must manifest the joy of the Christian life; the married man cannot forget mortification.

So our answer to the question, and the answer that More himself would probably give, is that involvement and detachment must be *balanced* in the life of every Christian. St Thomas More may not have said this in so many words, because the evolution of thought had not then formulated the problem in the terms we use today, but it is certainly the answer of More's life. His life was an attempt to balance the humanist ideals of investigation and appreciation of God's creatures with the traditional spirituality of self-denial and mortification. I suggest that the most important original element in his system is to be found, not on the side of ascetical writings or practice, but on the other side of the scales, that is, in his pursuit of holiness in the world. This originality is, I think, epitomized in what we have seen of his approach to law and duty. The context of his martyrdom, which was, in the circumstances, the logical outcome of his whole life and personality, is one of conflict of laws and duties. More is unique in the way he meticulously worked out the extent of his obligations to God, Church, country, his family and himself. He used his knowledge of moral, civil and canon law to the fullest extent to satisfy as far as possible the demands made upon him by these various duties. In the conflict he fulfilled them all as far as was allowable before God, but no more. He acutely examined his conscience in order to find the narrow course between his duty to God and the Church, on the one hand, and the obligation to try to save himself and to avoid treason on the other: that course was silence.

His case is surely singular in all history. Few people die on a matter of principle. But here was the greatest lawyer of his day, refusing to yield on a principle, and using all his skills, drawing from years of experience, making every conceivable manoeuvre in a great effort to show his innocence of the charge of treason, yet knowing all the time that the outcome would inevitably be against him. The man who conducted this amazing defence was not the hermit of the Tower, not the brooding meditator of *The Four Last Things:* it was rather the scintillating debater of Oxford, the incisive advocate of the law-courts, the King's trusty counsellor, the seeker after justice, the champion defender of the faith. His trial and death proclaimed to the world that he was 'the King's good servant, *and* God's first'.

More's loyalty to his country set a standard that was to be followed by most English Catholics for hundreds of years, particularly by the martyrs.[22] Even

22. See for example, Donald W. Wuerl, 'The Priest Martyrs of England', *Homiletic and Pastoral Review*, vol. LXXI, no. 7, April 1971, 24–33.

when the Pope relieved them of their allegiance to their Sovereign, they ignored the directive and protested themselves to be loyal Englishmen who would abide by the decisions of their countrymen and firmly uphold English law, except where it conflicted with the law of God. Like More they resisted unjust laws passively and by constitutional processes. There were unfortunate exceptions to this, but what has been said applies to the vast majority. St Thomas More initiated this policy.

III A CONTRIBUTION TO MODERN SPIRITUALITY

As was said in the introduction, the fact that the study of More's life and works is so much alive indicates that he has much to offer which is relevant to modern times. We must restrict our comments to our own theme. We suggest that More's example of loyalty contains a message which may help certain people find a solution to their difficulties. The Christian today finds himself debating again the ideals of obedience and freedom. We have dealt briefly with More's opinions on the matter. On the one hand we saw that he upheld the necessity of law and obedience; that he taught that law is necessary for the creation of that order which the social nature of man demands and which is needed if he is to fulfil his various duties. We saw also that More spurned minimalism, yet he made full use of such lowly motives as the fear of hell and of purgatory. This notion of the purpose and nature of law saves More from the charge of having a legalistic spirituality. Rather it could be said that he spiritualized law. Law was the course which he took to satisfy his hunger and thirst after justice, the means by which he endeavoured to be a peacemaker, and finally the cause for which he suffered persecution (Mt 5:6, 9, 10).

A Christian of today may find himself in a position similar to More in that the society in which he lives has laws which he cannot conscientiously support. More's example will be of assistance to such a person, not only as to the solution of the moral problem involved, but from the spiritual point of view. Be it understood however, that cases are so different that, as More would be the first to say, each man would have to resolve his own conscience.

Perhaps we may go even further. There are some today who find themselves conscientiously disagreeing with the *human* institutions of the Church itself – it may be a parish, a diocese, a curia, a religious congregation or even something involving the universal Church. The question of change in the Church is a source of crisis for many. Some disagree with the changes and prefer the old traditional ways; others think the Church is not changing quickly enough or is not introducing the right changes. More's thoughts on the reform of law, the care with which he avoided sedition, his solicitude for the common good, the search for objective norms for the formation of conscience, are considerations which he would offer for the determination of a practical course of action.

IV SUGGESTIONS FOR FUTURE INQUIRY

As this thesis was the first to investigate the spirituality of More on a theological level, it was inevitable that it should be rather exploratory. As often happens, the subject opened up many possibilities most of which could not be fully discussed. On our way we passed many interesting cross-roads and we trust that the sign-posts we have left will be of assistance to others who may care to investigate. Here are some suggestions of possible subjects of study in the field of More's Spirituality: the Passion of Christ; the Eucharist; the Mystical Body; martyrdom; liturgical and aliturgical practices of piety; prayer; liberal education; wealth and sanctity; More's criticism of the clergy and religious. Some essays have already been written on More's theology, but the possibilities in this wider field are still very great.[23]

23. See summary of doctrines discussed by More in section, 'Defence of the Church's Doctrine', p. 82.

APPENDIX

THE FOURTH COUNT OF THE INDICTMENT OF ST THOMAS MORE[1]

The fourth article, or count, in the Indictment of St Thomas More has been a source of difficulty from the very beginning. The unhappy start to its history has given rise, even in recent commentaries, to varying opinions. The earliest accounts of the trial, the *Paris News Letter*[2] and the *Expositio*,[3] do not even mention the fourth article. William Roper, More's son-in-law and the first biographer to deal with the trial, reports the matter but does not sufficiently distinguish what More denied and what he submitted as his own account of the allegedly treasonable words. Further evidence has been provided by Mr Reynolds' discovery of a written report of the conversation from which the words in the Indictment are taken.[4] This 'new' document is in English and appears to be anterior to the Indictment, which is in Latin: in fact it probably is the basis of this part of the charge.

The subject of the last count of the Indictment is a conversation held between More and Sir Richard Rich in the Tower of London on 21 June 1535. It is stated that on that occasion More deprived King Henry VIII of his title of Supreme Head of the Church of England. My object in writing this article is to suggest that Roper's account of the conversation is to be accepted as substantially that which More himself gave at his trial; that his words as recorded by Roper do not contain treason, and that More was telling the truth at his trial. Before giving my reasons for this position, I will set before the reader the two principal accounts of the conversation, viz. the fourth article of the Indictment and Roper's version.

THE FOURTH ARTICLE OF THE INDICTMENT[5]

Moreover, after all and each of the aforesaid deeds and words as

---

1. This article first appeared in *Moreana* no. 10, May 1966, 33–46, and is reproduced here with the editor's permission. It was a sequel to the following works: E. E. REYNOLDS, 'An Unnoticed Document', *Moreana no.* 1, Sep. 1963, 12–17; *The Trial of St Thomas More*, London 1964; J. DUNCAN M. DERRETT, 'The "New" Document on Thomas More's Trial', *Moreana no.* 3, June 1964, 5–19; 'The Trial of Sir Thomas More', *EHR* vol. LXXIX, no. 312, July 1964, 449–477. But for a later study of these events by REYNOLDS, see his book, *The Field is Won*, London 1968, 340 ff. and 385.
2. Published as an appendix in *Harpsfield's Life of More*, E.E.T.S., London, 1932, 258–266.
3. ALLEN, XI, 368–374.
4. REYNOLDS, *The Trial*, 109; also his article 'An Unnoticed Document'.
5. For the original Latin of this part of the Indictment see HARPSFIELD, p. 274, l. 14 to p. 276, l. 2. In making this translation I have made some use of the 'new' document.

stated above, namely, on the twelfth day of June in the aforesaid twenty-seventh year, Richard Rich, Solicitor-General of the said lord the King, came to the said Thomas More in the said Tower of London. During a conversation held then and there between the same Thomas More and Richard Rich concerning various matters touching the things already mentioned, the same Richard Rich charitably moved the said Thomas More to be conformable to the above mentioned Acts and Laws. To which the same Thomas said in reply to the said Richard Rich: 'Your conscience shall save you and my conscience shall save me.' And the said Richard Rich, protesting then and there that he had no commission or commandment to treat or communicate of that matter with the same Thomas More, then and there asked the same Thomas More: 'Supposing it were enacted by the authority of Parliament that the same Richard Rich were King and that it would be treason for anyone to deny it, what would be the offence in the said Thomas More if the same Thomas said that the said Richard Rich was King? Certainly, continued the same Richard, in his conscience there would be no offence. The same Thomas More was obliged to agree and to accept the same Richard for the reason that the consent of the said Thomas More was demanded by an Act of Parliament.' To which the said Thomas More then and there answered and said that he would offend if he refused because he would be bound by the Act since he could give his consent to it. But he said that that case was a simple case. Wherefore the same Thomas More then and there said to the said Richard Rich that he himself wished to put a higher case: 'Suppose it were enacted by Parliament that God were not God and that it should be treason for anyone to wish to impugn that Act,[6] if the question were asked of you, Richard Rich, would you say according to the statute that God is not God, and if you agreed, would you not offend?' To which the said Richard, replying to the said Thomas More, then and there said: 'Indeed, most certainly, because it is not possible to make God not God. And because your case is so exalted, I propose to you this middle case,[7] namely: You know that our lord the King has been made supreme Head on earth of the Church of England, and why ought not you, Master More, so to affirm and accept him, just as in the previous case, in which I was made King, you agreed that you would be bound to affirm and accept me as King?' To which the said Thomas More, falsely, traitorously and maliciously by words persisted in his treason and malice, and wishing to propose and defend his aforesaid treacherous and malicious intent and purpose, then and

6. In the Latin text in HARPSFIELD the comma appears before the words 'actum illum' – an evident mistake.
7. 'hunc casum mediocrem'; The 'new' document has 'to you a mi . . .' as against Mr Reynolds' reading 'to you & me'.

there replied accordingly to the said Richard Rich, namely 'that those cases are not like, because a King can be made by Parliament and can be deprived by Parliament, to which Act any subject being at the Parliament[8] may give his consent, but to the case of a primacy[9] the subject cannot be bound because he cannot give his consent from him[10] in Parliament; and although the King were accepted as such in England, yet most outer parts[11] do not affirm the same.'

ROPER'S VERSION [12]

Master Rich . . . said thus unto him:
'Forasmuch as it is well known, Master More, that you are a man both wise and well learned as well in the laws of the realm as otherwise, I pray you therefore, sir, let me be so bold as of goodwill to put unto you this case. Admit there were, Sir,' quoth he, 'an Act of Parliament that all the Realm should take me for King. Would not you, Master More, take me for King?'
'Yes, Sir' quoth Sir Thomas More, 'that would I.'
'I put case further,' quoth Master Rich, 'that there were an Act of Parliament that all the Realm should take me for Pope. Would not you then, Master More, take me for Pope?'
'For answer, sir,' quoth Sir Thomas More, 'to your first case, the Parliament may well, Master Rich, meddle with the state of temporal Princes. But to make answer to your other case: Suppose the Parliament would make a law that God should not be God. Would you then, Master Rich, say that God were not God.'
'No, Sir,' quoth he, 'that would I not, since no Parliament may make any such law.'
'No more,' said Sir Thomas More, as Master Rich reported of him, 'could the Parliament make the King Supreme Head of the Church.'

NOTE: There is a difference in the sequence of cases as related in the two versions. In the Indictment the cases run:
1. Rich to More: that Richard Rich was King.
2. More to Rich: that God was not God.
3. Rich to More: that the King was Supreme Head of the Church of England.

8. For 'ad parliamentum existens'; the 'new' document has 'being of the parliament'.
9. Following a reconstruction of the 'new' document, 'a' rather than 'the' primacy. The words 'of a prymacie' are almost totally deleted, but the bottom tail of 'f' is visible as well as the top loop of 'a' ('the' is impossible); 'p. .m. .e' are also decipherable.
10. 'ab eo' – the 'new' document has '. . . m hym.'
11. A literal translation of 'plurime tamen partes extere'; the 'new' document has 'yet most utter parts', i.e. 'outer parts' or foreign countries.
12. ROPER, *The Lyfe of Sir Thomas Moore*, E.E.T.S., London 1935, 85–6.

The 'new' document is seriously damaged, but as far as it can be understood, it gives the cases as they appear in the Indictment. The cases as proposed in Roper's version are:
1. Rich to More: that Rich was King.
2. Rich to More: that Rich was Pope.
3. More to Rich: that God was not God.

MORE'S ACCOUNT OF HIS CONVERSATION WITH RICH

As a comparison of the above extracts shows, Roper's version is quite different from that given in the Indictment. Since it differs from Rich's story (which More flatly contradicted), it seems probable that it is derived from the account that More himself gave at his trial. Roper was not present at the trial but he gathered his material from people who were there, such as his law-partner, Richard Heywood. The careful wording of the Roper version inclines me to think that the report which he used was a written one – probably notes taken at the trial itself or made soon afterwards. I do not think Roper was relying merely on memory because he himself seems puzzled by the last words of the conversation, possibly because he thought that they constituted treason and therefore that More was unlikely to have said them. He nevertheless recorded them but only as alleged by Rich. The other early biographers, Ro. Ba. (c. 1599) and Cresacre More (1631) make it clear that they do not believe that More said those last words: they are very indignant that Rich made such an allegation. Modern writers have been perplexed by the incompleteness of Roper's report as the following comments show: Rich 'detailed the conversation . . . with an addition which was a pure fabrication, namely that . . . Sir Thomas had replied, "No more, then, can Parliament make the King the head of the Church"' [13]; 'More gave his version of it but we do not know what this was' [14]; 'Had More, in fact, said that Parliament could not make the King Supreme Head he would have been placing his own head on the block.' [15]

An examination of Roper's story reveals a logically developed line of discussion: Rich advanced two cases for More's consideration, the first that Parliament should make him King, the second that Parliament should make him Pope. More answered the 'first case' by admitting the competence of Parliament, and then went on: 'But to make answer to your other case. . .' He did not answer directly but first proposed a case of his own, namely that Parliament enact that God should not be God. When Rich replied that such a law would be invalid, More applied the same criterion to the case they were discussing, namely, that Parliament should make Rich Pope. Logically the

13. Judge O'HAGAN, Introduction to *Utopia and Dialogue of Comfort*, London 1937, xxxi, originally an article in *Irish Monthly Magazine*, 1876.
14. PHILLIP INGRESS BELL, 'The Trial of Thomas More', *The Month*, vol. 23, 1960, 336.
15. REYNOLDS, *The Trial*, 112-3.

reply would have been: Neither 'can Parliament make you Pope.' Actually Roper gives it as Rich reported it: 'No more could the Parliament make the King Supreme Head of the Church.' The 'King' in question would be Rich after his election in the first case. Admittedly in another context the term 'Supreme Head of the Church' could refer to the Supremacy of the King in the English Church, but it does not necessarily do so: in itself and without any other qualification the term 'Church' means the universal Church. In *this* context it certainly means the universal Church because the case under discussion was the appointment of Rich as *Pope*. Nowhere did the conversation touch the King's title of Supreme Head of the Church of England, as according to Roper's account, this case was not raised by Rich. Hence there is no denial, even implicit, of the King's Supremacy of the Church of England and therefore no treason. There is not even an affirmation of a belief in the Papacy. There is only a denial that the Parliament of England could elect a Pope. In this version the cases discussed never left the realm of pure supposition.

Hence since Roper's version is one of entire innocence and since it is the only alternative to that given in the Indictment, which More stoutly denied, it may be argued that it is More's own account of the conversation.

Who was telling the Truth, Rich or More?

At the trial More accused Rich of distorting the evidence and gave his own description of the discussion. What is the evidence that Rich was lying? There were four other men in the small cell when the conversation took place. [16] At the trial two of them were called upon to testify in favour of the Crown. They declined to do so on the plea that they 'took no heed to their talk'. More was not allowed to call upon witnesses, [17] so we do not know whether any of the men present in the cell were prepared to support him. Hence we must look elsewhere to see if there are any indications of perjury by Rich.

More's assault on Rich at the trial was the most devastating personal attack that More ever made in his life. Was this simply a clever legal manoeuvre or was he telling the truth? Knowing More's meticulous honesty, I find it impossible to believe that he would so crushingly condemn Rich and his evidence if he were not telling the truth. More voluntarily added an oath (not legally recognized [18] but certainly morally binding) that Rich's evidence was false: and if he were the type of person who could take a false oath he would not have come to trial. More's views on perjury can be seen in his writings. [19] It is difficult to improve on More's own arguments of his innocence to this charge and of

16. Ibid. 109.
17. BELL, op. cit. 325–6.
18. Ibid. 336, states that More was not permitted to swear to the truth of his defence by a legal oath.
19. *EW* 345; *EW 1931*, II, 204–5.

the unlikelihood of his revealing his mind to Rich when he had steadfastly refused to discuss the matter with anyone else, even the King through his Councillors.

Is there any independent evidence of a plot by Rich to tamper with the evidence? The following comments may bring some understanding as to what took place.

1. The final words of the 'new' document describe Rich as saying to More as he takes his leave of the prisoner: 'Well, Sir, God comfort you, for I see your mind will not change which I fear will be very dangerous to you for I suppose your concealment to the question that hath been asked of you is as high offence as other that hath denied it.[20] And thus Jesu send you better grace.' Mr Reynolds argues that the word 'concealment' shows that More had not revealed his mind on the King's Supremacy. Dr Derrett replies that the word refers to an explicit denial as against the implicit one contained in More's denial of Parliament's competence. My own interpretation, however, is this: the words do not refer to the exchange of cases but refer back to the beginning of the conversation when More had declined to conform or to reveal his opinion on the statute. Rich is saying that More's silence is just as treasonable as a positive denial. It is worth recalling that Rich was trying to get a statement from More that could be used at the trial as evidence. But he did not wish to indicate to More that the exchange of cases was to be used against him because he wanted to surprise More at his trial. Indeed the element of surprise was a standard part of the prosecution's attack. The 'other' who had denied the Supremacy was undoubtedly Fisher who had been tricked into an absolute denial on 7 May. His Indictment was in process of preparation early in June; he was interrogated on 12 June, the same day as Rich's interview with More. Fisher was tried on 17 June: his case then must have occupied Rich's mind at the time of his conversation with More. This veiled allusion to Fisher is indicative that Rich was aware of the possibility of tricking More into saying something that could be used against him. His failure to comment on More's reply to the 'cases' is parallel to the deceit used on Fisher who was left under the impression until his trial that his opinion was given under the seal of professional secrecy. However, it should be admitted that the 'new' document does not furnish positive proof that Rich changed the final case that he put to More.

2. The fact that in the fourth article the allegedly incriminating words are given in Latin, whereas in the first three articles they are quoted in English, leads one to suspect that an effort was made to gloss over the changes which Rich had made in the report. It is true that Rich would have had to give verbal

20. I take the reading 'denyd it' as against REYNOLDS' blank (*The Trial*, corrected in *The Field is Won*) and DERRETT's 'semyd(?)'. I have used a photostat copy of the original document: the '. .nyd/. .t' is reasonably clear (the letter before 'y' is certainly an 'n' not an 'm'); the first two letters correspond with the 'de' of 'depryved' eight lines above except that the loop of the top of the 'd' is not clear; it seems to have been obscured by a fold in the document.

162

testimony in English, but he seems to have hoped that the witnesses would think his version near enough to the original to support it. More however was alert and pointed out the differences before the witnesses were called on. Confronted with this disagreement, they stated that they had not paid sufficient attention to the conversation to enable them to support Rich.

3. The Indictment, supported by the 'new' document, describes More as using the argument that 'although the King was accepted as such in England, yet most outer parts do not affirm the same.' This argument fits into More's version better than it does into Rich's. It is extremely unlikely that More would have argued that the English Parliament could not make the King Supreme Head of the English Church because other countries do not 'affirm the same'. Such a statement would have merely opened up an entirely new area of debate: why should the legislation of the English Parliament on an internal question be subject to the opinion of foreign countries? On the other hand, the opinion of foreign countries would have been *ad rem* and immediately conclusive if it were a question of the English Parliament attempting to elect a Pope. Such an election would evidently be void because the Supremacy of the whole Church could not be determined by England alone. The lack of recognition by other countries would show the absurdity of the suggestion.[21] It appears then that this argument in the Indictment is a part of the original conversation. Rich retained it because in its new context it seemed to serve his purpose as evidence of another denial of the Supremacy and also because it brought in a nationalistic element: More would be made to look as though he were appealing to foreign opinion on the domestic concerns of England. There is no mention of this argument in Roper because More did not challenge it: he merely put it into its proper context.

4. According to the Indictment, the last proposition made by More was his opinion about 'the case of a primacy'. The word 'primacy' was used to designate the office of the Pope but not that of the King. Hence the final case given by Rich and the one about which More was speaking was that which is given in Roper, viz. the competence of the English Parliament to make it obligatory on its subjects to accept its nominee, (King) Richard Rich as Pope.

---

21. This is a different argument from the one used by More before the Act of Supremacy (*SL* 221–2) and after the verdict (HARPSFIELD, 193 ff. and *Paris News Letter*, ibid, 263–4). viz. that England, a *part* of Christendom cannot make a law for itself that is *contrary* to the law of the *whole* of Christendom just as the City of London cannot make a law for itself which is contrary to a law passed by Parliament to bind the whole realm. Even during the danger period More cautiously pointed out that there is a difference between a law accepted throughout Christendom, including England, as the papacy had been, and 'a thing agreed in this realm and the contrary taken for truth in other realms' (*SL* 251). The argument in the Indictment does not mention the relation of part to whole nor the fact of a contrary general law: it is a case of something affirmed by the English Parliament but simply *not affirmed* by other countries and therefore void. Simple absence of recognition is sufficient proof of the incompetence of Parliament to elect a Pope, but it would not be sufficient proof of its incompetence to appoint the King Head of the Church of England: for that it would be necessary to bring in the essential unity of Christendom and the existence of a general law establishing papal jurisdiction over all Christians.

So it appears that Rich changed the cases according to a carefully pre-meditated plan. The jury could legally accept his word against More's, hence the need of More's alternative defence (which of course in no way weakened his main defence).

The theory I propose, then, is this: Rich imagined his cases with a view to getting from More a statement such as: 'A subject cannot be bound to consent to a King being made Head of the Church (Pope) by Parliament.' It was predictable (a) that More would answer these cases since they were not legally dangerous; (b) what his answer would be. Then after the conversation and according to plan the last question put to More was changed in the report from one about the papacy to one about the King's Supremacy of the Church of England. Few, if any, of the words in More's reply would have to be changed. [22] So the report, the 'new' document, has the cases as contained in the Indictment. As regards the words which Rich said to More as he left the cell: (a) Rich *said* them to allay suspicion by More that what he had said might be used against him; (b) they were *written* into the report so that Cromwell and others would be assured that Rich had not given any hint to More; (c) they were of course *omitted* from the Indictment as irrelevant. The prosecution was quite capable of using such deceit, as is shown in Fisher's case (to which Rich alluded in his parting words). This theory, I submit, does not contradict any of the known facts and is positively indicated by some of them.

It is not clear why More's defence has not been properly understood. It may have been due to the fact that readers have taken Roper's words 'Supreme Head of the Church' in the wider context of the historical moment rather than in the immediate context of the conversation. There has been apparently an unwarranted assumption that Roper's version attributes a third and real (i.e. not hypothetical) case to Rich: that the King had been made Head of the Church of England. One may also ask why the fourth count was not reported in the early descriptions of the trial. Quite contradictory suggestions have been offered: it has been said that More's sympathizers omitted the matter altogether because it seemed to go against him, and because it seemed the only count on which he was convicted; on the other hand it is said that More so annihilated Rich's testimony that it was completely disregarded by both the Court and the observers, especially when the two witnesses failed to give their support. At such a distance of time it is impossible to give more than a guess. Perhaps the observers were unable to follow the interchange of remarks. We simply do not know.

For anyone who accepts More's account of the conversation as understood in this essay, the question as to where the alleged treason is to be found in the fourth article of the Indictment becomes purely theoretical. However, let us

---

22. I would think that the words as given in the Indictment and the 'new' document are nearer the original than those in ROPER. ROPER was following More's version and More gave the gist of the conversation as he remembered it. Seeing that Rich was hoping for the support of witnesses he would try to keep as near to More's words as possible.

suppose for argument's sake that the account given in the Indictment is true. A denial of the competence of Parliament to *make* the King Supreme Head did not constitute treason, because Parliament did not profess that it *made* Henry Supreme Head. The Act of Supremacy was confirmatory and corroboratory of a supposed already existing fact.[23] To *declare* something to be true is not the same as *to make* something true. (This same argument applies also to Roper's version if it be understood as referring to the Church of England.) Moreover, even to have denied the competence of Parliament *to declare* the King to be Supreme Head would not necessarily have implied a denial of the Supremacy, because Parliament explicitly stated that the title did not rest upon its statute. If for example the French Parliament declared the Pope to be the Head of the Church of France, a person could challenge the competence of Parliament to make such a statement, yet still believe in the Supremacy of the Pope over the Church of France, because according to his belief the title is based on the law of Christ.

23. REYNOLDS, *The Trial*, 54, 113 footnote. Cf. Cromwell's interpretation as recorded by More in a letter to Margaret: 'Since it was now by Act of Parliament ordained that his Highness and heirs be, and *ever of right have been*, and perpetually should be, Supreme Head in earth of the Church of England under Christ . . .', *SL* 246; *Corr.* 552. *Of*, in the phrase we have italicized, though omitted by ROGERS, rightly appears in *EW* and in *Royal* 17 D XIV. I am indebted to Abbé MARC'HADOUR for bringing this latter detail to my attention.

INDEX

168

Linacre, Thomas, 146
Lucian of Samosata, 144, 151
Loyalty, 80, 83, 86, 115, ch III *passim*, 148, 154f
Luther, Martin, 30, 32f, 43ff, 56, 66, 75f, 79ff, 85, 87, 90, 148
Magisterium, 28
Magna Carta, 134
Marc'hadour, G., 29 n, 33 n, 44 n, 143 n, 165 n
Marcion, 82
Marius, Richard C., 32 n, 43 n, 110 n
Marriage, (Sacrament), 85f, 120, 153
Married State, 153ff
Martyrdom, More on, 49f, 64ff, 115, 132 149f, 156
Mary, (Mother of Christ), 45, 69, 70, 89, 106
Mary, Princess, later Queen, 53, 118, 122
Mass, 69 n, 75, 83, 84 n
Matthew, Gospel of, 155
Mayday Riots, 94
Merit, 83
Messenger, The, 48, 57f, 73, 85, 89
Miles, Leland, 52 n, 54 n, 95 n, 96, 132 n, 144 n
Miracles, 84ff
Misprision of Treason, 119, 128f
Morals, Catholic, 45, 90f
More, Alice, 101f, 107, 114n
More, Cecily, 107
More, Cresacre, 160
More, Jane, 101, 114 n, 148
More, John (Snr), 100f, 113, 147
More, John (Jnr), 107
More, Margaret, 38f, 64, 68, 102f, 105ff, 113, 124, 126, 127 n, 128ff, 144 n, 145 n, 147, 165 n
More, Thomas
  as humanist, 27, 71, 72, 80, 96, 146
  as thinker, 149ff
  anger, 103, 110, 124
  attitude to Education, 103f, 156
    Fathers, 27f, 31, 72, 88, 104, 108, 127, 144, 147, 150
    Indulgences, 56, 83
    King, 34, 64, 80, 92, 97ff, 105, ch III *Passim*
    Learning, 103f, 147
    Martyrdom, 49f, 64ff, 115, 132, 149f, 156
    Scripture, 26f, 72, 76, 88, 103f, 108, 127, 143f
    Sex, 106, 114, 152
    Theology, 76, 104, 143
    the world, 110f, 136, 152f, 156
  canonisation, 21
  eloquence, 76, 77
  epitaph, 96, 99, 101, 111, 115, 121 n
  execution, 68, 132f, 145, 151 n, 154
  resignation from Chancellorship, 95, 111, 121, 129

style, 76, 78ff, 150
trial, 107, 117, 131, 133f, 137, 139ff, 154, 157ff
vocation, 43, 91f, 100, 112ff, 147, 152ff
Works:
  Answer to a Poisoned Book, 78, 111 n
  Apology, 26, 33, 54, 71, 75 n, 76, 78, 81, 84 n, 86 n, 88 n, 90, 91 n, 95, 97 n
  Confutation, 46, 54
  Devout Prayer, A, 41
  Dialogue Concerning Heresies, 26f, 48, 57, 78, 81
  Dialogue of Comfort, 33, 37, 42, 48f, 63ff, 88 n, 102, 104f, 110f, 113, 132, 145, 149 n, 151f
  English Prayers and Treatise on the Holy Eucharist, 63 n
  Four Last Things, The, 37, 63, 104, 114, 154
  History of the Passion, 65, 67, 74, 84 n, 143, 149, 150
  Latin Epigrams, 72, 103 n
  Letter to a Monk, 72, 75 n, 84 n, 108
  Life of John Picus, The, 63, 146
  Responsio ad Lutherum, 31, 44f, 71 n, 79f, 82, 83 n, 84 n, 85, 87, 88 n, 90 n, 151
  Supplication of Souls, The, 69, 90, 102
  Treatise on the Holy Eucharist, 41
  Treatise on the Passion, The, 63, 84 n
  Treatise to Receive the Blessed Body of Our Lord, 114
  Utopia, 25f, 32f, 35f, 52f, 60, 65, 69, 71f, 75, 85 n, 87, 92, 99, 105, 108, 114 n, 144, 147, 148, 150
Morton, Cardinal John, 75, 108
Moses, 88
Mystical Body, 29, 36, 47, 65, 69, 74, 78, 83, 143, 149, 156
Norfolk, Duke of, 98
'Nun of Kent, The'
  see Barton, Elizabeth
Oath of Succession, 38f, 115, 119f, 124ff. 129f, 134, 142
Oaths, 141, 161
Oecolampadius, 77
O'Hagan, Judge, 160 n
Orders, Sacrament of, 83
Origen, 27, 144
O'Sullivan, Richard, 94 n
Oxford University, 104, 154
'Pacifier, The'
  see St German, Christopher
Papacy, 29ff, 35, 44, 55, 70f, 83, 90, 118, 120, 134, 149, 155
Paris News Letter, 64, 140, 157, 163 n
Parliament, 35, 39, 40, 58, 93, 96, 119, 121f, 124, 126, 128, 137ff, 148, 158ff
Parmiter, Geoffrey de C., 119 n, 124 n